THE END OF THE WORLD
AS WE KNOW IT

*The publication of this book was assisted by a bequest
from Josiah H. Chase to honor his parents,
Ellen Rankin Chase and Josiah Hook Chase,
Minnesota territorial pioneers.*

THE END OF THE WORLD AS WE KNOW IT

Social Science for the Twenty-First Century

Immanuel Wallerstein

University of Minnesota Press

Minneapolis

London

Published by the University of Minnesota Press
111 Third Avenue South, Suite 290
Minneapolis, MN 55401–2520
http://www.upress.umn.edu

Printed in the United States of America on acid-free paper

The University of Minnesota is an equal-opportunity educator and employer.

Library of Congress Cataloging-in-Publication Data

Wallerstein, Immanuel Maurice, 1930–
   The end of the world as we know it : social science for the twenty-
first century / Immanuel Wallerstein.
       p.   cm.
   Includes index.
   ISBN 0-8166-3397-5. – ISBN 0-8166-3398-3 (pbk.)
   1. Social sciences – Philosophy.   2. Sociology – Philosophy.
   I. Title.
   H61.W34   1999
   300 – dc21   99–26087

11 10 09 08 07 06 05 04 03 02 01 00 99   10 9 8 7 6 5 4 3 2

To Jacob, Jessie, Adam, and Joshua —
may they come to know a more useful social science
than the one I encountered when I came to study it

and

To Don Pablo González Casanova —
whose whole life's work has been an attempt to put
social science at the service of a more democratic world,
and who has inspired us all

Contents

Part II
THE WORLD OF KNOWLEDGE

Preface

From 1994 to 1998, I served as president of the International Sociological Association. I urged the ISA to place at the center of its concerns the need to reassess the collective social knowledge of social science in the light of what I argued would be a quite transformed world in the twenty-first century. Since, as president of the ISA, I was called upon to address many meetings of sociologists and other social scientists, I decided to follow my own urgings and use these occasions to lay out my views on the subject of a social science for the twenty-first century.

The title was furnished for me by Patrick Wilkinson, who read many of these essays as they were written. He told me one day that what I had been writing about was in fact "the end of the world as we know it," in the double sense of "know": as *cognoscere* and *scire*. I seized upon this insight as a way of organizing the collection of essays, divided into "The World of Capitalism" and "The World of Knowledge" — the world we have known in the sense that it framed our reality (the world of capitalism, or *cognoscere*) and the world we have known in the sense of acquiring understanding of it (the world of knowledge, or *scire*).

I believe we are in the midst of wandering through dark woods and have insufficient clarity about where we should be heading. I believe we need urgently to discuss this together, and that this discussion must be truly worldwide. I believe furthermore that this discussion is not one in which we can separate knowledge, morality, and politics into separate corners. I try to make this case briefly in the opening essay, "Uncertainty and Creativity." We are engaged in a singular debate, and a difficult one. But we shall not resolve the issues by avoiding them.

Uncertainty and Creativity
Premises and Conclusions

The first half of the twenty-first century will, I believe, be far more difficult, more unsettling, and yet more open than anything we have known in the twentieth century. I say this on three premises, none of which I have time to argue here. The first is that historical systems, like all systems, have finite lives. They have beginnings, a long development, and finally, as they move far from equilibrium and reach points of bifurcation, a demise. The second premise is that two things are true at these points of bifurcation: small inputs have large outputs (as opposed to times of the normal development of a system, when large inputs have small outputs); and the outcome of such bifurcations is inherently indeterminate.

The third premise is that the modern world-system, as a historical system, has entered into a terminal crisis and is unlikely to exist in fifty years. However, since its outcome is uncertain, we do not know whether the resulting system (or systems) will be better or worse than the one in which we are living, but we do know that the period of transition will be a terrible time of troubles, since the stakes of the transition are so high, the outcome so uncertain, and the ability of small inputs to affect the outcome so great.

It is widely thought that the collapse of the Communisms in 1989 marks a great triumph of liberalism. I see it rather as marking the definitive collapse of liberalism as the defining geoculture of our world-system. Liberalism essentially promised that gradual reform would ameliorate the inequalities of the world-system and reduce the acute polarization. The illusion that this was possible within the framework of the modern world-system has in fact been a great stabilizing element, in that it legitimated the states in the eyes of their populations and promised them a heaven on earth in the foreseeable future. The

Talk at "Forum 2000: Concerns and Hopes on the Threshold of the New Millennium," Prague, September 3–6, 1997.

1

collapse of the Communisms, along with the collapse of the national liberation movements in the Third World, and the collapse of faith in the Keynesian model in the Western world were all simultaneous reflections of popular disillusionment in the validity and reality of the reformist programs each propagated. But this disillusionment, however merited, knocks the props from under popular legitimation of the states and effectively undoes any reason why their populations should tolerate the continuing and increasing polarization of our world-system. I therefore expect considerable turmoil of the kind we have already been seeing in the 1990s, spreading from the Bosnias and Rwandas of this world to the wealthier (and assertedly more stable) regions of the world (such as the United States).

These, as I say, are premises, and you may not be convinced of them, since I have no time to argue them.[1] I wish therefore simply to draw the moral and political conclusions from my premises. The first conclusion is that progress, unlike what the Enlightenment in all its forms preached, is not at all inevitable. But I do not accept that it is therefore impossible. The world has not morally advanced in the last several thousand years, but it could. We can move in the direction of what Max Weber called "substantive rationality," that is, rational values and rational ends, arrived at collectively and intelligently.

The second conclusion is that the belief in certainties, a fundamental premise of modernity, is blinding and crippling. Modern science, that is, Cartesian-Newtonian science, has been based on the certainty of certainty. The basic assumption is that there exist objective universal laws governing all natural phenomena, that these laws can be ascertained by scientific inquiry, and that once such laws are known, we can, starting from any set of initial conditions, predict perfectly the future and the past.

It is often argued that this concept of science is merely a secularization of Christian thought, representing simply a substitution of "nature" for God, and that the requisite assumption of certainty is derived from and is parallel to the truths of religious profession. I do not wish here to start a theological discussion per se, but it has always struck me that the belief in an omnipotent God, a view common at least to the so-called Western religions (Judaism, Christianity, and Islam), is in fact both logically and morally incompatible with a belief in certainty, or at least in any human certainty. For if God is omnipotent, then humans cannot constrain him by edicting what they believe is eternally true, or God would not then be omnipotent. No doubt, the scientists of early modern times, many of whom were quite pious, may have thought they were arguing theses consonant with the reigning theology, and no doubt many theologians of the time gave them cause to think that, but it is simply not true that a belief in scientific certainty is a necessary complement to religious belief systems.

Furthermore, the belief in certainty is now under severe, and I would say very telling, attack within natural science itself. I need only refer you to Ilya Prigogine's latest book, *La fin des certitudes*,[2] in which he argues that, even in the inner sanctum of natural science, dynamic systems in mechanics, the systems are governed by the arrow of time and move inevitably far from equilibrium. These new views are called the science of complexity, partly because they argue that Newtonian certitudes hold true only in very constrained, very simple systems, but also because they argue that the universe manifests the evolutionary development of complexity, and that the overwhelming majority of situations cannot be explained by assumptions of linear equilibria and time-reversibility.

The third conclusion is that in human social systems, the most complex systems in the universe, therefore the hardest to analyze, the struggle for the good society is a continuing one. Furthermore, it is precisely in periods of transition from one historical system to another one (whose nature we cannot know in advance) that human struggle takes on the most meaning. Or to put it another way, it is only in such times of transition that what we call free will outweighs the pressures of the existing system to return to equilibria. Thus, fundamental change is possible, albeit never certain, and this fact makes claims on our moral responsibility to act rationally, in good faith, and with strength to seek a better historical system.

We cannot know what this would look like in structural terms, but we can lay out the criteria on the basis of which we would call a historical system substantively rational. It is a system that is largely egalitarian and largely democratic. Far from seeing any conflict between these two objectives, I would argue that they are intrinsically linked to each other. A historical system cannot be egalitarian if it is not democratic, because an undemocratic system is one that distributes power unequally, and this means that it will also distribute all other things unequally. And it cannot be democratic if it is not egalitarian, since an inegalitarian system means that some have more material means than others and therefore inevitably will have more political power.

The fourth conclusion I draw is that uncertainty is wondrous, and that certainty, were it to be real, would be moral death. If we were certain of the future, there could be no moral compulsion to do anything. We would be free to indulge every passion and pursue every egoism, since all actions fall within the certainty that has been ordained. If everything is uncertain, then the future is open to creativity, not merely human creativity but the creativity of all nature. It is open to possibility, and therefore to a better world. But we can only get there as we are ready to invest our moral energies in its achievement, and as we are ready to struggle with those who, under whatever guise and for whatever excuse, prefer an inegalitarian, undemocratic world.

I

The World of Capitalism

Chapter 1

Social Science and the Communist Interlude, or Interpretations of Contemporary History

A Communist interlude? Between what and what? And first of all, when? I shall consider it to be the period between November 1917 (the so-called Great October Revolution) and 1991, the year of the dissolution of the Communist Party of the Soviet Union in August, and of the USSR itself in December. This is the period in which there were states governed by Communist, or Marxist-Leninist, parties in Russia and its empire and in east-central Europe. To be sure, there are still today a few states in Asia that consider themselves to be governed by Marxist-Leninist parties, to wit, China, the Democratic Republic of Korea, Vietnam, and Laos. And there is Cuba. But the era in which there was a "socialist bloc of states" in any meaningful sense is over. So in my view is the era in which Marxism-Leninism is an ideology that commands significant support.

So we are talking of an interlude in the elementary sense that there was a point of time prior to the era in which there was a coherent bloc of states asserting that they were governed by Marxist-Leninist ideology and that today we are living in a period posterior to that era. Of course, its shadow was there before 1917. Marx and Engels had asserted in the *Manifesto* already in 1848 that "a spectre is haunting Europe, the spectre of Communism." And, in many ways, this spectre is still haunting Europe. Only Europe? Let us discuss that.

What was the spectre before 1917? What was it between 1917 and 1991? What is it today? I think it is not too difficult to come to an agreement on what the spectre was before 1917. It was the spectre that

Talk at International Sociological Association's regional colloquium, "Building Open Society and Perspectives of Sociology in East-Central Europe," Cracow, Poland, September 15–17, 1996.

7

somehow the "people" — seen as a largely uneducated, uncultivated, and unsophisticated mass of persons — would rise up in some disorderly manner, destroy and confiscate property, and redistribute it more or less, putting into power persons who would govern without respect for talent or initiative. And in the process, they would destroy what was seen as valuable in a country's traditions, including of course its religious traditions.

This was not a totally delusionary fear. There is a scene in the movie version of Pasternak's *Doctor Zhivago* when Dr. Zhivago, returning from the front shortly after the revolution to his relatively palatial home in Moscow, is greeted not merely by his family but by the very large collective of persons who have occupied his home as their new residence. His own family has been relegated to a single room in the vast house. Zhivago, representing the essential idealistic Russian intellectual, is asked somewhat aggressively what he thinks of this new reality, and he replies, "This is a better arrangement, comrades, more just."[1] To the end of his quite eventful life, Dr. Zhivago continues to believe that it is better, even if the reader/viewer is left to have more ambiguous sentiments.

We know the political and social history of nineteenth-century Europe fairly well. Let me summarize it. After the French Revolution, there was widespread and increasing acceptance in Europe of two concepts that would have been considered strange by most persons before the French Revolution. The first was that political change was an absolutely normal and expectable phenomenon. The second was that sovereignty, national sovereignty, resided not in rulers or legislatures but in something called the "people." These were not only new ideas; they were radical ideas, disturbing to most persons of property and power.

This new set of values that transcended particular states, what I call the emerging geoculture of the world-system, was accompanied by important changes in the demographic and social structuring of most European states. The rate of urbanization increased, and the percentage of wage labor increased. This sudden geographic concentration of sizable numbers of urban wageworkers in European cities, whose living conditions were generally abysmal, created a new political force composed of persons who were largely excluded from the benefits of economic growth: they suffered economically, were excluded socially, and had no say in the political processes, either at the national or the local levels. When Marx and Engels said, "Workers of the world, unite;

you have nothing to lose but your chains," they were both referring to and addressing this group.

Two things happened in Europe between 1848 and 1917 that affected this situation. First, the political leaders of the different states began to effectuate a program of reform, *rational* reform, designed to respond to the plaints of this group, palliate their miseries, and appease their sense of alienation. Such programs were put into effect within most European states, albeit at different paces and at different moments. (I include in my definition of Europe the principal White settler states: the United States, Canada, Australia, and New Zealand.)

The programs of reform had three main components. The first was suffrage, which was introduced cautiously but steadily expanded in coverage: sooner or later all adult males (and then women as well) were accorded the right to vote. The second reform was remedial workplace legislation plus redistributive benefits, what we would later call the "welfare state." The third reform, if reform is the right word, was the creation of national identities, largely via compulsory primary education and universal military service (for males).

The three elements together — political participation via the ballot, the intervention of the state to reduce the polarizing consequences of ungoverned market relations, and a transclass unifying national loyalty — comprise the underpinnings, and indeed in actuality the definition, of the liberal state, which by 1914 had become the pan-European norm and partial practice. After 1848, the pre-1848 differences between so-called liberal and so-called conservative political forces diminished radically as they tended to come together on the merits of a reform program, although of course there continued to be debate about the pace of reform and about the degree to which it was useful to preserve the veneration of traditional symbols and authorities.

This same period saw the emergence in Europe of what is sometimes called the social movement, composed on the one hand of the trade unions and on the other hand of socialist or labor parties. Most, although not all, of these political parties considered themselves to be "Marxist," though what this really meant has been a continuing matter of dispute, then and since. The strongest among these parties, and the "model" party for itself and for most of the others, was the German Social-Democratic Party.

The German Social-Democratic Party, like most of the other parties, was faced with one major practical question: Should it participate in parliamentary elections? (With the subsequent question, Should its members participate in governments?) In the end, the overwhelming majority of the parties and of the militants of parties answered yes to these questions. The reasoning was rather simple. They could thereby do some immediate good on behalf of their constituencies. Eventually, with extended suffrage and sufficient political education, the majority would vote them into total power, and once in power, they could legislate the end of capitalism and the installation of a socialist society. There were some premises that underpinned this reasoning. One was the Enlightenment view of human rationality: all persons will act in their own rational interest, provided they have the chance and the education to perceive it correctly. The second was that progress was inevitable, and that therefore history was on the side of the socialist cause.

This line of reasoning by the socialist parties of Europe in the pre-1914 period transformed them in practice from a revolutionary force, if they ever were one, into merely a somewhat more impatient version of centrist liberalism. Although many of the parties still talked a language of "revolution," they no longer really conceived of revolution as involving insurrection or even the use of force. Revolution had become rather the expectation of some dramatic political happening, say a 60 percent victory at the polls. Since at the time socialist parties were still doing quite poorly at the polls on the whole, prospective victory at the polls still bore the psychological flavor of revolution.

Enter Lenin, or rather enter the Bolshevik faction of the Russian Social-Democratic Party. The Bolshevik analysis had two main elements. First, the Bolsheviks said that the theorizing and praxis of the European social-democratic parties were not at all revolutionary but constituted at best a variant of liberalism. Second, they said that, whatever the justification for such "revisionism" might be elsewhere, it was irrelevant to Russian reality, since Russia was not a liberal state, and there was therefore no possibility that socialists could vote themselves into socialism. One has to say that these two assessments seem in retrospect absolutely correct.

The Bolsheviks drew from this analysis a crucial conclusion: Russia would never become socialist (and implicitly neither would any other state) without an insurrectionary process that involved seizing control of the state apparatus. Therefore, Russia's "proletariat" (the approved subject of history), which was in fact still numerically small, had to do this by organizing itself into a tightly structured cadre party that would plan and organize the "revolution." The "small" size of the urban industrial proletariat was more important to the implicit, not explicit, theorizing than Lenin and his colleagues admitted. For what we in effect got here was a theory of how to be a socialist party in a country that was neither wealthy nor highly industrialized, and was therefore not a part of the core zone of the capitalist world-economy.

The leaders of the October Revolution considered themselves to have led the first proletarian revolution of modern history. It is more realistic to say that they led one of the first, and possibly the most dramatic, of the national liberation uprisings in the periphery and semiperiphery of the world-system. What made this particular national liberation uprising different, however, from the others were two things: it was led by a cadre party that affected a universalist ideology and therefore proceeded to create a worldwide political structure under its direct control; and the revolution occurred in the particular country outside the core zone that was the strongest among them industrially and militarily. The whole history of the Communist interlude of 1917–91 derived from these two facts.

A party that proclaims itself a vanguard party, and then proceeds to achieve state power, cannot but be a dictatorial party. If one defines oneself as vanguard, then one is necessarily right. And if history is on the side of socialism, then the vanguard party is logically fulfilling the world's destiny by enforcing its will on everyone else, including those persons of whom it is supposed to be the vanguard, in this case, the industrial proletariat. Indeed, it would be remiss in its duty were it to act differently. If, in addition, only one of these parties in the entire world had state power, which was essentially the case between 1917 and 1945, then if one were to organize an international cadre structure, it does seem natural and plausible that the party of the state in power would become the leading party. In any case, this party had the material and political means to insist on this role against any opposition that arose. Thus it seems not unfair to state that the one-party regime of the USSR and its de facto control of the Comintern were almost inevitable consequences of the theory of the vanguard party. And with it came, if not quite inevitably then at least with high probability, what actually happened: purges, gulags, and an Iron Curtain.

No doubt the clear and continuous hostility of the rest of the world to the Communist regime in Russia played a big role in these developments. But it is surely specious to attribute these developments to that hostility, since Leninist theory predicted the hostility and therefore the hostility represented part of the constants of external reality with which the regime always knew it had to deal.

The hostility was to be expected. The internal structuring of the regime was to be expected. What was perhaps less to be expected was the geopolitics of the Soviet regime. There were four successive geopolitical decisions taken by the Bolsheviks that marked turning-points, and these do not seem to me to have been necessarily the only route that the Soviet regime could have taken.

The first was the reassembling of the Russian empire. In 1917, the Russian imperial forces were in military disarray, and vast segments of the Russian population were calling out for "bread and peace." This was the social situation within which the tsar was forced to abdicate, and in which, after a brief period, the Bolsheviks could launch their attack on the Winter Palace and seize state power.

At first, the Bolsheviks seemed to be indifferent to the fate of the Russian empire as such. After all, they were internationalist socialists, who were committed to a belief in the evils of nationalism, of imperialism, and of tsarism. They "let go" both Finland and Poland. One can be cynical and say that they were merely casting ballast overboard at a difficult moment. I think rather that it was a kind of immediate, almost instinctive, reaction in accord with their ideological prejudices.

What happened then was rational reflection. The Bolsheviks found themselves in a militarily difficult civil war. They were afraid that "letting go" meant the creation of actively hostile regimes on their borders. They wanted to win the civil war, and they decided that this required reconquest of the empire. It turned out to be too late for Finland and Poland, but not for the Ukraine and the Caucasus. And thus it was that, of the three great multinational empires that existed in Europe at the time of the First World War — the Austro-Hungarian, the Ottoman, and the Russian — only the Russian empire was to survive, at least until 1991. And thus it was that the first Marxist-Leninist regime became a Russian imperial regime, the successor to the tsarist empire.

The second turning-point was the Congress of the Peoples of the East in Baku in 1921. Faced with the reality that the long-awaited German revolution was not going to happen, the Bolsheviks turned inward and eastward. They turned inward insofar as they now proclaimed a new doctrine, that of building socialism in one country. And they turned eastward insofar as Baku shifted the world-systemic emphasis of the

Bolsheviks from a revolution of the proletariat in highly industrialized countries to an anti-imperialist struggle in the colonial and semicolonial countries of the world. Both seemed sensible as pragmatic shifts. Both had enormous consequences for the taming of Leninism as a world revolutionary ideology.

To turn inward meant to concentrate upon the reconsolidation of the Russian state and empire as state structures and to put forward a program of economic catching up, via industrialization, with the countries of the core zone. To turn eastward was to admit implicitly (not yet explicitly) the virtual impossibility of workers' insurrection in the core zone. It was also to join in the struggle for Wilson's self-determination of nations (under the more colorful banner of anti-imperialism). These shifts in objectives made the Soviet regime far less unpalatable to the political leadership of Western countries than its previous stance, and laid the basis for a possible geopolitical entente.

This led logically to the next turning-point, which came the very next year, 1922, in Rapallo, when Germany and Soviet Russia both reentered the world political scene as major players by agreeing to resume diplomatic and economic relations and to renounce all war claims on each other, thereby effectively circumventing the different kinds of ostracism each was suffering at the hands of France, Great Britain, and the United States. From that point on, the USSR was committed to a full integration in the interstate system. It joined the League of Nations in 1933 (and would have done so sooner, if permitted), allied itself with the West in the Second World War, cofounded the United Nations, and never ceased in the post-1945 world to seek recognition by everyone (and first of all, by the United States) as one of the world's two "great powers." Such efforts, as Charles de Gaulle was repeatedly to point out, might be hard to explain in terms of the ideology of Marxism-Leninism but were perfectly expectable as the policies of a great military power operating within the framework of the existing world-system.

And it was then not surprising that we saw the fourth turning-point, the often-neglected but ideologically significant dissolution of the Comintern in 1943. To dissolve the Comintern was first of all to recognize formally what had been a reality for a long time, the abandonment of the original Bolshevik project of proletarian revolutions in the most "advanced" countries. This seems obvious. What was less obvious is that this represented the abandonment of the Baku objectives as well, or at least in their original form.

Baku extolled the merits of anti-imperialist national liberation movements in the "East." But by 1943 the leaders of the USSR were no longer really interested in revolutions anywhere, unless they entirely controlled those revolutions. The Soviet leadership was not stupid, and it realized that movements that came to power through long national struggles were unlikely to surrender their integrity to someone in Moscow. Who would then? There was only one possible answer — movements that came to power because of and under the watchful eye of Russia's Red Army. Thus was born the Soviet policy toward the only part of the world of which this could possibly be true, at least at the time, east-central Europe. In the period 1944–47, the USSR was determined to place in power subservient Communist regimes in all areas where the Red Army found itself at the end of the Second World War, essentially Europe east of the Elbe. I say essentially because immediately there are three exceptions: Greece, Yugoslavia, and Albania. But we know what happened there. The Red Army was located in none of these three countries in 1945. In Greece, Stalin abandoned the Greek Communist Party dramatically. And both Yugoslavia and Albania, which had Marxist-Leninist regimes that had come to power through their own insurrectionary efforts, would openly break with the USSR. As for Asia, Stalin's foot-dragging was obvious to the world, not least of all to the Chinese Communist Party, which also broke dramatically with the USSR as soon as it could. Mao's meeting with Nixon is the direct outcome of this fourth Soviet turning-point.

After four turning-points, what was left? Not much of the old spectre of Communism. What was left was something quite different. The USSR was the second-strongest military power in the world. It was in fact strong enough to make a deal with the United States, which was the strongest power, and by far, that allowed it to carve out a zone of exclusive influence, from the Elbe to the Yalu, but not beyond. The deal was that this zone was its to control and that its free rein there would be respected by the United States, provided only that the USSR really stayed inside that zone. The deal was consecrated at Yalta and was essentially respected by the Western powers and the Soviet Union right up to 1991. In this, the Soviets played the game as the direct heirs of the tsars, performing their geopolitical role better.

Economically, the USSR had set out on the classic road to catching up, via industrialization. It did fairly well, considering all its handicaps and the costs of the destruction of the Second World War. If one looks at the 1945–70 figures, they are impressive on a world comparative scale. The USSR forced its satellite countries to pursue the same path, which made less sense for some of them, but these countries too did fairly well at first. But the economics were naive, not because they didn't leave enough place for private enterprise but because they assumed that steady "catching up" was a plausible policy and industrialization was the wave of the economic future. In any case, as we know, the USSR as well as the east-central European countries began to do badly in economic terms in the 1970s and 1980s and eventually collapsed. This was of course a period in which much of the world was also doing badly, and much of what happened in these countries was part of a larger pattern. The point, however, is that, from the point of view of people living in these countries, the economic failures were a sort of last straw, especially given the official propaganda that the greatest proof of the merits of Marxism-Leninism lay in what it could do immediately to improve the economic situation.

It was the last straw because the internal political situation in all these countries was one that virtually no one liked. Democratic political participation was nonexistent. If the worst of the terrorism was over by the mid-1950s, arbitrary imprisonment and control by the secret police were still the normal, ongoing reality of life. And nationalism was allowed no expression. This mattered perhaps least in Russia, where the reality was that Russians were on top of this political world, even if they were not allowed to say so. But for everyone else, Russian dominance was intolerable. Finally, the one-party system meant that, in all these countries, there was a very privileged stratum, the Nomenklatura, whose existence made the ideological claim of the Bolsheviks to represent egalitarianism seem a mockery.

There were always very many people in all these countries who in no sense shared the original Bolshevik objectives. What made the whole system collapse in the end, however, was that large numbers of those who did share these objectives became as hostile to the regimes as the others — perhaps even more hostile. The spectre that haunted the world from 1917 to 1991 had become transformed into a monstrous caricature of the spectre that had haunted Europe from 1848 to 1917. The old spectre exuded optimism, justice, morality, which were its strengths. The second spectre came to exude stagnation, betrayal, and ugly oppression. Is there a third spectre on the horizon?

The first spectre was one not for Russia or east-central Europe but rather for Europe (and the world). The second spectre was one for the whole world. And the third spectre will surely be that for the whole world again. But can we call it the spectre of Communism? Certainly not in the 1917–1991 use of the term. And only up to a point in the 1848–1917 usage of the term. But the spectre is nonetheless awesome and is not unrelated to the continuing problem of the modern world, its combination of great material and technological advance and extraordinary polarization of the world's populations.

In the ex-Communist world, many see themselves as having gone "back to normalcy." But this is no more realistic a possibility than it was when President Warren Harding launched that slogan for the United States in 1920. The United States could never go back to the pre-1914 world, and Russia and its ex-satellites cannot go back to the pre-1945 or pre-1917 world, neither in detail nor in spirit. The world has moved decisively on. And while most persons in the ex-Communist world are immensely relieved that the Communist interlude is behind them, it is not at all sure that they, or the rest of us, have moved into a safer or more hopeful or more livable world.

For one thing, the world of the next fifty years promises to be a far more violent one than the Cold War world out of which we have come. The Cold War was highly choreographed, highly constrained by the concern of both the United States and the Soviet Union that there be no nuclear war between them, and just as important by the fact that the two countries had between them the necessary power to ensure that such a war would not break out. But this situation has changed radically. Russia's military strength, while still great, is considerably weakened. But so, it must be said, is that of the United States, if less so. In particular, the United States no longer has three elements that ensured its military strength previously: the money, popular willingness within the United States to bear the losses of military action, and political control over western Europe and Japan.

The results are already clear. It is extremely difficult to contain escalating local violence (Bosnia, Rwanda, Burundi, and so on). It will be virtually impossible over the next twenty-five years to contain weapons proliferation, and we should anticipate a significant increase in the number of states that have nuclear weapons at their disposition, as well as biological and chemical weapons. Furthermore, given, on the one hand, the relative weakening of U.S. power and the emergence of a triadic division among the strongest states and, on the other hand, a continuing economic North-South polarization in the world-system, we should expect the likelihood that there will be more deliberate South-North military provocations (of the Saddam Hussein variety). Such provocations will be increasingly difficult to handle politically, and if several occur simultaneously, it is doubtful that the North will be able to stem the tide. The U.S. military has already moved into a mode of preparing to handle *two* such situations at the same time. But if there are three?

The second new element is South-North migration (which includes eastern Europe–western Europe migration). I say it is new, but of course such migration has been a feature of the capitalist world-economy for five hundred years now. Three things, however, have changed. The first is the technology of transport, which makes the process far easier. The second is the extensiveness of the global economic *and demographic* polarization, which makes the global push far more intensive. The third is the spread of democratic ideology, which undermines the political ability of wealthy states to resist the tide.

What will happen? It seems clear in the short run. In the wealthy states, we shall see the growth of right-wing movements that focus their rhetoric around keeping migrants out. We shall see the erection of more and more legal and physical barriers to migration. We shall nonetheless see a rise in the real rate of migration, legal and illegal — in part because the cost of real barriers is too high, in part because of the extensive collusion of employers who wish to utilize such migrant labor.

The middle-run consequences are also clear. There will come to be a statistically significant group of migrant families (including often the second-generation families) who will be poorly paid, not socially integrated, and almost certainly without political rights. These persons will constitute essentially the bottom stratum of the working class in each country. If this is the case, we shall be back to the pre-1848 situation in western Europe — an underclass concentrated in urban areas without rights and with very strong complaints, and this time clearly identifiable ethnically. It was this situation that led to the first spectre of which Marx and Engels spoke.

There is, however, now another difference with 1848. The world-system was riding a wave of enormous optimism about the future in the nineteenth century, and indeed up to about twenty years ago. We lived in an era in which everyone was sure that history was on the side of progress. Such faith had one enormous political consequence: it was incredibly stabilizing. It created patience, since it assured everyone that things would be better one day, one day soon, for at least one's children. It was what made the liberal state plausible and acceptable as a political structure. Today the world has lost that faith, and having lost it the world has lost its essential stabilizer.

It is this loss of faith in inevitable reform that accounts for the great turn against the state, which we see everywhere today. No one ever really liked the state, but the great majority had permitted its powers to grow ever greater because they saw the state as the mediator of reform. But if it cannot play this function, then why suffer the state? But if we don't have a strong state, who will provide daily security? The answer is we must then provide it ourselves, for ourselves. And this puts the world collectively back to the period of the beginning of the modern world-system. It was to get out of the necessity of constructing our own local security that we engaged in the construction of the modern state-system.

And one last, not so small, change. It is called democratization. Everyone speaks of it, and I believe it is really occurring. But democratization will not diminish, but add to, the great disorder. For, to most people, democratization translates primarily as the demand for three things as equal rights: a reasonable income (a job and later a pension), access to education for one's children, and adequate medical facilities. To the extent that there is democratization, people insist not merely on having these three, but on regularly raising the minimal acceptable threshold for each. But having these three, at the level that people are demanding each day, is incredibly expensive, even for the wealthy countries, not to speak of for Russia, China, India. The only way *everyone* can really have more of these is to have a radically different system of distribution of the world's resources than we have today.

So what shall we call this third spectre? The spectre of disintegration of the state structures, in which people no longer have confidence? The spectre of democratization, and the demand for a radically different system of distribution? The next twenty-five to fifty years will be a long political debate about how to handle this new spectre. It is not possible to predict the outcome of this worldwide political debate, which will be a worldwide political struggle. What is clear is that the responsibility of social scientists is to help in clarifying the historical choices that are before us.

Chapter 2

The ANC and South Africa

The Past and Future of Liberation Movements in the World-System

The African National Congress is one of the oldest national liberation movements in the world-system. It is also the latest movement to have achieved its primary objective, political power. It may well be the last of the national liberation movements to do so. And thus May 10, 1994, may mark not only the end of an era in South Africa but also the end of a world-systemic process that has been continuous since 1789.

"National liberation" as a term is of course recent, but the concept itself is much older. The concept in turn presumes two other concepts, "nation" and "liberation." Neither of these concepts had much acceptance or legitimacy before the French Revolution (although perhaps the political turmoil in British North America after 1765 that led to the American Revolution reflected similar ideas). The French Revolution transformed the geoculture of the modern world-system. It made widespread the belief that political change is "normal" rather than exceptional, and that sovereignty of states (itself a concept that dates at most from the sixteenth century) resides not in a sovereign ruler (whether a monarch or a parliament) but in the "people" as a whole.[1]

Since that time, these ideas have been taken seriously by many, many people — too many people as far as those in power are concerned. The principal political issue of the world-system for the past two centuries has been the struggle between those who wished to see these ideas implemented fully and those who resisted such a full implementation. This struggle has been a continuous one, hard fought, and it has assumed multiple forms in the different regions of the world-system. Early on, class struggles emerged in Great Britain, France, the United States, and

Keynote address at the annual meeting of the South African Sociological Association, Durban, South Africa, July 7–11, 1996.

elsewhere in the more industrialized zones of the world that pitted an enlarged urban proletariat against both its bourgeois employers and the aristocracies still in power. There were also numerous nationalist movements that pitted the people of a "nation" against an "outside" invader or against a dominant imperial center, as in Spain and Egypt during the Napoleonic era, or as in the case of the multiple movements in Greece, Italy, Poland, Hungary, and an ever-expanding list during the post–Napoleonic era. And there were still other situations in which the outside dominant force was combined with an internal settler population that made its own separate claims to autonomy, as in Ireland, Peru, and most significantly (though it is an often ignored case) Haiti. The movement in South Africa is basically a variant of this third category.

Even in the first half of the nineteenth century, as we can rapidly note, these movements were not limited to western Europe but included the peripheral zones of the world-system. And of course, as the years went by, more and more movements were to be founded in what we later came to call the Third World, or the South. In the period from circa 1870 to the First World War, a fourth variety emerged, that of movements in formally independent states in which the struggle against the *Ancien Régime* was considered simultaneously to be a struggle for the renaissance of national vitality and therefore against the dominance of outside forces. Such were the movements that came into existence, for example, in Turkey, Persia, Afghanistan, China, and Mexico.

What united all these movements was a sense that they knew who the "people" were and what "liberation" meant for the people. They also all shared the view that the people were not currently in power, that they were not truly free, and that there were concrete groups of persons who were responsible for this unjust, morally indefensible situation. Of course, the incredible variety of actual political situations meant that each of the detailed analyses made by the various movements was quite distinctive. And, as the internal situations changed over time, quite often the analyses of particular movements changed.

Nonetheless, despite the variety, all these movements shared a second common feature as well, their middle-run strategy. Or at least it was shared by those movements that came to be important politically. The successful movements, the dominant movements, all believed in what we speak of as the two-stage strategy: first attain political power, then transform the world. Their common motto was expressed most pithily by Kwame Nkrumah: "Seek ye first the political kingdom, and all things shall be added unto you." This was the strategy followed by the socialist movements that centered their rhetoric around the working class, by the ethnonational movements that centered their rhetoric around those who shared a particular cultural heritage, as well as by those nationalist movements that used common residence and citizenship as the defining feature of their "nation."

It is this last variety to which we have given the name of national liberation movements. The quintessential movement of this kind, and the oldest of them, is the Indian National Congress, founded in 1885 and still existing (at least nominally) today. When the ANC was founded in 1912, it named itself the South African Native National Congress, adapting that of the Indian movement. Of course, the Indian National Congress had one feature that few other movements shared. It was led throughout its most difficult and important years of its history by Mahatma Gandhi, who had elaborated a worldview and a political tactic of nonviolent resistance, *satyagraha*. He elaborated this tactic first, in fact, in the context of the oppressive situation of South Africa, and later transferred it to India.

Whether the Indian struggle was won because of *satyagraha*, or despite *satyagraha*, is something we can long debate. What is clear is that the independence of India in 1947 became a prime symbolic event for the world-system. It symbolized both the triumph of a major liberation movement situated in the world's largest colony and the implicit guarantee that the decolonization of the rest of the world was politically inevitable. But it symbolized also that national liberation, when it came, arrived in a form less than, and other than, that which the movement had sought. India was partitioned. Terrible Hindu-Muslim massacres followed in the wake of independence. And Gandhi was assassinated by a so-called Hindu extremist.

The twenty-five years following the Second World War were extraordinary on many counts. For one thing, they represented the period of clear U.S. hegemony in the world-system: unbeatable in terms of the efficiency of its productive enterprises, leader of a powerful political coalition that effectively contained world politics within a certain geopolitical order, imposing its version of the geoculture upon the rest of the world. This period was also remarkable for being that of the largest single expansion of world production and accumulation of capital that the capitalist world-economy has known since its inception four centuries ago.

These two aspects of that era — U.S. hegemony and the incredible expansion of the world-economy — are so salient in our minds that we often fail to notice that this was the era as well of the triumph of the historic antisystemic movements of the world-system. The movements of the Third International, the so-called Communist parties, came to control a third of the world's surface, that of the East. In the West, the movements of the Second International were de facto in power everywhere, to some extent literally and usually for the first time, and indirectly the rest of the time insofar as the parties of the right fully acceded to the principles of the welfare state. And in the South, one national liberation movement after another came to power — in Asia, in Africa, in Latin America. The only large zone in which this triumph was delayed was southern Africa, and this delay has now come to an end.

We do not discuss clearly enough the impact of this political triumph of the antisystemic movements. Looked at from the point of view of the middle of the nineteenth century, it was an absolutely extraordinary achievement. Compare the post-1945 period with that of the world-system in 1848. In 1848, we had in France the first attempt of a quasi-socialist movement to achieve power. The year 1848 is also called by historians the "springtime of the nations." But by 1851, all these quasi-insurrections had been easily suppressed everywhere. It seemed to the powerful people that the menace of the "dangerous classes" had passed. In the process, the quarrels between the old landowning strata and the new more industrial bourgeois strata, which had so dominated the politics of the first half of the nineteenth century, were put aside in the successful, unified effort to contain the "people" and the "peoples."

This restoration of order seemed to work. For some fifteen to twenty years thereafter, no serious popular movements could be discerned anywhere inside or outside of Europe. Furthermore, the upper strata did not merely sit on their laurels as successful suppressers of liberation movements. They pursued a political program not of reaction but of liberalism in order to ensure that the menace of popular revolt would be buried forever. They commenced down the road of slow but steady reformism: extension of suffrage, protection of the weak in the workplace, the beginnings of redistributive welfare, the building of an educational and health infrastructure that continuously extended its reach. They combined this program of reform, still limited during the nineteenth century to the European world, with the propagation and legitimation of a pan-European racism — the White man's burden, the civilizing mission, the Yellow Peril, a new anti-Semitism — that served to incrustate the European lower strata within the folds of a right-wing, nonliberatory, national identity and identification.

I shall not review here the whole history of the modern world-system from 1870 to 1945, except to say that it was during this period that the major antisystemic movements were first created as national forces, with an international vocation. The struggle of these antisystemic movements, singly and collectively, against the liberal strategy of an iron hand within a velvet glove was an uphill struggle all the way. We may thus be amazed that, between 1945 and 1970, they succeeded so swiftly and, when all is said and done, so easily. Indeed, we may be suspicious. Historical capitalism — as a mode of production, as a world-system, as a civilization — has proved itself remarkably ingenious, flexible, and hardy. We should not underestimate its ability to contain opposition.

Let us therefore start by looking at this protracted struggle of the antisystemic movements in general, and the movements of national liberation in particular, from the perspective of the movements. The movements had to organize within a political environment that was hostile to them, one that was quite often ready to suppress or constrain considerably their political activity. The states engaged in such repression both directly on the movements as such as well as on their members (particularly the leaders and the cadres), and indirectly by the intimidation of potential members. They also denied moral legitimacy to the movements and enlisted quite frequently the nonstate cultural structures (the churches, the world of knowledge, the media of communication) in the task of reinforcing this denial.

Against this massive barrage, each movement — which initially was almost always the work of small groups — sought to mobilize mass support and to canalize mass discontent and unrest. No doubt the movements were evoking themes and making analyses that resonated well with the mass of the population, but nonetheless effective political mobilization was a long and arduous task. Most people live day by day and are reluctant to engage in the dangerous path of defying authority. Many persons are "free riders," ready to applaud quietly the actions of the brave and the bold, but waiting to see whether others among their peers are joining in active support of the movement.

What mobilizes mass support? One cannot say it is the degree of oppression. For one thing, this is often a constant and does not explain therefore why people who have been mobilized at T_2 were not already mobilized at T_1. Furthermore, quite often acute repression works, keeping the less audacious from being ready to participate actively in the movement. No, it is not oppression that mobilizes masses, but hope and certainty — the belief that the end of oppression is near, that a better world is truly possible. And nothing reinforces such hope and certainty more than success. The long march of the antisystemic movements has been like a rolling stone. It gathered momentum over time. And the biggest argument that any given movement could use in order to mobilize support was the success of other movements that seemed comparable and reasonably close in geography and culture.

From this perspective, the great internal debate of the movements — reform versus revolution — was a nondebate. Reformist tactics fed revolutionary tactics, and revolutionary tactics fed reformist tactics, provided only that they worked, in the very simple sense that the outcome of any particular effort was applauded as positive by mass sentiment (as distinguished from the sentiment of leaders and cadres). And this because any success mobilized mass support for further action, as long as the primary objective of state power had not yet been achieved.

The passions that surrounded reform versus revolution debates were enormous. But they were passions that divided a small group of political tacticians. To be sure, these tacticians themselves believed that the differences in tactics mattered, both in the short run (efficacity) and in the middle run (outcome). It is not sure that history has proven them right in this belief, if one looks at what happened in the long run.

If one looks at this same process of mass mobilization from the point of view of those in power, those against whom the movements were mobilizing, one finds the obverse side of the coin. What those in power most feared was not the moral condemnation of the movements but their potential ability to disrupt the political arena by mass mobilization. The initial reaction to the emergence of an antisystemic movement was always therefore to seek to maintain the leadership in isolation from its potential mass support — physical isolation, political isolation, social isolation. The states precisely denied the legitimacy of movement leaders as "spokespersons" for larger groups, alleging that they came in fact from different class and/or cultural backgrounds. This was the well-known and well-used theme of the "outside agitators."

There came however a point where, in a given locality, this theme of the movement as being merely intrusive "agitators" no longer seemed to work. This turning-point was the consequence both of the patient labors of the movement (quite often, once it had turned to a "populist" mode) and of the contagious impact of the "rolling stone" within the world-system. At this turning-point, the defenders of the status quo were confronted with the identical dilemma of the movements, but in obverse form. As opposed to reform versus revolution, the defenders of the status quo debated concessions versus the hard line. This debate, which was constant, was also a nondebate. Hard-line tactics fed concessions, and concessions fed hard-line tactics, provided only that they worked, in the very simple sense that they altered the perspective of the movements on the one hand and of their mass support on the other.

The passions that surrounded hard line versus concession debates were enormous. But they were passions, once again, that divided a small group of political tacticians. These tacticians themselves believed that the differences in tactics mattered, both in the short run (efficacity) and in the middle run (outcome). But here too, it is not sure that history has proven them right in this belief, if one looks at what happened in the long run.

In the long run, what happened is that the movements came to power, just about everywhere, which marked a great symbolic change. Indeed, the moment of coming to power is everywhere well marked in general perception. It was seen at the time and remembered later as a moment of catharsis, marking the accession at last of the "people" to the exercise of sovereignty. It is also true, however, that the movements came to power almost nowhere on their full terms, and the real change everywhere has been less than they had wanted and expected. This is the story of the movements in power.

The story of the movements in power is parallel in some ways to the story of the movements in mobilization. The theory of the two-stage strategy had been that, once a movement achieved power and controlled the state, it could then transform the world, at least its world. But this was of course not true. Indeed, it was in hindsight extraordinarily naive. It took the theory of sovereignty at its face value and assumed that sovereign states are autonomous. But they are not autonomous, and they never have been. Even the most powerful among them, like for example the contemporary United States, are not truly sovereign. And when we come to very weak states, like for example Liberia, to speak of sovereignty is a bad joke. All modern states, without exception, exist within the framework of the interstate system and are constrained by its rules and its politics. The productive activities within all modern states, without exception, occur within the framework of the capitalist world-economy and are constrained by its priorities and its economics. The cultural identities found within all modern states, without exception, exist within a geoculture and are constrained by its models and its intellectual hierarchies. Shouting that one is autonomous is a bit like Canute commanding the tides to recede.

What happened when movements came to power? They found first of all that they had to make concessions to those in power in the world-system as a whole. And not just any concessions, but important concessions. The argument that they all used themselves was that of Lenin in launching the NEP (New Economic Policy): the concessions are temporary; one step backward and two steps forward. It was a powerful argument, since in those few cases where the movement did not make these concessions, it usually found itself ousted from power altogether soon thereafter. Still the concessions grated, leading to intra-leadership quarrels and puzzlement and questioning by the mass of the population.

If the movement was to remain in power, there seemed to be only one possible policy at this point, the postponement of truly fundamental change, substituting for it the attempt to "catch up" within the world-system. The regimes that the movements established all sought to make the state stronger within the world-economy and its standard of living nearer to that of the leading states. Since what the mass of the population usually really wanted was not fundamental change (which was hard to envisage) but rather precisely to catch up to the material benefits of the better-off (which was quite concrete), the switch in postcatharsis policies by the leaders of the movements was actually popular — provided it worked. There was the rub!

The first thing we need to know in order to determine whether a policy works is the period of time over which we shall measure this. Between instantaneous time and the Greek calends there is a long continuum of possibilities. Naturally, the leaders of movements in power pleaded with their followers for a longer rather than a shorter time-span of measure. But what arguments could they give the mass of the population for permitting them such leeway? There were two main kinds of arguments. One was material: the demonstration that there were some immediate, meaningful, measurable improvements, even if small ones, in the real situation. Some movements found it easier than others to achieve this, since the national situations varied. And it was easier to make such arguments at some moments in time than at others, given the fluctuating realities of the world-economy. There was only a limited degree to which it really was within the control of a movement in power to effectuate such meaningful, even if small, improvements.

There was, however, a second kind of argument, one about which movements in power found it easier to do something. It was the argument of hope and certainty. The movement could point to the rolling stone of the world's collectivity of liberation movements and use this to demonstrate that history was (visibly) on their side. They thereby proffered the promise that if not they then their children would live better, and if not their children then their grandchildren. This is a very powerful argument, and it did indeed sustain movements in power for a long time, as we now can see. Faith moves mountains. And faith in the future maintains antisystemic movements in power — as long as faith endures.

Faith, as we all know, is subject to doubt. Doubt about the movements has been fed from two sources. One source has been the sins of the Nomenklatura. Movements in power means cadres in power. And cadres are human. They too wish the good life and are often less patient about achieving it than the mass of the population. Consequently, corruption, arrogance, and petty oppressiveness have been virtually inevitable, especially as the glow of the moment of catharsis recedes. The cadres of the new regime seemed over time to look increasingly like the cadres of the *Ancien Régime,* indeed often worse. This may have happened in five years; it may have taken twenty-five years; but it did happen repeatedly.

Still what then, a revolution against the revolutionaries? Never right away. The same lethargy that made it a slow process to mobilize the mass of the population against the *Ancien Régime* operated here too. It takes something more than the sins of the Nomenklatura to undo movements in power. It takes a collapse in the immediate economy combined with a collapse in the certainty that the rolling stone is still rolling. When this has happened, we have had the end of the "postrevolutionary era," as has recently taken place in Russia and Algeria and many other countries.

Let us turn our look back to the worldwide rolling stone, the process within the world-system as a whole. I have already spoken of the long uphill struggle of the movements from 1870 to 1945, and the sudden breakthrough worldwide between 1945 and 1970. The sudden breakthrough led to considerable triumphalism and was inebriating.

It sustained the movements in the most difficult zones, like southern Africa. However, the biggest problem the movements have had to face was their success, not so much their individual successes but their collective worldwide success. When movements in power faced internal grumbling because of less than perfect performance, they could use the argument that their difficulties derived in large part from the hostility of powerful external forces, and in large part this was an absolutely true argument. But as more and more movements were in power in more and more countries, and as the movements themselves were using the argument of their growing collective strength, the attribution of their current difficulties to outside hostility seemed to lose its cogency. At the very least, it seemed in contradiction to the thesis that history was visibly on their side.

The failure of the movements in power was one of the underlying factors behind the worldwide revolution of 1968. All of a sudden, one heard voices everywhere wondering whether the limitations of the anti-systemic movements in power derived less from the hostility of the forces of the status quo than from the collusion of these movements themselves with the forces of the status quo. The so-called Old Left found itself under attack everywhere. Wherever the national liberation movements were in power, throughout the Third World, they did not escape this criticism. Only those not yet in power remained largely unscathed.

If the revolutions of 1968 shook the popular base of the movements, the stagnation in the world-economy in the following two decades continued the dismantlement of the idols. Between 1945 and 1970, the period of the great triumph of the movements, the great immediate promise was "national development," which many of the movements called "socialism." Indeed, the movements said that they and they alone could speed up this process and realize it fully in their respective states. And between 1945 and 1970, this promise seemed to be plausible, because the world-economy was expanding everywhere, and a rising tide was lifting all ships.

But when the tide began to recede, the movements in power in peripheral zones of the world-economy found that they could do little to prevent the very negative impact of world economic stagnation on their states. They were less powerful than they thought, and than their populations thought — far less powerful. Disillusionment with the prospects of catching up was translated in country after country into disillusionment with the movements themselves. They had sustained themselves in power by selling hope and certainty. They now were paying the price of dashed hopes and the end of certainty.

Into this moral crisis jumped the snake-oil salesmen, otherwise known as the "Chicago boys," who, with the massive support of a reinvigorated hard line on the part of the people in power in the world-system as a whole, offered everyone the magic of the market as a substitute. But the "market" can no more transform the economic prospects of the poorer 75 percent of the world's populations than taking vitamins can cure leukemia. It is a fake, and we will no doubt soon run the snake-oil salesmen out of town, but only once the damage is done.

In the middle of all this has occurred the miracle of South Africa, providing a glow of bright light in this dismal world scene. It is time out of joint. It is the 1960s triumph of national liberation movements all over again, and it occurred in the place everyone had always said had the worst situation and the most intractable. The transformation happened very fast, and with astonishing smoothness. In a way, it is an extraordinarily unfair burden the world has placed on South Africa and on the ANC. They have to succeed not only for their own sake, but for the sake of all the rest of us. After South Africa comes no other to serve as the still-optimistic mobilizer of popular forces, to be cheered on by the solidarity movements of the world. It is as though the very concept of antisystemic movements in the world were given one last chance, as if we all found ourselves at the decisive moment in purgatory before history draws its final verdict.

I am not sure what will happen in South Africa in the next ten to fifteen years. How can anyone be? But I do feel that neither South Africans nor the rest of us should put the burden of the world on their shoulders. The burden of the world belongs on the world. It is enough for South Africans to bear their own burdens, and to take their fair share of the world's burdens. I shall therefore reserve my remaining words to the burden of the world.

Antisystemic movements as a structure, and as a concept, were the natural product of the post-1789 transformation of the geoculture of the world-system. Antisystemic movements were a product of the system; they of course had to be. However critical a balance sheet we may now draw, and I fear that I have drawn such, I do not see any historic alternative that would have been better in the mid-nineteenth century than going down the path they took. There existed no other force for human liberation. And if the antisystemic movements did not achieve human liberation, they at the very least reduced some human suffering and held the banner high for an alternative vision of the world. What reasonable person does not believe that South Africa is a better place today than it was ten years ago? And whom should we credit other than the national liberation movement?

The basic problem lay in the strategy of the movements. They found themselves historically in a double bind. After 1848, there was only one objective that was politically feasible and offered some hope of immediate alleviation of the situation. This was the objective of taking power in the state structures, which provided the principal adjustment mechanism of the modern world-system. But taking power in the world-system was the one objective that ensured the eventual emasculation of the antisystemic movements and their incapacity to transform the world. They were in fact between Scylla and Charybdis: either immediate irrelevancy or long-term failure. They chose the latter, hoping it was avoidable. Who would not?

I want to argue that today, paradoxically, the very failure of the antisystemic movements collectively, including the failure of the national liberation movements to be truly and fully liberatory, provides the most hopeful element for positive developments in the coming twenty-five to fifty years. To appreciate this curious view, we must come to terms with what is happening in the present. We are living not the final triumph of world capitalism but its first and only true crisis.[2]

I want to point to four long-term trends, each of which is moving near to its asymptote and each of which is devastating from the point of view of capitalists pursuing the endless accumulation of capital. The first, and the least discussed of these trends, is the deruralization of the world. Only two hundred years ago, 80 to 90 percent of the world's population, and indeed of each country's population, was rural. Today worldwide, we are below 50 percent and rapidly going down. Whole areas of the world have rural populations less than 20 percent, some less than 5 percent. Well, so what, you may say? Are not urbanization and modernity virtually synonymous? Is this not what we hoped would happen with the so-called industrial revolution? Yes, that is indeed the commonplace sociological generalization we all have learned.

This is, however, to misunderstand how capitalism works. Surplus-value is always divided between those who have the capital and those who perform the labor. The terms of this division are in the final analysis political, the strength of the bargaining power of each side. Capitalists live with a basic contradiction. If worldwide the terms of remuneration of labor are too low, it limits the market, and, as Adam Smith already told us, the extent of the division of labor is a function of the extent of the market. But if the terms are too high, it limits the profits. Workers, for their part, naturally always want to increase their share and struggle politically to achieve this. Over time, wherever labor is concentrated, workers are able to make their syndical weight felt, and this leads eventually to one of the profit squeezes that have periodically occurred throughout the history of the capitalist world-economy. Capitalists can fight workers only up to a point, because after this point too much reduction of real wages threatens to cut into effective world demand for their products. The recurrent solution has been to allow the better-paid workers to supply the market and to draw into the world workforce new strata of persons who are politically weak and are willing for many reasons to accept very low wages, thereby reducing overall production costs. Over five centuries, capitalists have consistently located such persons in rural zones and transformed them into urban proletarians; however, these people remain low-cost workers only for a while, at which point others must be drawn into the labor supply. The deruralization of the world threatens this essential process and thereby threatens the ability of capitalists to maintain the level of their global profits.

The second long-term trend is what is called the ecological crisis. From the point of view of capitalists, this should be called the threat of ending the externalization of costs. Here again we have a critical process. A crucial element in the level of profits has always been that capitalists do not pay the totality of costs of their products. Some costs are "externalized," that is, spread pro rata over the whole of larger populations, eventually over the whole of the world population. When a river is polluted by a chemical plant, the clean-up (if there is one) is normally assumed by taxpayers. What the ecologists have been noticing is the exhaustion of zones to pollute, of trees to be cut down, and so forth. The world faces the choice of ecological disaster or of forcing the internalization of costs. But forcing the internalization of costs threatens seriously the ability to accumulate capital.

The third negative trend for capitalists is the democratization of the world. We have mentioned previously the program of concessions begun in the European zone in the nineteenth century, which we have these days labeled generically the welfare state. These involve expenditures on a social wage: money for children and the aged, education, health facilities. This could work for a long time for two reasons: the recipients had modest demands at first, and only the European workers were receiving this social wage. Today, workers everywhere expect it, and the level of their demands is significantly higher than it was even fifty years ago. Ultimately, these moneys can only come at the cost of accumulating capital. Democratization is not and has never been in the interest of capitalists.

The fourth factor is the reversal of the trend in state power. For four hundred years, the states have been increasing their power, both internally and externally, as the adjustment mechanisms of the world-system. This has been absolutely crucial for capital despite its anti-state rhetoric. States have guaranteed order, but just as importantly they have guaranteed monopolies, which are the one and only path to serious accumulation of capital.[3]

But the states can no longer perform their task as adjustment mechanisms. The democratization of the world and the ecological crisis have placed an impossible level of demands on the state structures, which are all suffering a "fiscal crisis." But if they reduce expenditures in order to meet the fiscal crises, they also reduce their ability to adjust the system. It is a vicious circle, in which each failure of the state leads to less willingness to entrust it with tasks, and therefore to a generic tax revolt. But as the state becomes less solvent, it can perform existing tasks even less well. We have entered into this vortex already.

It is here that the failure of the movements enters in. It has been the movements, more than anything else, that have in fact sustained the states politically, especially once they came to power. They served as the moral guarantor of the state structures. Insofar as the movements are losing their claims to support, because they can no longer offer hope and certainty, the mass of the population is becoming profoundly anti-state. But states are needed most of all not by reformers and not by movements but by capitalists. The capitalist world-system cannot function well without strong states (of course, always some stronger than others) within the framework of a strong interstate system. But capitalists have never been able to put forward this claim ideologically because their legitimacy derives from economic productivity and expansion of general welfare and not from either order or the guarantee of profits. In the last century, capitalists have relied ever increasingly on the movements to perform on their behalf the function of legitimating the state structures.

Today the movements are no longer able to do this. And, were they to try, they could not pull their populations along with them. Thus we see springing forth everywhere nonstate "groups" that are assuming the role of protecting themselves and even of providing for their welfare. This is the path of global disorder down which we have been heading. It is the sign of disintegration of the modern world-system, of capitalism as a civilization.

You can rest assured that those who have privilege will not sit back and watch this privilege go under without trying to rescue it. But you can rest equally assured that they cannot rescue it merely by adjusting the system once again, for all the reasons I have adduced. The world is in transition. Out of chaos will come a new order, different from the one we now know. Different, but not necessarily better.

That is where the movements come in once again. Those who have privilege will try to construct a new kind of historical system that will be unequal, hierarchical, and stable. They have the advantage of power, money, and the service of much intelligence. They will assuredly come up with something clever and workable. Can the movements, reinvigorated, match them? We are amid a bifurcation of our system. The fluctuations are enormous, and little pushes will determine which way the process moves. The task of the liberation movements, no longer necessarily national liberation movements, is to take serious stock of the crisis of the system, the impasse of their past strategy, and the force of the genie of world popular discontent that has been unleashed precisely by the collapse of the old movements. It is a moment for utopistics, for intensive, rigorous analysis of historical alternatives. It is a moment when social scientists have something important to contribute, assuming they wish to do so. But it requires for social scientists as well an unthinking of their past concepts, derived from the same nineteenth-century situation that resulted in the strategies adopted by the antisystemic movements.

Above all, it is a task neither on the one hand for a day or a week nor on the other hand for centuries. It is a task precisely for the next twenty-five to fifty years, one whose outcome will be entirely the consequence of the kind of input we are ready and able to put into it.

Chapter 3

The Rise of East Asia,
or The World-System in
the Twenty-First Century

Since about 1970, the so-called rise of East Asia has been a major topic of discussion among those interested in the evolution of the world-system, whether their emphasis was on the world-economy or on geopolitics. What most people have had in mind is, first, the extraordinary rise on all economic indicators of Japan, compared even with the 1960s; second, the subsequent rise of the so-called four dragons; and, most recently, the continuing pattern of economic growth in Southeast Asia and the People's Republic of China. The empirical reality seems quite clear; it is primarily its significance that is debated.

This worldwide discussion has centered around two questions: (1) What is the explanation of this growth, especially since it seemed to occur primarily at a point in time when growth elsewhere was much less significant, and in some regions even negative? (2) What does the economic growth of the East Asian region portend for the world-system in the twenty-first century?

I propose to discuss these two questions successively, as ways into the analysis of the structure and trajectory of the modern world-system. Structure and trajectory are of course intimately linked. Hence to discuss the trajectory, it is necessary to start with a review of some of the general premises about the structure of the capitalist world-economy. I will here summarize views that I have explicated at length elsewhere by means of a list of the propositions most relevant to these questions:

Keynote address at a symposium entitled "Perspective of the Capitalist World-System in the Beginning of the Twenty-First Century," sponsored by the Perspectives on International Studies project, Institute of International Studies, Meiji Gakuin University, Tokyo, January 23–24, 1997.

- The modern world-system is a capitalist world-economy, which means that it is governed by the drive for the endless accumulation of capital, sometimes called the law of value.

- This world-system came into existence in the course of the sixteenth century, and its original division of labor included in its bounds much of Europe (but not the Russian or Ottoman Empires) and parts of the Americas.

- This world-system expanded over the centuries, successively incorporating other parts of the world into its division of labor.

- East Asia was the last large region to be incorporated, and this occurred only in the middle of the nineteenth century, after which the modern world-system could be said to have become truly worldwide in scope, the first world-system ever to include the entire globe.

- The capitalist world-system is constituted by a world-economy dominated by core-peripheral relations and a political structure consisting of sovereign states within the framework of an interstate system.

- The fundamental contradictions of the capitalist system have been expressed within the systemic process by a series of cyclical rhythms, which have served to contain these contradictions.

- The two most important cyclical rhythms have been the 50/60-year Kondratieff cycles in which the primary sources of profit alternate between the sphere of production and the financial arena, and the 100/150-year hegemonic cycles consisting of the rise and decline of successive guarantors of global order, each one with its particular pattern of control.

- The cyclical rhythms resulted in regular slow-moving but significant geographical shifts in the loci of accumulation and power, without however changing the fundamental relations of inequality within the system.

- These cycles were never perfectly symmetrical, but rather each new cycle brought about small but significant structural shifts in particular directions that constitute the secular trends of the system.

- The modern world-system, like all systems, is finite in duration and will come to an end when its secular trends reach a point such that the fluctuations of the system become sufficiently wide and erratic that they can no longer ensure the renewed viability of the system's institutions. When this point is reached, a bifurcation will occur, and via a period of (chaotic) transition the system will come to be replaced by one or several other systems.

Within this set of premises, one can analyze the so-called rise of East Asia quite easily. It occurred during a Kondratieff B-phase, a period that was also the beginning of the decline (or B-phase) of U.S. hegemony. Whether this same period constituted also the beginning of the age of transition is the subject of strenuous debate.[1] This description allows us to discuss more clearly the two questions at hand: the explanation of the present-past situation of East Asia; and the import of East Asia's rise for the future.

What can we say about Kondratieff B-phases in general? They normally have several general features if one compares them to A-phases: profits from production are down, and large capitalists tend to shift their profit-seeking activities to the financial realm, which is the realm of speculation. Worldwide, wage employment is down. The squeeze on production profits leads to significant relocation of production activity, the priority of low transactions costs yielding to the priority of reduced wage levels and more efficient management. The squeeze on employment leads to acute competition between the states that are centers of accumulation, which seek to export the unemployment to each other to the degree that they can. This leads in turn to fluctuating exchange rates. It is not difficult to show that all this has been occurring in the period from about 1967–73 to today.[2]

For the majority of areas of the world, such a Kondratieff B-phase is perceived as a downturn, or "bad times," in comparison with the previous A-phase. However, it is never the case that such a period is bad for everyone. For one thing, large capitalists, or at least some large capitalists, may be able to find alternative profitable outlets such that their individual level of accumulation rises. And second, since one of the features of a Kondratieff B-phase is the relocation of productive activity, it is normally the case that some zone in the world-system sees a significant improvement in its overall economic standing, and therefore perceives the period as "good times."

I speak of "some economic zone" because it is seldom inscribed beforehand exactly which zone this will be, and usually at first several zones compete vigorously to be the prime beneficiary of this relocation. But it is also normally the case that only one such zone is in fact able to do very well, since there is only so much production activity to relocate, and there are economic advantages for producers in concentrating the relocation in one area. The basic picture thus is one of opportunity for several zones, but great success for only one of them. I remind you that as recently as the 1970s, when the term NICs (newly industrialized countries) was invented, most commentators listed four countries as the most significant examples: Mexico, Brazil, South Korea, and Taiwan. But by the 1980s, Mexico and Brazil began to be dropped from the list of examples, and in the 1990s we hear talk only of "the rise of East Asia." It is thus clear that it is East Asia that has been the great beneficiary of the geographical restructuring of this Kondratieff B-phase.

Of course, we must also explain why it is that East Asia was the great beneficiary rather than, say, Brazil or South Asia. Some scholars attribute the present rise of East Asia to its history over the past five hundred years: either the Meiji Revolution, accounted for in turn by the commercial development of the Edo period (Kawakatsu Heita), or the China-centered tributary system (Takeshi Hamashita). However, it can be plausibly argued that, as of 1945, the economic situation of Brazil or South Asia was not in fact all that different from that of East Asia, and that therefore one could reasonably have expected either of them to have made a surge forward in the post-1945 world. The great difference between East Asia on the one hand and both Brazil and South Asia on the other was the geography of the Cold War. East Asia was on the front line, and the other two were not. Hence the view of the United States was quite different. Japan was a very great economic beneficiary of the Korean War as well as of direct U.S. assistance. Both South Korea and Taiwan were supported (and indulged) economically, politically, and militarily for Cold War reasons. This difference in the 1945–70 period translated itself into the crucial advantage for the 1970–1995 period.

The economic consequence of the rise of East Asia has been to transform the economic geography of the postwar world. In the 1950s, the United States was the only major center of capital accumulation. By the 1960s, western Europe had become again a major center. And by the 1970s, Japan (and more generally East Asia) had become the third. We had arrived at the so-called triad. The rise of western Europe and East Asia meant necessarily a lessened role for U.S.-based economic structures, and the finances of the United States state suffered accordingly. In the 1980s, the United States acquired a huge external debt to pay for its military Keynesianism, and in the 1990s the United States has given priority to reducing state expenditure. This has had in turn a major impact on its ability to conduct military activities. For example, the U.S. military victory in the Gulf War was dependent on the fact that its forces were financed by four other states: Saudi Arabia, Kuwait, Germany, and Japan.

If one looks at a somewhat longer period, the two centuries that run from 1789 to 1989, one observes another fundamental reality of the modern world-system, and here also East Asia played a notable role. It is the story of the political stabilization of the world-system. The story starts with the French Revolution.[3] The French Revolution transformed the capitalist world-system by its cultural impact. The most significant lasting consequence of the revolutionary turmoil and its Napoleonic aftermath was the widespread acceptance, for the first time, of two basic themes associated with it: the normality of political change and hence its fundamental legitimation; and the view that a state's sovereignty was incarnated not in the person of the ruler or in the legislature but rather in the "people," and hence the denial of moral legitimacy to nondemocratic regimes.

These were truly revolutionary and dangerous ideas, and threatened all established authority. Ever since, all those who enjoy privilege within the existing system have had to contend with these ideas and to seek to contain their effects. The principal way in which this has been done has been by the erection and propagation of ideologies, which are in fact political strategies to deal with the massive spread of these values. Historically, three major ideologies were put forth, as modes of containment. The first, most immediate, and most obvious was conservatism, which sought initially simply to reject outright these populist values as heretical. Liberalism arose as an ideology to counter conservatism, its proponents considering conservatism to be a rigid and self-defeating response to the challenge. In its place, liberals argued the necessity of channeling these populist values, by accepting their legitimacy in theory but slowing down the pace of realizing them in practice. They did this by insisting that the rational implementation of these values required the intermediation of specialists. Radicalism/socialism arose as the third ideology, a breakaway from liberalism. The radicals were appalled by the timidity of the liberals, and deeply suspicious of the motives and intentions of the specialists. They insisted therefore on the importance of popular control of the administration of change. They argued further that only rapid transformation could stem the underlying popular pressure to destabilize social life and make possible the re-creation of a harmonious social reality.

The battle between the advocates of the three ideologies has been the central political story of the nineteenth and twentieth centuries. Two things are clear about these battles in retrospect. The first is that none of the ideologies *in practice* was anti-state, despite the rhetoric that all three employed. The movements formed in the name of these ideologies all sought political power in the states, and they all pursued their political aims by using and augmenting state power when they had it. The result was a continuous and significant increase in the administrative apparatus and effective reach of the state machineries, and in the scope of the legislative interventions that governments made. The justification offered has regularly been the implementation of the values made popular by the French Revolution.

The second thing to note is that for a long period — to be precise, between 1848 and 1968 — liberalism was the dominant ideology of the three and put its stamp on the geoculture of the world-system. This can be seen in the fact that after 1848 (and until 1968) both conservatives and radicals modified their views in practice, and even in rhetoric, to offer versions of their ideology that turned out to be mere variants of the political program of the liberal center. The differences between the two of them and the liberals, originally ones of fundamental principle, were increasingly reduced to arguments about the rapidity of change: slow if possible, said the conservatives; fast if possible, said the radicals; and at just the right speed, decreed the liberals. This reduction of the debates to one more about the pace of change than about its content is the source of the complaint, which became ever more accentuated over the period, about the minimal difference that the repeated changes in government almost everywhere have really made, if analyzed over a medium term, even when such changes were proclaimed as "revolutionary."

To be sure, this is not the whole political story of the nineteenth and twentieth centuries. We need also to explain how it is that the populist ideas that had gotten such a strong hold in the wake of the French Revolution, a hold strong enough to force all major political forces eventually to pay lip service to these values, could have been so well contained in practice. For it was not at all easy to do this. The same period (1848–1968), which I have suggested was the era of the triumph of liberalism within the geoculture of the world-system (and therefore the triumph of a program of very moderate political change controlled by elites), was also after all the period of the birth, rise, and yes triumph of the so-called Old Left. Now the members of this Old Left had always asserted that their objectives were antisystemic, that is, that they were continuing the battle of the French Revolution to achieve, but this time truly and fully, the trinity of liberty, equality, and fraternity.

While the values of the French Revolution had indeed become widespread in the early nineteenth century, the extensive and growing inequalities of the real world made it in fact extremely difficult for popular forces to organize politically. At first, they had neither votes nor money nor trained cadres. It was a long, arduous, and uphill battle to create the organizational structures that eventually would become a global network of radical-popular movements.

The second half of the nineteenth century saw the slow creation of bureaucratic structures — trade unions, socialist and labor parties, and nationalist parties — primarily in Europe and North America at this point, but there were already some in the non-European world. At this stage, to get even one person elected to Parliament or to win even one important strike seemed an achievement. The antisystemic organizations concentrated on creating a cadre of militants, mobilizing larger groups for collective activities, and educating them for political action.

This period was simultaneously the moment of the last great geographical expansion of the world-economy, including the incorporation of East Asia. It was the moment as well of the last great direct political subordination of the periphery — the colonization of Africa, Southeast Asia, and the Pacific. It was in addition the moment of the first great demonstration of the real possibilities of technological advances that could affect the quality of everyday life: the railroad, then the automobile and airplane; the telegraph and telephone; the electric light; the radio; household appliances — all of which seemed dazzling and seemed to confirm the plausibility of the liberal promise of the gradual improvement of the conditions for everyone.

If one puts these elements together — the effective organization of the working classes in Europe and North America and their entry (however marginal) into ordinary parliamentary politics; the beginning of a material payoff for the European working classes; and the acme of European dominance of the non-European world — one has no difficulty understanding why the threefold liberal political program for the European working classes (universal suffrage; the welfare state; and the creation of a national identity, one that was combined with White racism) was able by the early twentieth century to tame these European dangerous classes.

It is precisely at this point, however, that the "Orient" raised its political head in the world-system. The Japanese defeat of Russia in 1905 was the first sign that there could be a rollback of European expansion. The Chinese Revolution of 1911 commenced the process of the reconstitution of the Middle Kingdom, the world's oldest and demographically largest entity. In a sense, East Asia, last to be incorporated, was first to begin the process of bringing down European triumphalism.[4] The great African-American leader W. E. B. Du Bois had said in 1900 that the twentieth century was to be the century of the color line. He was proved entirely right. The dangerous classes of Europe might have been tamed, but the much larger dangerous classes of the non-European world posed a problem for world order for the twentieth century to replace the nineteenth-century dangers that had been resolved.

The liberals made a valiant, and at first seemingly successful, attempt to repeat their successful strategy and to tame the dangerous classes of the non-European world as well. On the one hand, the national liberation movements of the non-European world gained organizational and political strength and put increasing pressure on the colonial and imperialist powers. This process reached a point of maximum strength in the twenty-five years following the end of the Second World War. On the other hand, the liberals offered a world program of the self-determination of nations (the parallel to universal suffrage) and the economic development of underdeveloped nations (the parallel to the welfare state), which they argued met the essential demands of the non-European world.

Throughout the world, in the period 1945–1970, the Old Left came to power basically on the basis of these liberal political programs. In Europe/North America the Old Left obtained the full political legitimation of its parties and the implementation of full employment and a welfare state that went much further than anything that had been constructed previously. In the rest of the world, national liberation and/or Communist movements came to power in a large number of countries, achieving their immediate political objectives and launching a program of national economic development.

What the members of the Old Left had achieved by this point was, however, not at all what they had originally set out to achieve in the mid–nineteenth century. They had not brought down the system. They had not obtained a truly democratic, egalitarian world. What they had achieved was at most half a pie, exactly what the liberals had set out to offer them in the first half of the nineteenth century. If they were "tamed" at this point, that is, if they were ready to work within the world-system pursuing developmentalist, reformist objectives, it is not because they were satisfied with half a pie. Far from it. It was that the popular forces truly believed that they were en route to getting the whole pie. It was because of the incrementalist hope (and faith) of the mass of the populations that their children would inherit the world that the movements were able to channel their revolutionary ardors into this reformist cul-de-sac. For if the populations had such a hope and faith, it was not at all based on the promises of the liberals/centrists who were hoping to contain their democratic ardors and in whom the populations had little trust, but it was based rather on two other considerations: one, the fact that the popular movements had in fact obtained half a pie through a century of struggle and, two, the fact that their own movements were promising them that history was on their side and therefore, implicitly, that incrementalism was indeed possible.

The genius of the liberals was that they had been able to constrain the popular forces on the one hand by flimflam (the hope that the half a pie they offered would one day be the whole pie) and on the other hand by transforming the movements of their opponents (and in particular their radical/socialist opponents) into their avatars, which in effect were spreading the liberal doctrine of incremental reform as managed by specialist/experts. The limitations of the liberals were nonetheless the same as their genius. One day, it would inevitably become clear that half a pie could never be the whole pie, since if the popular forces were given the whole pie, capitalism could no longer exist. And on that day the movements of the Old Left, the radical/socialist avatars of liberalism, would inevitably lose their credibility.

The day of which we have been speaking has already come. It is called 1968/1989. And here once again we find the particularity of East Asia. The world revolution of 1968 struck everywhere — in the United States and France, in Germany and Italy, in Czechoslovakia and Poland, in Mexico and Senegal, in Tunisia and India, in China and Japan. The specific griefs and demands were particular to each place, but the two repeated themes were these: one, a denunciation of the world-system dominated by the United States, in collusion with its rhetorical opponent, the USSR; and, two, a critique of the Old Left for its failures, and in particular for the fact that its multiple movements had become mere avatars of the liberal doctrine.

The immediate dramatic effects of 1968 were suppressed or were frittered away in the two or three following years. But the world revolution of 1968 had one lasting immediate effect, and one effect that came to be felt in the succeeding two decades. The immediate lasting effect was the destruction of the liberal consensus and the liberation of both conservatives and radicals from the siren of liberalism. After 1968, the world-system reverted to the ideological picture of 1815–48 — a struggle between the three ideologies. Conservatism has been resurgent, often under the false name of neoliberalism. It has proved itself so strong that, far from it presenting itself as an avatar of liberalism today, it is liberalism that is beginning to present itself as an avatar of conservatism. At first, radicalism/socialism sought to revive itself in various guises: as the multiple, short-lived Maoisms of the early 1970s and as the so-called New Left movements (Greens, identity movements, radical feminism, and others) that have been longer lived but that have not entirely shed the image of being avatars of the pre-1968 liberalism. The collapse of the Communisms in east-central Europe and in the ex-USSR was simply the last phase in the critique of the false radicalism that was an avatar of the pre-1968 liberalism.

The second post-1968 change, the one that took two decades to be fully realized, was the loss of popular faith in incrementalism, or rather in the Old Left movements that had preached it in a revolutionary guise. The hope (and faith) that the children of the mass of the populations would inherit the world has been shattered, or at least severely weakened. The two decades since 1968 have been precisely the moment of the latest Kondratieff B-phase. The period 1945–70 had been the most spectacular A-phase in the history of the capitalist world-economy and was also the moment of the coming to power of all sorts of antisystemic movements across the globe. The two together had admirably fed the illusion (the hope and faith) that all parts of a capitalist world-economy could in fact "develop," meaning that the popular forces could look forward to an early drastic reduction in the economic and social polarities of the world-economy. The subsequent letdown of the B-phase was therefore all the more dramatic.

What this Kondratieff B-phase made clear was the narrow limits within which the so-called economic development of underdeveloped nations could occur. Industrialization, even when possible, was no remedy per se. For most of the industrialization of the peripheral and semiperipheral zones has been a hand-me-down industrialization, the shift of activities that could no longer be monopolized and therefore could no longer give rise to very high profit rates from the erstwhile core zone to other countries. This is true, for example, of steel production, not to speak of textiles, which in the late eighteenth century had been a leading industry. This is true of those aspects of the service sector that are most routinized.

The game of capitalists jumping from one activity to another in search of relatively monopolizable, highly profitable sectors has not ended. Meanwhile, the overall economic and social polarization has not only not diminished; it has been rapidly intensifying. As fast as the so-called underdeveloped countries or regions run, the others run faster. To be sure, some individual countries and regions may shift positions, but the rise of some has always meant the relative decline of others, to maintain the same approximate percentages in the various zones of the world-economy.

The immediate impact of the Kondratieff B-phase was felt most sharply in the most defenseless areas, such as Africa. But it was felt quite severely as well in Latin America, the Middle East, east and central Europe, the ex-USSR, and South Asia. It was even felt, albeit much less severely, in North America and western Europe. The one zone that substantially escaped from the negative impact was East Asia. Of course, when one says that a geographic region was affected negatively, it does not mean that all its residents lost in equal proportions. Not at all. Within each of these areas, there was increased internal polarization, which means that even in those areas the Kondratieff B-phase has been very positive for a minority of the populations in terms of their income levels and possibilities of capital accumulation; but not for the majority. Again, East Asia, or at least parts of East Asia, has seen less of this increased internal polarization.

Let us ponder the political consequences of the world economic difficulties of the period 1970–95. First and foremost, it has meant the serious discrediting of the Old Left, the erstwhile antisystemic movements — the national liberation movements in the ex-colonial world, the populist movements in Latin America, but also the Communist parties in Europe (east and west) and the social-democratic/labor movements in western Europe and North America. Most of them have felt that, in order to survive electorally, they needed to become even more centrist than before. Their mass appeal has as a result seriously diminished, and their self-confidence has declined to the same degree.

In any case, they can scarcely any longer serve as guarantors of liberal reformism for impatient and impoverished populations. They are therefore unable to serve as a mechanism of control (previously they were the principal mechanism of control) of the political reactions of such populations, many of whom have turned elsewhere — to political apathy (which, however, is always a temporary way station), to fundamentalist movements of all kinds, and in some cases to neofascist movements. The point is that these populations have become volatile once again, and therefore dangerous once again from the point of view of the privileged strata in the world-system.

The second political consequence has been that, across the world, populations have as a result turned against the state. They have, to be sure, been considerably encouraged in this attitude by resurgent conservative forces who are seeking to take advantage of the opportunity, as they see it, to destroy the last vestiges of the liberal/centrist political program that had dominated world politics from 1848 to 1968. But these populations, by taking this position, are for the most part not expressing their support of some reactionary utopia. Rather they are expressing their disbelief in the idea that incrementalist reformism is any solution for their miseries. And thus they have turned against the state, which has been the instrument par excellence of such incrementalist reformism.

The anti-state attitude is reflected not merely in a rejection of the state's role in economic redistribution, but also in a general negative view of taxation levels and of the efficacy and motivation of the state's security forces. It is reflected as well in a renewed active disparagement of the experts/specialists who had for so long been the intermediaries of liberal reformism. It is expressed in an increased open flouting of legal processes, and indeed of criminality as a form of protest. The politics of such anti-statism is cumulative. The populations complain of inadequate security and begin to take security functions back into private hands. They are consequently ever more reticent to pay the taxes that are assessed. Each such step weakens the state machinery and makes it still more difficult for the states to fulfill their functions, which makes the original complaints seem still more valid, leading to still more rejection of the state. We are living today in the first period of significant decline of state power in the various states that has occurred since the creation of the modern world-system.

The only area that has not yet seen the spread of anti-statism is precisely East Asia, since it is the only area that has not yet lived through a serious decline in economic prospects during the period 1970–95, and therefore the only area where disillusionment with incrementalist reformism has not taken place. The relative internal order of the East Asian states reinforces the sense of the rise of East Asia, both in East Asia and elsewhere. It may indeed also be the explanation of the fact that the East Asian Communist states are the only ones that have so far escaped the collapse that the others experienced circa 1989.

I have tried thus far to account for the present/past of East Asia within the world-system. What does this portend for the future? Nothing is less sure. There are basically two possible scenarios. The world-system can continue more or less as before and enter into another set of cyclical changes. Or the world-system has reached a point of crisis and therefore will see drastic structural change, an explosion or an implosion, that will end with the constitution of some new kind of historical system. The consequences for East Asia might well be different in the two scenarios.

If we follow scenario number 1, and assume that whatever is going on in the world-system right now is merely a variant of the situation that occurs repeatedly with the early stages of the decline of a hegemonic power, then we may expect the following "normal" set of developments, which I will resume briefly in a few quick propositions:[5]

- A new Kondratieff A-phase should begin shortly, based on the new leading products that have come to the fore in the last twenty years.

- There will be an acute competition between Japan, the European Union, and the United States to become the primary producers of these new leading products.

- There will simultaneously be the beginning of a competition between Japan and the European Union to be the successor hegemonic power to the United States.

- Since a triad in ferocious mutual competition usually reduces to a duo, the most likely combination is Japan plus the United States versus the European Union, a combination that is undergirded by both economic and paradoxically cultural considerations.

- This pairing would return us to the classical situation of a sea-air power supported by the ex-hegemonic power versus a land-based power, and suggests for both geopolitical and economic reasons the eventual success of Japan.

- Each member of the triad would continue to reinforce its economic and political links with particular regions: the United States with the Americas, Japan with East and Southeast Asia, the European Union with east-central Europe and the former USSR.

- The most difficult political problem in this geopolitical regrouping would be the inclusion of China in the Japan-U.S. zone and of Russia in the E.U. zone, but there are no doubt terms on which both of these matters could be arranged.

In such a scenario, we could expect considerable tension between the European Union and East Asia about fifty years from now, and a probable triumph of East Asia. Whether at that point China would be able to wrest from Japan the dominant role within this new structure is very difficult to say.

I do not wish to spend further time on this scenario because I do not expect it to occur. Or rather I believe that it has indeed begun and will continue, but will not come to the "natural" conclusion one might expect because of the underlying structural crisis of the capitalist world-system as a system. Here too, I shall summarize my views succinctly because I have elaborated them elsewhere in some detail:[6]

- We cannot be sure whether the present Kondratieff B-phase will end with a bang or a whimper, that is, whether there will be a deflationary crash or not. I do not think it much matters, except that the crash would dramatize the issue. In any case, I believe we are probably moving into a deflationary era, swiftly or slowly.

- Restarting a Kondratieff A-phase requires, among other things, expanding real effective demand. That means that some sector of the world's populations must obtain buying power over and above what they presently have. This segment could be disproportionately located in East Asia.

- In any case, an upswing will require considerable productive investment, and it is easy to predict that this will be located disproportionately again in the North, as such investment as is going to peripheral and semi-peripheral zones in search of cheap labor will diminish significantly. The result will be a further marginalization of the South.

- The deruralization of the world has virtually eliminated the traditional compensatory mechanism of opening up new primary production zones, and therefore the worldwide cost of labor will rise to the detriment of capital accumulation.

- The serious ecological dilemmas will create enormous pressure on governments either to draw from other expenditures to handle the costs of restoring a sufficient level of biotic equilibrium and preventing a further deterioration or to impose on productive enterprises the internalization of such costs. The latter alternative will place enormous constraints on the accumulation of capital. The former alternative will require either higher taxation on enterprises with the same result or higher taxes/lowered services for the mass of the population with very negative political consequences, given the disillusionment with the state that I have discussed previously.

- The level of popular demand on state services, especially for education, health, and income floors, will not diminish, despite the turn against the state. This is the price of "democratization."

- The excluded South will become politically far more restive than at present, and the level of global disorder will increase markedly.

- The collapse of the Old Left will have eliminated the most effective moderating forces on these disintegrative forces.

We can anticipate from this a longish period of dark times, the increase of civil wars (local, regional, and perhaps worldwide). And here the scenario ends. For the outcome of this process will force the "search for order" in contradictory directions (a bifurcation), whose outcome is inherently unpredictable. Furthermore, the geography of this conflict is not easy to ascertain in advance. Some areas may well profit from it more than others, or suffer from it more than others. But which? East Asia? I cannot say.

So, has there been a rise of East Asia? Undoubtedly. But for how long? a decade? a century? a millennium? And is a rise of East Asia good for the world, or only for East Asia? Nothing, I repeat, is less clear.

Coda

The So-called Asian Crisis
Geopolitics in the *Longue Durée*

Politicians, journalists, and too many scholars are repeatedly over-whelmed by the latest headlines. This is unfortunate because it leads to curious and unsatisfactory analyses of the meaning and importance of even large events. Thus it has been with the collapse of the Com-munisms; thus it has been with the geopolitical challenge of Saddam Hussein; and thus it is with the so-called Asian financial crisis. To make sense of this "event," it is useful to have recourse to the multiple social times that Fernand Braudel insisted are the crucible within which we may be able to analyze reality realistically.

Let me start with an interesting editorial comment from the *Financial Times* (February 16, 1998, p. 15) on the situation:

> Why have [the east Asian countries] sunk now? A big part of the ex-planation has to do with the fickleness of external investors, who first behaved as if east Asian economies could do nothing wrong and, shortly thereafter, as if they could do nothing right....
>
> Panic-stricken lenders. The inflows offered more temptation than in-experienced businessmen, guaranteed financial institutions, or corrupt and incompetent politicians could resist. The outflows worsened the sub-sequent punishment; a domestic asset bubble can be managed by domestic institutions. As the capital flooded out, exchange rates collapsed and bankruptcy engulfed the private sector, countries found themselves at the mercy of panic-stricken private lenders and demanding official ones....
>
> This is a world of panic. Once panic begins, each investor rationally wants to escape before all the others. Vastly more damage is then done than the underlying economic situation would warrant.

There are several things to be noted about this analysis. The financial slump in East Asia is looked at from the point of view of investors,

Address at the International Studies Association meeting, Minneapolis, March 20, 1998.

primarily external investors, and the editorial suggests that a prime consideration in explaining the extent of the problem was their panic. If
one reads closely, one sees that we are talking especially of comparatively smaller investors, who have the least political clout and the most
reason to need "to escape before all the others." The second thing to
note is that geopolitical considerations do not seem to enter the analysis. The third thing to note is the almost left-wing policy conclusion
of the *Financial Times:*

> The wisdom of over-hasty integration of emerging economies into global
> financial markets must be reconsidered. Foreign direct investment is in-
> valuable. But easy private-sector access to short-term borrowing can be
> lethal. Only the prepared and skillful can navigate this ocean. Lacking a
> true global lender of last resort, fragile emerging economies should stay
> close to shore.

First, the article attacks recent neoliberal wisdom by speaking of "over-
hasty integration of emerging economies into global financial markets."
Then it suggests that the world-economy (always? only at present?) is an
"ocean" that only "the prepared and skillful can navigate." Beware, I suppose, the "inexperienced businessmen, guaranteed financial institutions,
or corrupt and incompetent politicians." Perhaps the corrupt politicians
need to be more competent. Finally, the conclusion notes the absence of
a "true global lender of last resort," an allusion (I would suggest) to the
structural financial weakness of the United States, which, far from being
a global lender of last resort, is a global borrower dependent currently
on Japan.

For all its limitations, this editorial is sounder than many a prognostic
on the current situation because it is bereft of the illusions that all that
is needed is a little more IMF mercurochrome and because, above all, it
underlines the issue of "panic." Panic is never an issue of the so-called
real economy. Panic occurs when there is speculation, that is to say, when
large groups of people are making money not primarily out of the profits from production but out of financial manipulations. The alternating
or cyclical relationship between an emphasis on profits derived from
production and one on profits derived from financial manipulations is a
basic element of the capitalist world-economy[1] and reminds us that the
first place we should look for an explanation of what is going on is in
the fact that we are located within a B-phase of a Kondratieff cycle, one
that has in fact been going on since 1967/73.

It would be worthwhile to remind ourselves of some recent economic history of the world-system. We can look at what has happened since 1967/73 in two zones: on the one hand, in the core countries, which are the United States, western Europe (collectively), and Japan (Japan, not East Asia); and, on the other hand, in the semiperipheral and peripheral areas, which include the so-called East Asian tigers, China, and Southeast Asia. Let us start with the core zone. The basic meaning of a Kondratieff B-phase is that there is too much production for the available effective demand, so that the rate of profit from production is down. An immediate global solution might be to reduce production. But who wants to put himself forward as the sacrificial loser? The real reaction ordinarily, since the rate of profit is down, is for aggressive producers either to seek to *increase* production (thus maintaining their overall real profit, albeit at a reduced *rate* of profit) or to relocate to an area of lower real wage rates, thereby increasing their rate of profit. Increasing production (the first solution) is of course globally counterproductive and collapses after a while. Relocation (the second solution) does solve the global problem for longer than increasing production, but only until it too leads to increasing the global production without simultaneously increasing the effective demand, or at least increasing it sufficiently.

This is what has been happening over the past thirty years. Global production of all sorts (automobiles, steel, electronics, among others, and more recently computer software) has been relocating from North America, western Europe, and Japan to other areas. This has led to considerable unemployment in the core zones. The unemployment, however, does not need to be evenly spread. Indeed, a typical feature of a Kondratieff downturn is the effort of governments in core zones to export unemployment to each other. If we look at the pattern of the past thirty years, the United States suffered most at the beginning, in the 1970s and especially the early 1980s; then it was Europe's turn and still is; and only recently has it been that of Japan, whose difficulties since 1990 have permitted the U.S. employment rates to go up again.

In the meantime, investors everywhere have been engaged in all kinds of financial speculations. The OPEC oil price rises of the 1970s led to global accumulations that were recycled as loans to Third World countries. These loans eventually impoverished the borrowers, but, for a decade or so, they did maintain core zone incomes globally, until the Ponzi game finally gave out with the so-called debt crisis of the early

1980s. This manipulation was followed by a second game, the combination in the 1980s of borrowing by the U.S. government (the military Keynesianism of Reagan) and by private capitalists (junk bonds), until that Ponzi game also gave out with the so-called crisis of the U.S. deficit.[2] The Ponzi game of the 1990s has been the inflows of global capital via "short-term borrowing" to East and Southeast Asia, which, as the *Financial Times* says, "can be lethal."

In all of this, of course, some people have made a lot of money (and others have lost their shirts). And one level down from the great capitalists, there is the level of overpaid yuppies who have also done very well, provided they were in the right country in the right decade. The point is, however, that, by and large, most of the profit has been made from financial manipulations. Probably the only arena in which significant profits have been made out of production has been in computers, a "new" industry, and even here we are reaching the point of overproduction and hence of a falling rate of profit, at least in hardware. If we turn to the peripheral and semiperipheral countries as a group, a Kondratieff B-phase offers both disaster and opportunity. The disastrous side is the reduction of market for their exports, especially their primary products, because of the reduction in global production that occurs. The oil price increase also affected them severely, in that, while it resulted in reduced world production, it also resulted in increased costs of imports for non-core countries. The combination of decreased exports and increased costs of imports created acute balance of payments difficulties for most of these countries, especially in the 1970s, which made their governments receptive to loans (the recycling of the OPEC superprofits) and led within a decade to the so-called debt crisis.

But a Kondratieff B-phase also offers opportunities. Because one major effect is the relocation of industries from the core countries, non-core countries are the beneficiaries of this relocation, that is, *some* non-core countries. It is crucial to bear in mind that there is just so much relocation possible and that all non-core countries are in competition with each other to be the site. In the 1970s, a new term was invented. We began to speak of NICs, that is, of "newly industrializing countries." The literature of the time gave four major examples: Mexico, Brazil, (South) Korea, and Taiwan. By the 1980s, Mexico and Brazil tended to disappear from the lists, and we began to speak of the Four Dragons (Korea, Taiwan, Hong Kong, and Singapore). By the 1990s, there were indications of further relocation, beyond the Four Dragons, to Thailand, Malaysia, Indonesia, the Philippines, Vietnam, and (mainland) China. And now, there is a so-called financial crisis, first of all in this last group, but in the Four Dragons as well. Of course, Japan has been experiencing some economic difficulties since the early 1990s, and the pundits suggest that the current crisis might "spread" to Japan, and then possibly elsewhere, for example, to the United States.

Into this picture has stepped the IMF, supported strongly by the U.S. government, with its "solution" invented for the debt crisis of the early 1980s: the recommendation that governments in crisis practice a combination of fiscal austerity and opening the market for investors even more widely. As the chief economist of the Deutsche Bank in Tokyo has pointed out, and as cited approvingly by no less than Henry Kissinger, the IMF is acting "like a doctor specializing in measles [who] tries to cure every illness with one remedy."[3]

Kissinger points out that the Asian countries had in fact been doing exactly what "conventional wisdom" had recommended and that neither the countries nor the world's financial centers "had foreseen the current crisis." Who then is to blame? It's a combination, says Kissinger, of "domestic shortcomings and exuberant foreign investors and lenders, [who] had been making] large windfall profits . . . [via] unsound investments." In any case, Kissinger warns that the IMF remedies, forcing "the complete crippling of the domestic banking system [in countries] which have no social safety net," are disastrous, causing what is in essence a "political" crisis with potentially very negative impact on the U.S. position in the world-system. Kissinger draws this lesson for the powerful of this world:

> [I]t is clear that world leaders need a better understanding of global capital flows and their potential impact on the economies of both industrialized and developing countries. And they must become more aware of the potential international impact of decisions often taken largely for domestic reasons.

Kissinger is speaking at this point as a political economist, concerned with maintaining the stability of the capitalist world-economy as a historical system, and well aware of the limitations of the degree of polarization that is politically tolerable, especially when the immediate cause of increased suffering can be traced to financial speculations. But, of course, he is operating also as a plumber advising how to stop the leak, and in this capacity, he is not making a long-term analysis.

Let us look at the so-called East Asian crisis in three temporalities, two of them conjunctural and one structural. We have just recounted the story as a story of the current Kondratieff cycle, one still not quite terminated. In the Kondratieff B-phase, for some reason (to be suggested shortly), the East/Southeast Asian region of the world-system was the major beneficiary of the relocation caused by the Kondratieff downturn. This meant that, unlike other parts of the periphery and semiperiphery, the countries of the region had a major growth spurt and seemed to be prospering, until the effects of the downturn hit even them. In this sense, there is nothing unusual or unexpected about what has happened. Of course, to appreciate this, we have to put aside all the glowing explanations of East Asia's virtues, which have now given place to all the sour and reproving clucking about "crony capitalism." East Asia did do exactly the right things in the 1970s and 1980s to attract to itself the relocation of world industry. What the recent crisis proves is that even doing all of this is not enough to sustain a long-term fundamental improvement in a region's comparative economic status in the world-system.

But there is another conjunctural cycle, one that is longer-term than the Kondratieff. This is the cycle of hegemony. That cycle goes back in the present instance not to 1945 but to circa 1873, and traces the rise and now the decline of U.S. hegemony in the world-system. It started with a long competition between the United States and Germany to become the successor hegemonic power to Great Britain. This struggle culminated in the Thirty Years War between the two contenders that went on between 1914 and 1945, a war that the United States won. The period of true hegemony followed, from 1945 to 1967/73. True hegemony, however, cannot last. Its base, which is economic productive superiority, must inevitably be undermined by the entry into a strong competitive position of other powers, in this case western Europe and Japan. The relative economic decline of the United States has been going on apace since then, to the advantage of its economic competitors. The United States has been able, up to a point, to contain them politically, primarily by using the menace of the Cold War to keep its allies in line. This weapon, however, disappeared with the collapse of the Soviet Union between 1989 and 1991.

For various reasons, Japan has been able to do even better than western Europe in this period, in part because its economic apparatuses were "newer" (the Gerschenkron effect) and in part because U.S. firms seemed more interested in making long-term arrangements with Japan than with western Europe. Whatever the explanation, Japan, which as late as the 1960s was being compared by U.S. scholars with Turkey,[4] became an economic superpower. The ability of the Four Dragons and later Southeast Asia to perform so well in the 1980s was due to their geographical and economic linkage with Japan (the so-called flying geese effect). In five years, Thailand may look no better than Venezuela, and Korea no better than Brazil, but Japan will continue to be an economic superpower, and will probably emerge in the early twenty-first century, in the wake of the next Kondratieff upturn, as the leading locus of capital accumulation in the world-system. How large a role a resurgent China will play in this economic centrality of Japan/East Asia is one of the great uncertain factors of this geoeconomic, geopolitical restructuring, the start of a new hegemonic cycle and of competition between Japan or Japan/China and western Europe for the new top role. From this perspective, the so-called East Asian financial crisis is a minor, temporary event of limited importance that will probably change nothing of the underlying rise of Japan or Japan/China or Japan/East Asia.

If the East Asian crisis forces a serious world depression, the United States is likely to be the worst hit of all. And even if everyone comes out of the final subphase of the Kondratieff B-phase and into a new A-phase, it will probably be the start of a secular deflation, such as the world-economy saw in the seventeenth and nineteenth centuries.

Finally, there is the structural temporality. The capitalist world-economy has been in existence as a historical system since the long sixteenth century. Every historical system has three moments: the moment of genesis, the moment of normal life or development, and the moment of structural crisis. Each must be analyzed separately. There is much reason to believe that the modern world-system, the one in which we all live, has entered into its structural crisis.[5] If this is so, we are unlikely to see the full acting out of another hegemonic cycle. Japan may never have its moment in the sun, as the historic successor to the United Provinces, the United Kingdom, and the United States. To be sure, we may have one more Kondratieff cycle, but its glorious A-phase would no doubt only make more acute the structural crisis, rather than annulling it.

In this case, we may consider ourselves to be in what the scientists of complexity call a "bifurcation," during which the world-system will be "chaotic," in the technical sense that there will be many simultaneously possible solutions to all the equations of the world-system, and therefore no predictability about the short-term patterns. But out of this system will come some new "order," absolutely indeterminate (in the sense that it is impossible to predict), but subject to much agency (in the sense that even small pushes may have enormous impact on the path of the system in crisis).

From this point of view, the East Asian crisis is an annunciatory sign. It is not the first. The first was the world revolution of 1968. But insofar as the neoliberals claimed to have found the secret of restabilizing the system, the East Asian crisis will have demonstrated how barren is their ideology and how irrelevant. This is what is panicking those who, like the *Financial Times* and Henry Kissinger, are worrying about the political impact of the "panic" of the financial investors. The sages are right in their critiques of the IMF, but they in turn have little to offer us, because they feel they have to argue that the historical system in which we live is immortal, and thus they must forswear analyzing its dilemmas. No system, however, is immortal, and certainly not the one that has generated the greatest economic and social polarization in the history of humanity.

Chapter 4

States? Sovereignty?

The Dilemmas of Capitalists
in an Age of Transition

There have long been debates, as we all know, about the relationship of the individual states to the capitalists. Views range from those who emphasize the degree to which states are manipulated by capitalists to serve their individual and collective interests to those who emphasize the degree to which states are autonomous actors that deal with capitalists as one interest group among several or many. There has also been debate about the degree to which capitalists can escape control by the state machinery, and there are many who are arguing that their ability to do this has increased considerably in recent decades, with the onset of the transnational corporation and so-called globalization.

In addition, there have long been debates about the relationship of so-called sovereign states to each other. Views range from those who emphasize the effective sovereignty of the various states to those who are cynical about the ability of so-called weak states to resist the pressures (and blandishments) of so-called strong states. This debate is often kept separate from the debate about the relationship of individual states to capitalists, as though we were dealing with two different questions. It seems to me difficult, however, to discuss these issues intelligently without looking at them in tandem, because of the peculiar structure of the modern world-system.

The modern world-system, in existence in at least part of the globe since the long sixteenth century, is a capitalist world-economy. This means several things. A system is capitalist if the primary dynamic of social activity is the endless accumulation of capital. This is sometimes

Keynote address at the conference, "State and Sovereignty in the World Economy," University of California, Irvine, February 21–23, 1997.

called the law of value. Not everyone, of course, is necessarily motivated to engage in such endless accumulation, and indeed only a few are able to do so successfully. But a system is capitalist if those who do engage in such activity tend to prevail in the middle run over those who follow other dynamics. The endless accumulation of capital requires in turn the ever-increasing commodification of everything, and a capitalist world-economy should show a continuous trend in this direction, which the modern world-system surely does.

This then leads to the second requirement, that the commodities be linked in so-called commodity chains, not only because such chains are "efficient" (meaning that they constitute a method that minimizes costs in terms of output), but also because they are opaque (to use Braudel's term). The opacity of the distribution of the surplus-value in a long commodity chain is the most effective way to minimize political opposition, because it obscures the reality and the causes of the acute polarization of distribution that is the consequence of the endless accumulation of capital, a polarization that is more acute than in any previous historical system.

The length of the commodity chains determines the boundaries of the division of labor of the world-economy. How long they are is a function of several factors: the kind of raw materials that need to be included in the chain, the state of the technology of transport and communications, and perhaps most important the degree to which the dominant forces in the capitalist world-economy have the political strength to incorporate additional areas into their network. I have argued that the historical geography of our present structure can be seen to have three principal moments. The first was the period of original creation, between 1450 and 1650, during which time the modern world-system came to include primarily most of Europe (but neither Russia nor the Ottoman Empire) plus certain parts of the Americas. The second moment was the great expansion from 1750 to 1850, when primarily the Russian empire, the Ottoman Empire, South Asia and parts of Southeast Asia, large parts of West Africa, and the rest of the Americas were incorporated. The third and last expansion occurred in the period 1850–1900, when primarily East Asia but also various other zones in Africa, the rest of Southeast Asia, and Oceania were brought inside the division of labor. At that point, the capitalist world-economy had become truly global for the first time. It became the first historical system to include the entire globe within its geography.

Though it is fashionable to speak of globalization today as a phenomenon that began at the earliest in the 1970s, in fact transnational commodity chains were extensive from the very beginning of the system, and global since the second half of the nineteenth century. To be sure, the improvement in technology has made it possible to transport more and different kinds of items across great distances, but I contend that there has not been any fundamental change in the structuring and operations of these commodity chains in the twentieth century, and that none is likely to occur because of the so-called information revolution.

Still, the dynamic growth of the capitalist world-economy over five hundred years has been extraordinary and very impressive, and of course we are dazzled by the ever more remarkable machines and other forms of applied scientific knowledge that have come into existence. The basic claim of neoclassical economics is that this economic growth and these technological accomplishments are the result of capitalist entrepreneurial activity, and that, now that the last remaining barriers to the endless accumulation of capital are being eliminated, the world shall go from glory to glory, wealth to wealth, and therefore satisfaction to satisfaction. Neoclassical economists, and their associates in other disciplines, paint a very rosy picture of the future, provided their formulas are accepted, and a quite dismal one if these formulas are rejected or even hampered.

But even neoclassical economists will admit that the last five hundred years have not been in reality ones of unlimited "free flow of the factors of production." Indeed, that is what the talk about "globalization" tells us. Seemingly, it is only today, and not even yet, that we are seeing this truly free flow. If so, one has to wonder how the capitalist entrepreneurs have been able to do so well prior to the last few decades, since persons of virtually every intellectual and political persuasion seem to agree that capitalist entrepreneurs have indeed, as a group, done quite well over the past few centuries in terms of their ability to accumulate capital. To explain this seeming anomaly, we have to turn to that part of the story that the neoclassical economists since Alfred Marshall have been strenuously excluding from consideration, the political and social story. And here is where the states come in.

The modern state is a peculiar creature, since these states are so-called sovereign states within an interstate system. I contend that the political structures that existed in noncapitalist systems did not operate in the same way and that they constituted qualitatively a different kind of institution. What then are the peculiarities of the modern state? First and foremost, that it claims sovereignty. Sovereignty, as it has been defined since the sixteenth century, is a claim not about the state but about the interstate system. It is a double claim, looking both inward and outward. Sovereignty of the state, inward-looking, is the assertion that, within its boundaries (which therefore must necessarily be clearly defined and legitimated within the interstate system), the state may pursue whatever policies it deems wise, that it may decree whatever laws it deems necessary, and that it may do this without any individual, group, or sub-state structure inside the state having the right to refuse to obey the laws. Sovereignty of the state, outward-looking, is the argument that no other state in the system has the right to exercise any authority, directly or indirectly, within the boundaries of the given state, since such an attempt would constitute a breach of the given state's sovereignty. No doubt, earlier state forms also claimed authority within their realms, but "sovereignty" involves in addition the mutual recognition of these claims of the states within an interstate system. That is, sovereignty in the modern world is a reciprocal concept.

However, as soon as we put these claims on paper, we see immediately how far they are from a description of how the modern world really works. No modern state has ever been truly inwardly sovereign de facto, since there has always been internal resistance to its authority. Indeed in most states this resistance has led to institutionalizing legal limitations on internal sovereignty in the form, among others, of constitutional law. Nor has any state even been truly outwardly sovereign, since interference by one state in the affairs of another is common currency, and since the entire corpus of international law (admittedly a weak reed) represents a series of limitations on outward sovereignty. In any case, strong states notoriously do not fully reciprocate recognition of the sovereignty of weak states. So why is such an absurd idea put forth? And why do I say that this claim to sovereignty within an interstate system is the peculiar political characteristic of the modern world-system, in comparison to other kinds of world-systems?

The concept of sovereignty was in fact formulated in western Europe at a time when state structures were very weak in reality. States had small and ineffective bureaucracies, armed forces they did not control very well, and all sorts of strong local authorities and overlapping jurisdictions with which to deal. It is only with the so-called new monarchies of the late fifteenth century that the balance begins, just begins, to be redressed. The doctrine of the absolute right of monarchs was a theoretical claim of weak rulers for a far-off utopia they hoped to establish. Their arbitrariness was the mirror of their relative impotence. Modern diplomacy, with its recognition of extraterritoriality and the safe passage of diplomats, was an invention of Renaissance Italy and spread Europewide only in the sixteenth century. The establishment of a minimally institutionalized interstate system took over a century to realize, with the Peace of Westphalia in 1648.

The story of the past five hundred years has been the slow but steady linear increase, within the framework of the capitalist world-economy, of the internal power of the states and of the authority of the institutions of the interstate system. Still, we should not exaggerate. These structures went from a very low point on the scale to somewhere further up the scale, but at no point have they approached anything that might be called absolute power. Furthermore, at all points in time, some states (those we call strong) had greater internal and greater external power than most other states. We should of course be clear what we mean by power here. Power is not bombast, and it is not a theoretically (that is, legally) unlimited authority. Power is measured by results; power is about getting one's way. The truly powerful can be (and usually are) soft-spoken, respectful, and quietly manipulative; the truly powerful succeed. The powerful are those who are heeded, even when their legitimacy is only partially accorded. Their threat of force most often obviates the need to use it. The truly powerful are Machiavellian. They know that their ability to use force in the future usually is diminished by the very process of actually using it in the present, and they are therefore quite sparing and prudent in such use.

This political system of sovereign states within an interstate system, of states and an interstate system both having as intermediate degree of power, suited perfectly the needs of capitalist entrepreneurs. For what do persons whose goal is the endless accumulation of capital need in order to realize their objectives? Or, another way of asking this is: Why isn't the free market sufficient for their purposes? Could they really do better in a world in which no political authority existed at all? To ask the question is to see that no capitalist or capitalist apologist — not even Milton Friedman, not even Ayn Rand — has ever quite asked for this. They have insisted at the very least on having the so-called night watchman state.

Now what does a night watchman do? He sits in relative darkness, twiddling his thumbs in boredom, occasionally twirling his baton or revolver when not asleep, and waiting. His function is to ward off intruders who intend to pilfer property. He does this primarily just by being there. So here we are at basics, the universally noted demand for securing property rights. There's no point in accumulating capital if you can't hold on to it.

There are three major ways in which entrepreneurs can lose accumulated capital outside market operations. Capital can be stolen; it can be confiscated; it can be taxed. Theft in one form or another is a persistent problem. Outside the modern world-system, the basic defense against serious theft had always been to invest in private security systems. This was even true of the capitalist world-economy in its early days. There exists, however, an alternative, which is to transfer the role of providing antitheft security to the states; generically this is called the police function. The economic advantages of shifting the security role from private to public hands is admirably laid out in Frederic Lane's *Profits from Power*, in which he invents the term "protection rent" to describe the increased profits that resulted from this historic shift, a benefit from which some entrepreneurs (those in strong states) drew far greater advantage than others.

For the truly rich, however, theft has probably been a smaller problem, historically, than confiscation. Confiscation always was a major political and economic weapon in the hands of rulers, especially of powerful rulers, in noncapitalist systems. Confiscation has undoubtedly been one of the major mechanisms whereby capitalists were prevented from making the priority of the endless accumulation of capital prevail. This is why institutionalizing the illegitimacy of confiscation via the establishment not only of property rights but of the "rule of law" has been a necessary condition of constructing a capitalist historical system. Confiscation remained widespread in the early days of the modern world-system, if not directly then indirectly via state bankruptcies (see the four successive ones of the Spanish Hapsburgs), and confiscation via socialization has been a phenomenon of the twentieth century. Nonetheless, the remarkable thing is not how much but how little confiscation there has been. There has been no comparable level of security for capitalists in any other world-system, and this security against confiscation has actually grown with time. Even the socialization processes have been frequently effectuated "with compensation," and, furthermore, as we know, they have often been reversed and, therefore, from a systemic point of view, have been only temporary. In any case, the pervasiveness of the rule of law has tended to make future levels of income more predictable, which allows capitalists to make more rational investments and therefore ultimately more profit.

As for taxation, no one wants to be taxed of course, but capitalists as a class have never been opposed to what they think of as reasonable taxation. From their point of view, reasonable taxation is the purchase of services from the state. As with all other purchases, capitalists prefer to pay the lowest rates available, but they do not expect to get these services gratis. In addition, as we know, taxes on paper are not the same as taxes really paid. Still, it is fair to say that the rate of real taxation has grown over the centuries of the capitalist world-economy, but this is because the services have grown. It is not at all sure that it would be less costly for capitalists to assume the costs of these necessary services directly. Indeed, I would argue that relatively high rates of taxation are a plus for large capitalists, since much, even most, of the money is recycled to them in one way or another, which means that state taxation tends to be a way of shifting surplus-value from small enterprises and the working classes to the large capitalists.

What are the services that capitalists need of the state? The first and greatest service they require is protection against the free market. The free market is the mortal enemy of capital accumulation. The hypothetical free market, so dear to the elucubrations of economists, one with multiple buyers and sellers, all of whom share perfect information, would of course be a capitalist disaster. Who could make any money in it? The capitalist would be reduced to the income of the hypothetical proletarian of the nineteenth century, living off what might be called "the iron law of profits in a free market," just enough barely to survive. We know that this is not how it works, but that is because the real existing market is by no means free.

Obviously, any given producer will be able to increase his returns to the extent that he monopolizes the market. But the free market does tend to undermine monopolies, which is of course what the spokespersons of capitalists have always said. If an operation is profitable, and monopolized operations are by definition so, then other entrepreneurs will enter the market if they can, thereby reducing the price at which a given item is sold on the market. "If they can!" The market itself puts only very limited constraints on entry. These constraints are called efficiency. If an entrant can match the efficiency of existing producers, the market says welcome. The really significant constraints on entry are the doing of the state, or rather of the states.

The states have three major mechanisms that transform the economic transactions on the market. The most obvious one is legal constraint. The states can decree or forbid monopolies, or create quotas. The most utilized methods are import/export prohibitions and, even more important, patents. By relabeling such monopolies "intellectual property," the hope is that no one will notice how incompatible this notion is with the concept of a free market, or perhaps it lets us see how incompatible the concept of property is with that of a free market. After all, the classic mugger's opening gambit, "Your money or your life," offers a free market alternative. So does the classic terrorist menace, "Do x or else."

Prohibitions are important for entrepreneurs, but they do seem to violate grossly much of the rhetoric. So there exists a certain amount of political hesitation to use them too frequently. The state has other tools in the creation of monopolies that are somewhat less visible and hence probably more important. The state can distort the market very easily. Since the market presumably favors the most efficient, and efficiency is a question of reducing cost for comparable output, the state can quite simply assume part of the cost of the entrepreneur. It assumes part of the costs whenever it in any way subsidizes the entrepreneur. The state can do this directly for a given product. But more importantly the state can do this on behalf of multiple entrepreneurs simultaneously in two ways. It can build so-called infrastructure, which of course means that given entrepreneurs do not have to assume those costs. This is usually justified on the grounds that the costs are too high for any single entrepreneur and that such state expenditure represents a collective sharing of the cost that benefits everyone. But this explanation assumes that all entrepreneurs benefit equally, which is seldom the case, certainly not transnationally and most often not even within the boundaries of the state. In any case, the costs of the infrastructure are not usually imposed on the collectivity of beneficiaries but on all taxpayers, and even disproportionately on nonusers.

Nor is such direct assumption of costs via infrastructure the largest single assistance given by the states. The states offer the entrepreneurs the possibility of not paying the costs of repairing the damage they do to what is not their property. If an entrepreneur pollutes a stream and doesn't pay the costs either of avoiding the pollution or of restoring the stream to a pristine state, de facto the state is permitting the transmission of the cost to society at large, a bill that is often not paid for generations thereafter, but which eventually must be paid by someone. In the meantime, the absence of constraint on the entrepreneur, his ability to "externalize" his costs, is a subsidy of considerable importance.

Nor does this end the process. There is a special advantage of being an entrepreneur in a strong state that entrepreneurs in other states do not enjoy to the same degree. And here we see the advantage of the location of states in an interstate system from the point of view of the entrepreneurs. Strong states can prevent other states from conferring monopolistic advantages against certain entrepreneurs, usually citizens of their own state.

The proposition is very simple. Real profit, the kind that permits a serious endless accumulation of capital, is possible only with relative monopolies, for however long they last. And such monopolies are not possible without the states. Furthermore, the system of multiple states within an interstate system offers the entrepreneurs great assistance in making sure that the states restrict themselves to helping them and do not overstep their bounds and hurt them. The curious interstate system permits entrepreneurs, particularly large ones, to circumvent states that get too big for their britches, by seeking the patronage of other states, or using one state mechanism to curb another state mechanism.

This brings us to the third way in which states can prevent the free market from functioning freely. The states are major purchasers in their national markets, and large states command an impressive proportion of purchases in the world market. They are frequently monopsonists, or near-monopsonists, for certain very expensive goods; for example, today, for armaments or superconductors. They could of course use this power to lower prices for themselves as purchasers, but instead they seem for the most part to use this power to permit the producers to monopolize a roughly equal share of the market, and to raise their prices scandalously.

But, you will think, about what then was Adam Smith so agitated? Did he not inveigh against the state's role in creating monopolies? Did he not call for laissez-faire, laissez-passer? Yes, he did, up to a point. The reason why, however, is the crucial thing to see. Obviously, one man's monopoly is another man's poison. And entrepreneurs are always competing first of all with each other. So, naturally, those who are out are always screaming against state-induced monopolies. Adam Smith was the spokesman of these poor, benighted underdogs. To be sure, once the underdogs have undone the monopolies in which they did not participate, they happily proceed to try to create new ones of their own, at which point they tend to cease citing Adam Smith and instead bankroll neoconservative foundations.

Of course, monopoly is not the only advantage capitalists obtain from the state. The other main advantage, regularly noted, is the maintenance of order. Order within the state means first of all order against insurgency by the working classes. This is more than the police function against theft; it is the state's role in reducing the efficacy of class struggle by workers. This is done through a combination of force, deception, and concessions. What we mean by a liberal state is one in which the amount of force is reduced and the amount of deception and concessions increased. This works better, to be sure, but it is not always possible, especially in peripheral zones of the world-economy, where there is too little surplus available to permit the state to allocate much of it to concessions. Even in the most liberal state, however, there are serious legal constrictions on the modes of action by the working classes, and on the whole these constrictions are greater, usually far greater, than those reciprocally imposed on employers. No legal system is class-blind, although, as a result of workers' political activity over the past two centuries, the situation did tend to get somewhat better after 1945 than it previously had been. It is this improvement in the position of the working classes that the resurgent conservative ideology around the world since the 1970s has been contesting.

What, however, about interstate order? Schumpeter, in one of his few naive moments, insisted that interstate disorder was a negative from the point of view of entrepreneurs and a social atavism. Perhaps it was not naïveté that led Schumpeter to insist on this — perhaps it was merely his desperate need not to accept the economic logic of Lenin's *Imperialism*. In any case, it seems to me quite clear that capitalists generally feel about war what they feel about taxation. Their attitude depends on the particular circumstances. War against Saddam Hussein may seem positive in terms of preserving certain possibilities of capital accumulation for certain capitalists. Even world wars are useful for particular capitalists, usually provided they are serving the winning side and are located somewhat out of the direct line of fire, or if their production is particularly geared to wartime needs of either side.

Still, Schumpeter has a point in general, in that too much or too persistent interstate disorder makes it difficult to predict the market situation and leads to capricious destruction of property. It also makes impossible, or at least very difficult, certain kinds of economic transactions, interfering with previous routes of commodity chains. In short, if the world-system were continuously in a state of "world war," capitalism probably wouldn't work very well. So the states are needed to prevent this. Or rather it is useful to have a hegemonic power that can institute a certain degree of regulation in the system, which increases predictability and minimizes capricious losses. But once again the order a hegemonic power imposes is always better for some capitalists than for others. Collective unity of the capitalist classes is not too strong in this domain. We could sum this up by saying that waging war is, at many points in time and for certain capitalists, a great service, even if this is not always true. I certainly do not wish to suggest that capitalists, singly or collectively, call wars on and off. Capitalists are powerful in a capitalist world-economy, but they do not control everything. Others get into the picture of deciding on wars.

It is at this point that we must discuss the so-called autonomy of the states. Capitalists seek to accumulate capital. Politicians, for the most part, primarily seek to obtain, and remain in, office. One might think of them as petty entrepreneurs who, however, exercise considerable power beyond their own capital. Remaining in office is a function of support — support of capitalist strata to be sure, but also support of voters/citizens/popular strata. This latter support is what makes possible the minimal legitimacy of a state structure. Without this minimal legitimacy, the cost of remaining in office is very high, and the long-run stability of the state structure is limited.

What legitimates a state within the capitalist world-economy? Surely it is not the fairness of the distribution of the surplus-value or even of the application of the laws. If one says it is the myths that every state uses about its history or origins or special virtues, one still needs to ask why people buy into these myths. It is not self-evident that they will. And in any case we know that popular insurrections occur repeatedly, some of which even involve cultural revolutionary processes that call into question these basic myths.

So legitimacy needs explaining. The Weberian typology allows us to understand the different fashions in which people legitimate their states. What Weber calls rational-legal legitimation is of course the form that liberal ideology preaches. In much of the modern world, this form has come to prevail, if not all of the time, at least for a good deal of the time. But why does it prevail? I insist not only on the importance of this question but on the fact that an answer is far from self-evident. We live in a highly unequal world. We live in one in which polarization is constantly increasing and in which even the middle strata are not keeping up proportionately with the upper strata, despite any and all improvements in their absolute situation. So why do so many persons tolerate this situation, even embrace it?

There are, it seems to me, two kinds of answers one might give. One is relative deprivation. *We* may be badly off, or at least not well enough off, but *they* are really badly off. So let us not rock the boat, and above all let us prevent them from rocking the boat. That this kind of collective psychology plays a major role seems to me to be very widely accepted, whether one applauds it by talking of a sizable middle class as the basis of democratic stability or deplores it by talking of a labor aristocracy having false consciousness, and whether one thinks of it as operating primarily within states or within the world-system as a whole. This explanation is a structural one; that is to say, it is an argument that a certain collective psychology derives from the very structure of the capitalist world-economy. If this aspect of the structure remains intact, that is, if we continue to have a hierarchical structure that has many positions on the ladder, then the degree of legitimation resulting from this structure should remain constant. At the moment, the reality of a hierarchical ladder of positions does seem to have remained intact, and therefore the structural explanation cannot explain any variation in legitimation.

There does, however, seem to be a very important second factor that accounts for continuing legitimation of state structures. This factor is more conjunctural and therefore can vary; and it has indeed varied. The degree of legitimation of the capitalist world-economy before the nineteenth century was undoubtedly quite low, and it has remained low in most of the peripheral zones right into the late twentieth century. The continuous commodification of productive transactions seemed to bring changes, many or even most of which were negative from the point of view of the direct producers. Still, after the French Revolution, the situation began to change. It is not that the impact of commodification became less negative, at least for the large majority. It is that their restiveness took the form of insisting that sovereignty could not be discussed merely as a definition of authority and lawful power. One had to ask the question, Who exercised this power? Who was the sovereign? If the answer were not to be the absolute monarch, what alternative was there? As we know, the new answer that began to be widely accepted was "the people."

To say that the people are sovereign is not to say anything very precise, since one then has to decide who are the people and by what means they can collectively exercise this authority. But just suggesting that there was such an entity as "the people" and that they might exercise sovereign power had very radical implications for those exercising de facto authority. The result has been the great politico-cultural turmoil of the nineteenth and twentieth centuries surrounding the question of how to interpret, and tame, the exercise by the people of their sovereignty.

The story of the taming of the exercise of popular sovereignty is the story of liberal ideology — its invention, its triumphal ascendancy in the nineteenth century as the geoculture of the capitalist world-economy, its ability to transform the two competitor ideologies (conservatism on the one hand and radicalism/socialism on the other) into avatars of liberalism. How this was done I have discussed at length in my book *After Liberalism*. Let me just resume here the essentials.

Liberalism presented itself as a centrist doctrine. The liberals preached that progress was desirable and inevitable and could best be achieved if a process of rational reform were instituted, one controlled by specialists, who could, on the basis of an informed analysis, implement the necessary reforms throughout the historical system, using the authority of the states as their basic political lever. Faced with the impetuous demands of the "dangerous classes" of the nineteenth century — the urban proletariat of western Europe and North America — the liberals offered a three-pronged program of reforms: suffrage, the beginnings of a welfare state, and a politically integrating, racist nationalism.

This three-pronged program worked exceptionally well, and, by 1914, the original dangerous classes, the urban proletariat of western Europe and North America, were no longer dangerous. Just then, however, the liberals found themselves confronted with a new set of "dangerous classes" — the popular forces in the rest of the world. In the twentieth century, the liberals sought to apply a similar reform program at the interstate level. The self-determination of nations served as the functional equivalent of universal suffrage. The economic development of underdeveloped nations was offered as the equivalent of the national welfare state. The third prong, however, was unavailable because, once one was trying to include the entire world, there was no outside group against whom one could construct an integrating, racist nationalism.

Nonetheless, the twentieth-century version of world-level liberalism seemed also to work up to a point and for a while, especially in the "glorious" years after 1945. But the formula came unstuck as of 1968. To be sure, the self-determination of nations offered little problem. But world-level redistribution, even to a modest degree, threatened to put an enormous strain on the possibilities of endlessly accumulating capital. And the third prong was entirely absent. As of the 1970s, global liberalism no longer seemed to be viable.

To understand why this is so devastating to the system, we have to understand what it was that liberalism had offered and why therefore it had successfully stabilized the system politically for a long while. The three-pronged program that the liberals had used to tame the dangerous classes did not offer the dangerous classes what they wanted and had initially demanded — easily enough summarized in the classic slogan of the French Revolution: "Liberty, equality, fraternity." If these demands had been met, there would no longer have been a capitalist world-economy, since it would have been impossible to ensure the endless accumulation of capital. What the liberals offered therefore was half a pie, or more exactly about one-seventh of a pie: a reasonable standard of living for a minority of the world's population (those famed middle strata). Now this small pie was doubtless a lot more than this one-seventh had had before, but it was far less than an equal share of the pie, and it was almost nothing at all for the other six-sevenths.

Giving this much did not significantly diminish the possibilities of accumulating capital for the large capitalists, but it did accomplish the political objective of pulling the plug on revolutionary ferment over the middle run. The one-seventh who benefited materially were for the most part quite grateful, all the more so when they saw the conditions of those they left behind. (Remember Tawney's image of the talented "scrambl[ing] to shore, undeterred by the thought of drowning companions!"[1]) What is more interesting is the reaction of the drowning companions. They came to interpret the ability of the talented to swim to shore as evidence of hope for them. This was understandable psychologically if imprudent analytically.

Liberalism offered the opiate of hope, and it was swallowed whole. It was swallowed not least by the leaders of the world's antisystemic movements, who mobilized on the promise of hope. They claimed that they would achieve the good society by revolution, but of course they in fact meant by reform, which they, as substitute specialists for those offered by the current authorities, would administer once they gained control of the levers of state power. I suppose that if you are drowning, and someone offers hope, it is not irrational to grab hold of whatever is extended as a lifesaver. One cannot retrospectively reprimand the popular masses of the world for offering their support and their moral energy to the multiple antisystemic movements that voiced their grievances.

Those in authority, faced with voluble, vigorous, and denunciatory antisystemic movements, could react in one of two ways. If they were frightened, and they often were, they could try to cut off the heads of what they saw as vipers. But since the beasts were in fact hydra-headed, the more sophisticated defenders of the status quo realized that they needed more subtle responses. They came to see that the antisystemic movements actually served in a perverse way the interests of the system. Mobilizing the masses meant channeling the masses, and state power for the leaders had very conservatizing effects. Furthermore, once such movements were in power, they moved themselves against the impetuous demands of their followers, and tended to do so with as much, even more, severity than their predecessors. Furthermore, the sedative of hope was even more efficacious when the peddler was a certified revolutionary leader. If the future was theirs, the popular masses reasoned that they could afford to wait a while, especially if they had a "progressive" state. Their children, at least, would inherit the earth.

The shock of 1968 was more than momentary. The shock of 1968 was the realization that the whole geoculture of liberalism, and especially the construction of historical optimism by the antisystemic movements, was tainted, nay fraudulent, and that the children of the popular masses were not scheduled to inherit the earth; indeed, their children might be even worse off than they. And so these popular masses began to abandon the antisystemic movements, and beyond the movements all of liberal reformism, and therefore abandoned the state structures as vehicles of their collective betterment.

To abandon a well-worn path of hope is not done with lightness of heart. For it does not follow that the six-sevenths of humanity were ready to accept quietly their fate as oppressed and unfulfilled human beings. Quite the contrary. When one abandons the accepted promises of hope, one searches for other paths. The problem is that they are not so easy to find. But there is worse. The states may not have offered long-term betterment for the majority of the populations of the world, but they did offer a certain amount of short-term security against violence. If, however, the populations no longer legitimate the states, they tend neither to obey its policemen nor to pay its tax-collectors. And thereupon the states are less able to offer short-term security against violence. In this case, individuals (and firms) have to return to the ancient solution, that of providing their own security.

As soon as private security becomes once again an important social ingredient, confidence in the rule of law tends to break down, and therefore so does civil (or civic) consciousness. Closed groups emerge (or reemerge) as the only safe haven, and closed groups tend to be intolerant, violent, and inclined toward zonal purifications. As intergroup violence rises, the leadership tends to become more and more Mafioso in character — Mafioso in the sense of combining muscular insistence on unquestioning intragroup obedience and venal profiteering. We see this all around us now, and we shall see much more of it in the decades to come.

Hostility to the state is fashionable now, and spreading. The anti-state themes common to conservatism, liberalism, and radicalism/ socialism, which had been ignored in practice for over 150 years, are now finding deep resonance in political behavior in all camps. Should not the capitalist strata be happy? It seems doubtful that they are, for they need the state, the strong state, far more than their official rhetoric has ever admitted.

No doubt they don't want peripheral states to interfere with the transactions flows of the world-economy, and now that the antisystemic movements are in deep trouble, the big capitalists are currently able to use the IMF and other institutions to enforce this preference. It is, however, one thing for the Russian state no longer to keep out foreign investors; it is quite another thing for the Russian state to be unable to guarantee the personal safety of the entrepreneurs who visit Moscow.

In a recent issue of *CEPAL Review*, Juan Carlos Lerda makes a very cautious assessment of the loss of autonomy of state authorities in the face of globalization. He does, however, stress what he believes to be a bright side in the increased vigor of world market forces:

> The globalization phenomenon effectively restricts national governments'
> freedom of movement. However, the disciplining force of international
> competition which underlies at least a large part of the process may have

considerable beneficial effects on the future course of public policy in the countries of the region. Thus, when talking about "loss of autonomy," care must be taken to check whether it is not rather a matter of a welcome "reduction in the level of arbitrariness" with which public policy is sometimes applied.[2]

Here we see what one might call the official line. The market is objective and therefore "disciplining." What it disciplines, it seems, is everyone's perverse instincts to make social decisions on any basis other than the maximization of profits. When states make social decisions on such grounds, they are being arbitrary.

But let the states try not to be "arbitrary" when important capitalist interests are at stake, and you will hear the shouting. When in 1990, major U.S. financial institutions were in danger of bankruptcy, Henry Kaufman wrote an op-ed piece in the *New York Times* in which he said:

> Financial institutions are the holders, and therefore, the guardians of Americans' savings and temporary funds, a unique public responsibility. Truly letting the marketplace discipline the financial system would mean acquiescing in an avalanche of potential failures.[3]

So there we have it, clearly outlined. It is welcome for the market to discipline the states when they are arbitrary, but irresponsible if the states allow the same market to discipline the banks. A social decision to retain social welfare is irresponsible, but a social decision to save banks is not.

We must always keep clearly in mind not only that one man's monopoly (or arbitrary decision) is another man's poison, but that capitalists depend on the intervention of the states in such a multitude of ways that any true weakening of state authority is disastrous. The case we have been arguing here is that globalization is not in fact significantly affecting the ability of the states to function, nor is it the intention of large capitalists that it do so. The states are, however, for the first time in five hundred years, on a downward slide in terms of their sovereignty, inward and outward. This is not because of a transformation of the world-economic structures but because of a transformation of the geoculture, and, first of all, because of the loss of hope by the popular masses in liberal reformism and its avatars on the left.

Of course, the change in the geoculture is the consequence of transformations in the world-economy, primarily the fact that many of the internal contradictions of the system have reached points where it is no longer possible to make adjustments that will resolve once again the issue such that one sees a cyclical renewal of the capitalist process. These critical dilemmas of the system include among others the deruralization of the world, the reaching of limits of ecological decay, and the fiscal crises of the states brought on by the democratization of the political arena and the consequent rise in the levels of minimum demand for education and health services.[4]

The sovereignty of the states — their inward and outward sovereignty within the framework of an interstate system — is a fundamental pillar of the capitalist world-economy. If it falls, or seriously declines, capitalism is untenable as a system. I agree that it is in decline today, for the first time in the history of the modern world-system. This is the primary sign of the acute crisis of capitalism as a historical system. The essential dilemma of capitalists, singly and as a class, is whether to take full short-run advantage of the weakening of the states, or to try short-run repair to restore the legitimacy of the state structures, or to spend their energy trying to construct an alternative system. Behind the rhetoric, intelligent defenders of the status quo are aware of this critical situation. While they are trying to get the rest of us to talk about the pseudo-issues of globalization, some of them at least are trying to figure out what a replacement system could be like and how to move things in that direction. If we don't want to live in the future with the inegalitarian solution that they will promote, we should be asking the same question. Let me thus resume my position. A capitalist world-economy requires a structure in which there are sovereign states linked in an interstate system. Such states play crucial roles to sustain entrepreneurs. The principal ones are the assumption of part of the costs of production, the guarantee of quasi-monopolies to increase profit ratios, and their efforts both to restrain the capacity of the working classes to defend their interests and to soften discontent by partial redistributions of surplus-value.

However, this historical system, like any other, has its contradictions, and when these contradictions reach a certain point (otherwise put, when the trajectory has moved far from equilibrium), then the normal functioning of the system becomes impossible. The system reaches a point of bifurcation. There are many signs that, today, we have reached this point. Deruralization, ecological exhaustion, and democratization, each in different ways, reduce the ability to accumulate capital. So does the fact that the states are, for the first time in five hundred years, declining in strength — not at all because of the rising strength of the transnational corporations, as is often asserted, but because of the declining legitimacy accorded to the states by their populations, the result of having lost faith in the prospects of gradual amelioration. The state still matters — to the entrepreneurs above all. And because of the declining strength of the states, the transnationals find themselves in acute difficulty, faced as they are with a long-term profits squeeze for the first time and with states that are no longer in a position to bail them out.

We have entered a time of troubles. The outcome is uncertain. We cannot be sure what kind of historical system will replace the one in which we find ourselves. What we can know with certainty is that the very peculiar system in which we live, and in which the states have played a crucial role in supporting the processes of the endless accumulation of capital, can no longer continue to function.

Chapter 5

Ecology and Capitalist Costs of Production

No Exit

Today, virtually everyone agrees that there has been a serious degradation of the natural environment in which we live, by comparison with thirty years ago, a fortiori by comparison with one hundred years ago, not to speak of five hundred years ago. And this is the case despite the fact that there have been continuous significant technological inventions and an expansion of scientific knowledge that one might have expected would have led to the opposite consequence. As a result, today, unlike thirty or one hundred or five hundred years ago, ecology has become a serious political issue in many parts of the world. There are even reasonably significant political movements organized centrally around the theme of defending the environment against further degradation and reversing the situation to the extent possible.

Of course, the appreciation of the degree of seriousness of the contemporary problem ranges from those who consider doomsday as imminent to those who consider that the problem is one well within the possibility of an early technical solution. I believe the majority of persons hold a position somewhere in-between. I am in no position to argue the issue from a scientific viewpoint. I will take this in-between appreciation as plausible and will engage in an analysis of the relevance of this issue to the political economy of the world-system.

The entire process of the universe is of course one of unceasing change, so the mere fact that things are not what they were previously is so banal that it merits no notice whatsoever. Furthermore, within this constant turbulence, there are patterns of structural renewal we call life.

Keynote address at PEWS XXI, "The Global Environment and the World-System," University of California, Santa Cruz, April 3–5, 1997.

Living, or organic, phenomena have a beginning and an end to their individual existence, but in the process procreate, so that the species tends to continue. But this cyclical renewal is never perfect, and the overall ecology is therefore never static. In addition, all living phenomena ingest in some way products external to them, including most of the time other living phenomena, and predator/prey ratios are never perfect, so that the biological milieu is constantly evolving.

Furthermore, poisons are natural phenomena as well and were playing a role in the ecological balance sheets long before human beings got into the picture. To be sure, today we know so much more chemistry and biology than our ancestors did that we are perhaps more conscious of the toxins in our environment; although perhaps not, since we are also learning these days how sophisticated the preliterate peoples were about toxins and antitoxins. We learn all these things in our primary and secondary school education and from the simple observation of everyday living. Yet often we tend to neglect these obvious constraints when we discuss the politics of ecological issues.

The only reason it is worth discussing these issues at all is if we believe that something special or additional has been happening in recent years, a level of increased danger, and if at the same time we believe that it is possible to do something about this increased danger. The case that is generally made by the green and other ecology movements precisely comprises both these arguments: increased level of danger (for example, holes in the ozone layer, or greenhouse effects, or atomic meltdowns); and potential solutions.

As I said, I am willing to start on the assumption that there is a reasonable case for increased danger, one that requires some urgent reaction. However, in order to be intelligent about how to react to danger, we need to ask two questions: For whom does the danger exist? And what explains the increased danger? The "danger for whom" question has in turn two components: whom, among human beings; and whom, among living beings. The first question raises the comparison of North-South attitudes on ecological questions; the second is the issue of deep ecology. Both in fact involve issues about the nature of capitalist civilization and the functioning of the capitalist world-economy, which means that before we can address the issue of "for whom," we had better analyze the source of the increased danger.

The story begins with two elementary features of historical capitalism. One is well known: capitalism is a system that has an imperative need to expand — expand in terms of total production, expand geographically — in order to sustain its prime objective, the endless accumulation of capital. The second feature is less often discussed. An essential element in the accumulation of capital is for capitalists, especially large capitalists, not to pay their bills. This is what I call the "dirty secret" of capitalism.

Let me elaborate these two points. The first, the constant expansion of the capitalist world-economy, is admitted by everyone. The defenders of capitalism tout it as one of its great virtues. Persons concerned with ecological problems point to it as one of its great vices, and in particular often discuss one of the ideological underpinnings of this expansion, which is the assertion of the right (indeed duty) of human beings "to conquer nature." Now, to be sure, neither expansion nor the conquest of nature was unknown before the onset of the capitalist world-economy in the sixteenth century. But, like many other things that were social phenomena prior to this time, neither had existential priority in previous historical systems. What historical capitalism did was to push these two themes — the actual expansion and its ideological justification — to the forefront, and thus capitalists were able to override social objections to this terrible duo. This is the real difference between historical capitalism and previous historical systems. All the values of capitalist civilization are millennial, but so are other contradictory values. What we mean by historical capitalism is a system in which the institutions that were constructed made it possible for capitalist values to take priority, such that the world-economy was set upon the path of the commodification of everything in order that there be ceaseless accumulation of capital for its own sake.

Of course, the effect of this was not felt in a day or even a century. The expansion had a cumulative effect. It takes time to cut down trees. The trees of Ireland were all cut down in the seventeenth century. But there were other trees elsewhere. Today we talk about the Amazon rain forest as the last real expanse, and it seems to be going fast. It takes time to pour toxins into rivers or into the atmosphere. A mere fifty years ago, "smog" was a newly invented word to describe the very unusual conditions of Los Angeles. It was thought to describe life in a locale that showed a heartless disregard for the quality of life and high culture. Today, smog is everywhere; it infests Athens and Paris. And the capitalist world-economy is still expanding at a reckless rate. Even in this Kondratieff downturn, we hear of remarkable growth ratios of

East and Southeast Asia. What may we expect in the next Kondratieff upturn?

Furthermore, the democratization of the world, and there has been a democratization, has meant that this expansion remains incredibly popular in most parts of the world. Indeed, it is probably more popular than ever. More people are demanding their rights, and this includes quite centrally their rights to a piece of the pie. But a piece of the pie for a large percentage of the world's population necessarily means more production, not to mention the fact that the absolute size of the world population is still expanding as well. So it is not only capitalists but ordinary people who want this. This does not stop many of these same people from also wanting to slow down the degradation of the world environment. But that simply proves that we are involved in one more contradiction of this historical system. That is, many people want to enjoy both more trees and more material goods for themselves, and a lot of them simply segregate the two demands in their minds.

From the point of view of capitalists, as we know, the point of increasing production is to make profits. In a distinction that does not seem to me in the least outmoded, it involves production for exchange and not production for use. Profits on a single operation are the margin between the sales price and the total cost of production, that is, the cost of everything it takes to bring that product to the point of sale. Of course, the actual profits on the totality of a capitalist's operations are calculated by multiplying this margin by the amount of total sales. That is to say, the "market" constrains the sales price, in that, at a certain point, the price becomes so high that the total sales profits is less than if the sales price were lower.

But what constrains total costs? The price of labor plays a very large role in this, and this of course includes the price of the labor that went into all of the inputs. The market price of labor is not merely, however, the result of the relationship of supply and demand of labor but also of the bargaining power of labor. This is a complicated subject, with many factors entering into the strength of this bargaining power. What can be said is that, over the history of the capitalist world-economy, this bargaining power has been increasing as a secular trend, whatever the ups and downs of its cyclical rhythms. Today, this strength is at the verge of a singular ratchet upward as we move into the twenty-first century because of the deruralization of the world.

Deruralization is crucial to the price of labor. Reserve armies of labor are of different kinds in terms of their bargaining power. The weakest group has always been those persons resident in rural areas who come to urban areas for the first time to engage in wage employment. Generally speaking, for such persons the urban wage, even if extremely low by world, or even local, standards, represents an economic advantage over remaining in the rural area. It probably takes twenty to thirty years before such persons shift their economic frame of reference and become fully aware of their potential power in the urban workplace, such that they begin to engage in syndical action of some kind to seek higher wages. Persons long resident in urban areas, even if they are unemployed in the formal economy and living in terrible slum conditions, generally demand higher wage levels before accepting wage employment. This is because they have learned how to obtain from alternative sources in the urban center a minimum level of income higher than that which is being offered to newly arrived rural migrants.

Thus, even though there is still an enormous army of reserve labor throughout the world-system, the fact that the system is being rapidly deruralized means that the average price of labor worldwide is going up steadily. This means in turn that the average rate of profits must necessarily go down over time. This squeeze on the profits ratio makes all the more important the reduction of costs other than labor costs. But, of course, all inputs into production are suffering the same problem of rising labor costs. While technical innovations may continue to reduce the costs of some inputs, and governments may continue to institute and defend monopolistic positions of enterprises permitting higher sales prices, it is nonetheless absolutely crucial for capitalists to continue to have some important part of their costs paid by someone else.

This someone else is of course either the state or, if not the state directly, then the "society." Let us investigate how this is arranged and how the bill is paid. The arrangement for states to pay costs can be done in one of two ways. The governments can accept the role formally, which means subsidies of some kind. However, subsidies are increasingly visible and increasingly unpopular. They are met with loud protests by competitor enterprises and by similar protests by taxpayers. Subsidies pose political problems. There is another, more important, way, which has been politically less difficult for governments, because all it requires is nonaction. Throughout the history of historical capitalism, governments have permitted enterprises not to internalize many of their costs, by failing to require them to do so. They do this in part by underwriting infrastructure and in part, probably in larger part, by not insisting that a production operation include the cost of restoring the environment in such a way that it is "preserved."

There are two different kinds of operations in preserving the environment. The first is the cleaning up of the negative effects of a production exercise (for example, combating chemical toxins that are a by-product of production or removing nonbiodegradable waste). The second is investment in the renewal of the natural resources that have been used (for example, replanting trees). Once again, the ecology movements have put forward a long series of specific proposals that would address these issues. In general, these proposals meet with considerable resistance on the part of the enterprises that would be affected by such proposals, on the grounds that these measures are far too costly and would therefore lead to the curtailment of production.

The truth is that the enterprises are essentially right. These measures are indeed too costly, by and large, if we define the issue in terms of maintaining the present average worldwide rate of profit. They are too costly by far. Given the deruralization of the world and its already serious effect upon the accumulation of capital, the implementation of significant ecological measures, seriously carried out, could well serve as the coup de grâce to the viability of the capitalist world-economy. Therefore, whatever the public relations stance of individual enterprises on these questions, we can expect unremitting foot-dragging on the part of capitalists in general. We are in fact faced with three alternatives. One, governments can insist that all enterprises internalize all costs, and we would be faced with an immediate acute profits squeeze. Or, two, governments can pay the bill for ecological measures (cleanup and restoration plus prevention) and use taxes to pay for this. But if one increases taxes, one either increases the taxes on the enterprises, which would lead to the same profits squeeze, or raises taxes on everyone else, which would probably lead to an acute tax revolt. Or, three, we can do virtually nothing, which will lead to the various ecological catastrophes of which the ecology movements warn. So far, the third alternative has been carrying the day. In any case, this is why I say that there is "no exit," meaning by that that there is no exit within the framework of the existing historical system.

Of course, if governments refuse the first alternative of requiring the internalization of costs, they can try to buy time. That is, in fact, what many have been doing. One of the main ways to buy time is to try to

shift the problem from the politically stronger to the backs of the politically weaker, that is, from the North to the South. There are two
ways in turn to do this. One is to dump the waste in the South. While
this buys a little time for the North, it doesn't affect global cumulation and its effects. The other is to try to impose upon the countries of
the South a postponement of "development" by asking them to accept
severe constraints on industrial production or the use of ecologically
sounder but more expensive forms of production. This immediately
raises the question of who is paying the price of global restraints and
whether in any case these partial restraints will work. If China were to
agree, for example, to reduce the use of fossil fuels, what would this do
to the prospects of China as an expanding part of the world market,
and therefore the prospects for capital accumulation? We keep coming
back to the same issue.

Frankly, it is probably fortunate that dumping on the South provides
in fact no real long-term solution to the dilemmas. One might say that
such dumping has been part of the procedure all along, for the past
five hundred years. But the expansion of the world-economy has been
so great, and the consequent level of degradation so severe, that we no
longer have the space to adjust the situation significantly by exporting it
to the periphery. We are thus forced back to fundamentals. It is a matter
of political economy first of all, and consequently a matter of moral and
political choice.

The environmental dilemmas we face today are directly the result
of the fact that we live in a capitalist world-economy. While all prior
historical systems transformed the ecology, and some prior historical
systems even destroyed the possibility of maintaining a viable balance in
given areas that would have assured the survival of the locally existing
historical system, only historical capitalism, by the fact that it has been
the first such system to englobe the earth and by the fact that it has expanded production (and population) at a previously unimaginable rate,
has threatened the possibility of a viable future existence for mankind.
It has done this essentially because capitalists in this system succeeded in
rendering ineffective the ability of all other forces to impose constraints
on their activity in the name of values other than that of the endless accumulation of capital. It is precisely Prometheus unbound that has been
the problem.

But Prometheus unbound is not inherent in human society. The un-
bounding, of which the defenders of the present system boast, was

itself a difficult achievement, whose middle-term advantages are now being overwhelmed by its long-term disadvantages. The political economy of the current situation is that historical capitalism is in fact in crisis precisely because it cannot find reasonable solutions to its current dilemmas, of which the inability to contain ecological destruction is a major one, if not the only one.

I draw from this analysis several conclusions. The first is that reformist legislation has built-in limits. If the measure of success is the degree to which such legislation is likely to diminish considerably the rate of global environmental degradation in say the next ten to twenty years, I would predict that this type of legislation will have very little success. This is because the political opposition can be expected to be ferocious, given the impact of such legislation on capital accumulation. It doesn't follow, however, that it is therefore pointless to pursue such efforts. Quite the contrary, probably. Political pressure in favor of such legislation can add to the dilemmas of the capitalist system. It can crystallize the real political issues that are at stake, provided, however, that these issues are posed correctly.

The entrepreneurs have argued essentially that the issue is one of jobs versus romanticism, or humans versus nature. To a large degree, many of those concerned with ecological issues have fallen into the trap by responding in two different ways, both of which are, in my view, incorrect. The first is to argue that "a stitch in time saves nine." That is to say, some persons have suggested that, within the framework of the present system, it is formally rational for governments to expend x-amounts now in order not to spend greater amounts later. This is a line of argument that does make sense within the framework of a given system. But I have just argued that, from the point of view of capitalist strata, such "stitches in time," if they are sufficient to stem the damage, are not at all rational, in that they threaten in a fundamental way the possibility of continuing capital accumulation.

There is a second, quite different, argument that is made, one that I find equally politically impractical. It is the argument on the virtues of nature and the evils of science. This translates in practice into the defense of some obscure fauna of whom most people have never heard, and about which most people are indifferent, and thereby puts the onus of job destruction on flaky middle-class urban intellectuals. The issue becomes entirely displaced from the underlying ones, which are, and must remain, two. The first is that capitalists are not paying their bills. And the second is that the endless accumulation of capital is a substantively irrational objective, and that there does exist a basic alternative, which is to weigh various benefits (including those of production) against each other in terms of collective substantive rationality.

There has been an unfortunate tendency to make science the enemy and technology the enemy, whereas it is in fact capitalism that is the generic root of the problem. To be sure, capitalism has utilized the splendors of unending technological advance as one of its justifications. And it has endorsed a version of science — Newtonian, determinist science — as a cultural shroud, which permitted the political argument that humans could indeed "conquer" nature, should indeed do so, and that thereupon all negative effects of economic expansion would eventually be countered by inevitable scientific progress.

We know today that this vision of science and this version of science are of limited universal applicability. This version of science is today under fundamental challenge from within the community of natural scientists themselves, from the now very large group who pursue what they call "complexity studies." The sciences of complexity are very different from Newtonian science in various important ways: the rejection of the intrinsic possibility of predictability; the normality of systems moving far from equilibrium, with their inevitable bifurcations; the centrality of the arrow of time. But what is perhaps most relevant for our present discussion is the emphasis on the self-constituting creativity of natural processes and the nondistinguishability of humans and nature, with a consequent assertion that science is of course an integral part of culture. Gone is the concept of rootless intellectual activity, aspiring to an underlying eternal truth. In its place we have the vision of a discoverable world of reality, but one whose discoveries of the future cannot be made now because the future is yet to be created. The future is not inscribed in the present, even if it is circumscribed by the past.

The political implication of such a view of science seems to me quite clear. The present is always a matter of choice, but as someone once said, although we make our own history, we do not make it as we choose. Still, we do make it. The present is a matter of choice, but the range of choice is considerably expanded in the period immediately preceding a bifurcation, when the system is furthest from equilibrium, because at that point small inputs have large outputs (as opposed to moments of near equilibrium, when large inputs have small outputs).

Let us return therefore to the issue of ecology. I placed the issue within the framework of the political economy of the world-system. I explained that the source of ecological destruction was the necessity of entrepreneurs to externalize costs and the lack of incentive therefore to make ecologically sensitive decisions. I explained also, however, that this problem is more serious than ever because of the systemic crisis into which we have entered. For this systemic crisis has narrowed in various ways the possibilities of capital accumulation, leaving as the one major crutch readily available the externalization of costs. Hence, I have argued it is less likely today than ever before in the history of this system to obtain the serious assent of entrepreneurial strata to measures fighting ecological degradation.

All this can be translated into the language of complexity quite readily. We are in the period immediately preceding a bifurcation. The present historical system is in fact in terminal crisis. The issue before us is what will replace it. This will be the central political debate of the next twenty-five to fifty years. The issue of ecological degradation, but not of course only this issue, is a central locus of this debate. I think what we all have to say is that the debate is about substantive rationality and that we are struggling for a solution or for a system that is substantively rational.

The concept of substantive rationality presumes that in all social decisions there are conflicts between different values as well as between different groups, often speaking in the name of opposing values. It presumes that there is never any system that can realize fully all these sets of values simultaneously, even if we were to feel that each set of values is meritorious. To be substantively rational is to make choices that will provide an optimal mix. But what does optimal mean? In part, we could define it by using the old slogan of Jeremy Bentham, the greatest good for the greatest number. The problem is that this slogan, while it puts us on the right track (the outcome), has many loose strings.

Who, for example, are the greatest number? The ecological issue makes us very sensitive to this issue. For it is clear that, when we talk of ecological degradation, we cannot limit the issue to a single country. We cannot even limit it to the entire globe. There is also a generational issue. On the one hand, what may be the greatest good for the present generation may be very harmful to the interests of future generations. On the other hand, the present generation also has its rights. We are already in the midst of this debate concerning living persons: percentage of total social expenditures on children, working adults, and the aged. If we now add the unborn, it is not at all easy to arrive at a just allocation.

But this is precisely the kind of alternative social system we must aim at building, one that debates, weighs, and collectively decides on such fundamental issues. Production is important. We need to use trees as wood and as fuel, but we also need to use trees as shade and as aesthetic beauty. And we need to continue to have trees available in the future for all these uses. The traditional argument of entrepreneurs is that such social decisions are best arrived at by the cumulation of individual decisions, on the grounds that there is no better mechanism by which to arrive at a collective judgment. However plausible such a line of reasoning may be, it does not justify a situation in which one person makes a decision that is profitable to him at the price of imposing costs on others, without any possibility for the others to intrude their views, preferences, or interests into the decision. But this is what the externalization of costs precisely does.

No exit? No exit within the framework of the existing historical system? But we are in the process of exit from this system. The real question before us is where we shall be going as a result. It is here and now that we must raise the banner of substantive rationality, around which we must rally. We need to be aware that once we accept the importance of going down the road of substantive rationality, this is a long and arduous road. It involves not only a new social system, but new structures of knowledge, in which philosophy and sciences will no longer be divorced, and we shall return to the singular epistemology within which knowledge was pursued everywhere prior to the creation of the capitalist world-economy. If we start down this road, in terms of both the social system in which we live and the structures of knowledge we use to interpret it, we need to be very aware that we are at a beginning, and not at all at an end. Beginnings are uncertain and adventurous and difficult, but they offer promise, which is the most we can ever expect.

Chapter 6

Liberalism and Democracy

Frères Ennemis?

Both liberalism and democracy have been sponge terms. Each has been given multiple, often contradictory, definitions. Furthermore, the two terms have had an ambiguous relationship to each other ever since the first half of the nineteenth century when they first began to be used in modern political discourse. In some usages, they have seemed identical, or at least have seemed to overlap heavily. In other usages, they have been considered virtually polar opposites. I shall argue that they have in fact been *frères ennemis*. They have been members in some sense of the same family, but they have represented pushes in very different directions. And the sibling rivalry, so to speak, has been very intense. I will go further. I would say that working out today a reasonable relationship between the two thrusts, or concepts, or values is an essential political task, the prerequisite for resolving positively what I anticipate will be the very strong social conflicts of the twenty-first century. This is not a question of definitions, but first and foremost one of social choices.

Both concepts represent responses, rather different responses, to the modern world-system. The modern world-system is a capitalist world-economy. It is based on the priority of the ceaseless accumulation of capital. Such a system is necessarily inegalitarian, indeed polarizing, both economically and socially. At the same time, the very emphasis on accumulation has one profoundly equalizing effect. It puts into question any status obtained or sustained on the basis of any other criteria, including all criteria that are acquired through filiation. This ideological contradiction between hierarchy and equality that is built into the very rationale for capitalism has created dilemmas, from the beginning, for all those who have privilege within this system.

Fourth Daalder Lecture, Rijksuniversiteit Leiden, Interfacultaire Vakgroep Politieke Wetenschappen, March 15, 1997.

87

Let us look at this dilemma from the point of view of the quintessential actor of the capitalist world-economy, the entrepreneur, sometimes called the bourgeois. The entrepreneur seeks to accumulate capital. To do this, he acts *through* the world market, but seldom exclusively *by means of* the market. Successful entrepreneurs necessarily depend on the aid of the state machinery's to help them create and retain relative sectorial monopolies, which are the only source of truly substantial profits in the market.[1]

Once the entrepreneur has accumulated substantial amounts of capital, he must worry about retaining it — against the vagaries of the market to be sure, and also against the attempts of others to steal it, confiscate it, or tax it away. But his problems do not end there. He must also worry about passing it on to heirs. This is not an economic necessity, but rather a sociopsychological necessity, one however that has serious economic consequences. The need to ensure that capital is bequeathed to heirs is an issue not primarily of taxation (which can be treated as an issue of defending the market against the state) but of the competency of heirs as entrepreneurs (which means that the market becomes the enemy of inheritance). Over the long run, the only way to ensure that incompetent heirs can inherit and retain capital is to transform the source of renewal of capital from profits to rents.[2] But while this solves the sociopsychological need, it undermines the social legitimacy of entrepreneurial accumulation, which is competency in the market. And this in turn creates a continuing political dilemma.

Now, let us look at the same problem from the point of view of the working classes, those who are not in a position to accumulate capital in any serious way. The development of the productive forces under capitalism leads as we know to vastly increased industrialization, urbanization, and geographical concentration of wealth and higher-wage employment. We are not concerned here with why this is so or how it occurs, but merely with its political consequences. Over time, and especially in the core or "more developed" countries, this process leads to a reconfiguration of the state-level stratification pattern, with increasing percentages of middle strata and higher-waged employees, and therefore to the increasing political strength of such persons. The primary geocultural consequence of the French Revolution and its Napoleonic aftermath was to legitimate the political demands of such persons via the argument that national sovereignty resided in the "people." While popular sovereignty was possibly compatible with the hypothetical egalitarianism of market accumulation, it was absolutely at odds with any and all attempts to create rentier sources of income.

Reconciling the ideology of market legitimacy with the socio-psychological need to create rentier income has always been a matter of fast talk for the entrepreneurs. The contradictory language of liberals is one of the results. It is this attempt to juggle the language that set the stage for the ambiguous relationship during the last two centuries of "liberalism" and "democracy." At the time that liberalism and democracy first began to be political terms in common usage, in the first half of the nineteenth century, it was the case that the basic political cleavage was between conservatives and liberals, the party of order and the party of movement. Conservatives were those fundamentally opposed to the French Revolution in all its guises — Girondin, Jacobin, Napoleonic. Liberals were those who saw the French Revolution as something positive, at the minimum in its Girondin version, which was believed to represent something akin to the English evolution of parliamentary government. This positive view of the French Revolution, cautious at first in 1815 in the wake of the Napoleonic defeat, became bolder as the years went by.

In the years between 1815 and 1848, in addition to the conservatives and the liberals, there were persons sometimes called democrats, quite often republicans, sometimes radicals, even occasionally socialists. These persons represented, however, not much more than a small left appendage of the liberals, sometimes playing the role of its ginger element, more often seen as an embarrassment by the mainline contingent of liberals. It is only later that this left appendage emerged as a full-fledged independent ideological thrust, at this later point usually under the label of socialists. After 1848, the ideological horizon became stabilized; we had arrived at the trinity of ideologies that have framed the political life of the nineteenth and twentieth centuries: conservatism, liberalism, and socialism/radicalism (otherwise known as right, center, and left). I shall not repeat here my argument about how and why liberalism after 1848 gained the upper hand over its rivals as an ideological construct, creating a consensus around it that became consecrated as the geoculture of the modern world-system and transforming both conservatism and socialism in the process into avatars of liberalism. Nor shall I repeat the argument that this consensus held firm until 1968, when it was once again called into question, allowing both conservatism and radicalism to reemerge as distinctive ideologies.[3]

What is crucial, I think, for the purposes of this discussion is to understand that, after 1848, the central concern of liberals ceased being to argue against the *Ancien Régime*. Rather, their central concern came to be at the other end of the political spectrum: how to counter the growing demand for democracy. The revolutions of 1848 showed, for the first time, the potential strength of a militant left force, the beginnings of a real social movement in the core zones and of national liberation movements in the more peripheral zones. The strength of this upsurge was frightening to the centrist liberals, and even though the revolutions of 1848 all petered out or were suppressed, liberals were determined to reduce the volubility of what they saw as the too radical, antisystemic demands of the dangerous classes.

Their counterefforts came in three forms. First, they put forward over the next half-century a program of "concessions" that they thought would satisfy these demands sufficiently to calm the situation but in such a way that the concessions would not threaten the basic structure of the system. Second, they quite openly replaced the de facto political coalition with the left (which they had pursued in the 1815–48 period, when the left seemed tiny and they thought their primary opponent was the conservatives) with a priority to political coalition on the right, whenever and wherever the left seemed threatening. Third, they developed a discourse that subtly distinguished liberalism from democracy.

The program of concessions — the suffrage, the beginnings of a welfare state, an integrative racist nationalism — was magnificently successful in the European/North American world and laid the basis for the ability of the capitalist system to surmount all its storms, at least until the last twenty years or so. The second measure, the political coalition with the right, turned out to be all the easier to achieve in that the right had drawn a similar conclusion as a consequence of 1848. "Enlightened conservatism" became the dominant version of right politics, and, since it was essentially an avatar of liberalism, there was no longer a real obstacle to a form of parliamentary life that involved the regular shift of formal power between parties whose real politics revolved around a centrist consensus, never swinging too far in either direction.

It is the third tactic, the discourse, that created some problems. This was because liberals wanted to have it both ways. They wanted to distinguish liberalism from democracy, but they wished at the same time to appropriate the theme of democracy, indeed the very term of democracy, as an integrative force. It is on the discourse and its problems that I wish to concentrate this discussion.

Liberalism, as is often noted, starts its analysis from the individual, whom it takes to be the primary subject of social action. The liberal metaphor is that the world consists of a multitude of independent individuals who have somehow, at some time, entered into an accord (social contract) to establish common ties for the common good. They have also pictured this accord as a quite limited accord. The source of this emphasis is obvious. Liberalism had its origins in the attempt to remove those persons whom liberals defined as "competent" from the arbitrary control of institutions (the church, the monarchies, and the aristocracy, and therefore the state) that they saw as being essentially in the hands of less competent persons. The concept of a limited social contract provided exactly the rationale for such a putative liberation of the competent.

This explains of course such traditional slogans identified with the French Revolution as "la carrière ouverte aux talents." The combination of the word "open" and the word "talent" gave the essential message. This quite precise language however soon slid into the vaguer, more fluid language of the "sovereignty of the people." The problem with this latter phrase, which was widely legitimated in the wake of the French Revolution, is that the "people" are a group far more difficult to bound than the "talented people." Talented people constitute a measurable group with logical boundaries. All we need to do is decide on some indicators of talent, no matter whether they are plausible or spurious, and we can identify who these persons are. But who constitute the "people" is not really a matter of measurement at all, but a matter of public, collective definition; that is, it is a political decision, and acknowledged as such.

Of course, if we were ready simply to define the "people" as truly everyone, there would be no problem. But the "people" as a political concept is primarily used to refer to rights within a state, and thereupon it becomes contentious. What is obvious is that virtually no one was, or is, prepared to say that the "people" is everyone, that is, that truly everyone should have full political rights. There are some widely agreed-upon exclusions: not children, not the insane, not criminals, not foreign visitors — all these exceptions being considered more or less obvious to almost everyone. But then to add to this list other categories of exceptions — not migrants, not the propertyless, not the poor, not the ignorant, not women — seemed to many just as obvious, especially to those who were not themselves migrants, propertyless, poor, ignorant, or women. Who the "people" are constitutes to this day a continuing and major source of political controversy, everywhere.

For the last two hundred years, throughout the world, those who have no rights, or less rights than others, have been constantly knocking at the door, pushing and shoving the door open, always asking for more. Let some in, and others have been coming right behind them requesting entry as well. Faced with this political reality, which is evident to everyone, the responses have been varied. In particular, the tonalities of the responses associated with liberalism and with democracy have been quite different, almost opposite.

Liberals have tended to seek to constrain the flow. Democrats have tended to applaud it and to push it. Liberals have asserted a primary concern with process; bad process leads to bad outcome. Democrats have asserted a primary concern with outcome; bad outcome indicates bad process. Liberals pointed to the past and stressed how much had been achieved. Democrats looked to the future and talked of how much was yet to be fulfilled. Cup half full? Cup half empty? Perhaps, but perhaps also a difference in objective.

The mantra of liberals is rationality. Liberals are the most loyal scions of the Enlightenment. They believe in the *potential* rationality of all persons, a rationality that is achieved, not ascribed, and achieved through education, *Bildung*. What education can create is not, however, merely intelligent citizens endowed with civic virtue. Liberals in the modern world have been well aware that the town meeting model of democracy, derived from the Greek city-state, is unmanageable in the physically large entities that are modern states, which are furthermore required to decide upon a wide range of complex matters. Liberals share the metaphor of Newtonian science: that complexity is best handled by reducing it to smaller parts, by differentiation and specialization. It follows that, in order to perform their role as intelligent citizens endowed with civic virtue, individuals have need of expert counsel to guide them, to delimit the alternatives, and to suggest criteria by which to judge political alternatives.

If rationality, to be exercised, requires expertise, it also then requires the civic culture of giving the specialists pride of place. The modern educational system, whether in its humanistic or scientific form, has been intended to socialize citizens into accepting the edicts of experts. This is the nexus around which all the debates about suffrage and other forms of political participation has revolved: who has the necessary expertise, who has the cultural frame of mind to allow themselves to be informed by these experts. In short, although all persons are potentially rational, not all persons are actually rational. Liberalism is the call to accord rights to the rational in order that the irrational not be those who make crucial social decisions. And if, under pressure, one is obliged politically to accord formal rights to the many who are not yet rational, it then becomes essential that the formal rights be circumscribed in such a way that no hasty foolishness occur. This is the source of the concern with process. What is meant by process is slowing down decisions long enough and in such a way that experts have an excellent chance of prevailing.

Exclusions of the irrational are always effectuated in the present. It is, however, always promised that the excluded will be included in the future, once they have learned, once they have passed the tests, once they have become rational *in the same way as those presently included.* While unfounded discrimination is anathema to the liberal, the liberal sees a world of difference between unfounded and founded discrimination.

The discourse of the liberal hence tends to be fearful of the majority, fearful of the unwashed and unknowing, of the mass. The discourse of the liberal no doubt is always full of praise for the potential integration of the excluded, but it is always a controlled integration of which the liberal is speaking, an integration into the values and structures of those who are already included. Against the majority, the liberal is constantly defending the minority. But it is not the group minority that the liberal defends, but the symbolic minority, the heroic rational individual against the crowd — that is, himself.

This heroic individual is both competent and civilized. The concept of the competent is not in fact very different from the concept of the civilized. Those who are civilized are those who have learned how to adjust themselves to the social needs of the *civis,* how to be both civil and civic, how to enter into a social contract and be responsible for the obligations that thereupon are incumbent upon them. It is always we who are civilized and they who are not. The concept is almost necessarily a universalist one, in the sense that the values involved are asserted to hold universally, but it is also a developmentalist one. One learns to be civilized; one is not born civilized. And individuals, groups, and nations can *become* civilized. Competence is a more instrumentalist notion. It refers to the ability to function socially, especially in work. It is linked to the idea of a *métier,* a profession. It is the result of education, but of more formal education than is the case for civilization, which is first and foremost a matter of childhood socialization within the family. Still, it is always assumed that there is a high correlation between the two, that those who are competent are also civilized and vice versa. A disjunction is surprising and anomalous and most of all disturbing. Liberalism is as much as anything a code of manners. That such definitions, however formally abstract, are always class-based or class-biased seems to me obvious.

The minute however we invoke civilization and competence, it is clear in any case that we are not speaking of everyone — not of all individuals, of all groups, of all nations. "Civilized" and "competent" are inherently comparative concepts, which describe a hierarchy of persons: some are more so than others. At the same time, they are universal concepts: everyone can become so in theory, eventually. Indeed, the universalism is closely related to the other inherent connotation of liberalism: paternalism toward the weak, the uncivilized, the incompetent. Liberalism implies a social duty to improve the others, by individual efforts to be sure, but most of all by collective efforts of the society and of the state. It is therefore perpetually the call for more education, more *Bildung*, more social reform.

The very term "liberal" has built into it not only the political meaning but the usage of largesse, of *noblesse oblige*. Powerful individuals can be liberal in their distribution of material and social values. And here we see quite openly the link with the concept of aristocracy, to which liberalism purports to be opposed. In reality, what liberals have opposed is not the concept of aristocracy per se, but the idea that aristocrats are persons defined by certain external signs of status, derived from past achievements of an ancestor, of titles that accord privileges. In his theorizing, the liberal is in that sense extremely present-oriented. It is the achievement of the current individual with which the liberal is concerned, at least theoretically. The aristocrats, the best, are really, can only really be, those who have proved in the present that they are the most competent. This is expressed in the twentieth-century usage of "meritocracy" as the defining legitimation of social hierarchy.

Meritocracy, unlike nobility, is presented as an egalitarian concept because formally it can be made open to everyone to take the tests that accord or define merit. One presumably does not inherit merit. But of course one inherits the advantages that improve considerably the possibility for a child to acquire the skills that are tested. And this being the fact, the results are never really egalitarian, which is the recurrent complaint of those who do poorly in the formal testing, and the allocation of position and status that is its consequence. These then are the complaints both of the democrats and of the "minorities," meaning by "minority" here any group (whatever its size) that has been persistently and historically treated as a socially inferior group and that is presently at the lower end of the social hierarchy.

The competent defend their advantage on the basis of formal rules that are universalist. They therefore defend the importance of formal rules in political controversy. They are by nature fearful of anything that can be called or considered "extreme." But what is "extreme" in modern politics? It is anything and everything that can be labeled "populist." Populism is the appeal to the people in terms of the outcome: the outcome in legislation; the outcome in social distribution of roles; the outcome in wealth. The liberal center has been for the most part viscerally antipopulist, although on rare occasions, when the threat of fascism was on the horizon, it has accepted for brief periods the legitimacy of popular demonstrations.

Populism has normally been a game of the left. At one level, the political left has been traditionally populist, or at the very least has traditionally pretended to be populist. It is the left that has spoken in the name of the people, of the majority, of the weaker and the excluded. It is the political left that has sought repeatedly to mobilize popular sentiment and to utilize this mobilization as a form of political pressure. And when this popular pressure emerged spontaneously, the leadership of the political left has usually run to catch up with it. Democrats have given priority to including the excluded, in specific opposition to the liberal notion that the good society is one in which the competent prevail.

There has also been right-wing populism. However, populism as played by the left and by the right are not quite the same game. Right-wing populism has never been truly populist, since it is right-wing, and what characterizes the right conceptually is that it puts no faith in the people except as followers. Right-wing populism has in practice combined hostility to experts with some social welfare concerns but always on the basis of great exclusionism, that is, limiting these benefits to an ethnically delimited group and often defining the experts as members of the out-group. Right-wing populism is therefore not democratic at all in the sense that we are using the term, as a concept that gives priority to including the excluded.

What we have meant by democracy is in fact quite opposed to right-wing populism, but it is also quite opposed to what we have meant by liberalism. Democracy precisely implies suspicion of the experts, of the competent — of their objectivity, of their disinterestedness, of their civic virtue. The democrats have seen in liberal discourse the mask for a new aristocracy, all the more pernicious in that it has claimed a universalist basis that somehow tended always to result in maintaining largely the existing patterns of hierarchy. Liberalism and democracy have thus been very much at odds with each other, standing for deeply diverging tendencies.

This is sometimes openly admitted. We find it in the discourse concerning the famous slogan of the French Revolution, about which it is often said that liberals give priority to liberty, meaning individual liberty, and that democrats (or socialists) give priority to equality. This, it seems to me, is a deeply misleading way to explain the difference. Liberals do not merely give priority to liberty; they are opposed to equality, because they are strongly opposed to any concept measured by outcome, which is the only way the concept equality is meaningful. Insofar as liberalism is the defense of rational government, based on the informed judgment of the most competent, equality appears as a leveling, anti-intellectual, and inevitably extremist concept.

However, it is not true that democrats are in a parallel manner opposed to liberty. Far from it! What democrats have refused is the distinction between the two. On the one hand, democrats have traditionally argued that there can be no liberty except within a system based on equality, since unequal persons cannot have equal ability to participate in collective decisions. They have also argued that unfree persons cannot be equal, since this implies a political hierarchy that thereby translates itself into social inequality. This has recently been given the conceptual label of egaliberty (or equaliberty) as a singular process.[4] On the other hand, it is true today that few on the self-proclaimed left have been ready to make egaliberty their theme of popular mobilization, out of the very same fear that has made liberals insist on process and competence: fear that the people, given full rein, will act irrationally, meaning in a fascist or racist fashion. What we can say is that the popular demand for democracy has been constant, whatever the formal position of left parties. Indeed, over the long run, left parties that have refused to embrace egaliberty have found that their popular base of support has eroded, and found that their erstwhile base came to classify them for this reason as "liberals" rather than as "democrats."

The tension between liberalism and democracy is not an abstract issue. It returns to us constantly as a set of political dilemmas and political choices. The world-system was engulfed by this tension and these dilemmas between the two world wars, with the rise of fascist movements in a large number of countries. We can remember the hesitations and indecision that were the mark of both centrist and left politics in this era. These hesitations have become visible and acute once again in the 1990s with the rise of multiple destructive racisms masking as nationalisms and the attempts, within the Western world, to build new exclusionary politics on the basis of anti-immigrant, antioutsider rhetoric.

At the same time, there is a second, quite different issue that emerged in the post-1968 era with the great upsurge of movements of the excluded, who were framing their demands for political rights in terms of group rights. This has taken the form of calls for "multiculturalism." Originally an issue primarily in the United States, it has now come to be discussed in most of the other countries with long-standing pretensions to being liberal states. This issue is often confounded with the issue of opposition to what the French call the *lepénisation* of society, but it is not the identical issue.

The relationship of the *frères ennemis* is thus once again today very much at the center of debates about political tactics. I don't think we are going to make any significant progress on this issue, unless we can cut through the rhetoric.

Let us start with some contemporary realities. I think there are four elements in the post-1989 situation that are basic, in the sense that they form the parameters within which political decisions are necessarily being made. The first is the profound disillusionment, worldwide, with the historic Old Left, in which I group not only the Communist parties, but the social-democratic parties and the national liberation movements as well. The second is the massive offensive to deregulate constraints on the movement of capital and commodities and to dismantle simultaneously the welfare state. This offensive is sometimes called "neoliberalism." The third is the constantly increasing economic, social, and demographic polarization of the world-system, which the neoliberal offensive promises to fuel further. The fourth is the fact that, despite all of this or perhaps because of all of this, the demand for democracy — for democracy, not liberalism — is stronger than it has been at any time in the history of the modern world-system.

The first reality, the disillusionment with the Old Left, is primarily, in my view, the result of the fact that, over time, the Old Left abandoned the struggle for democracy and advanced in fact a liberal program, in the very simple sense that they built their programs around the crucial role of the competent people. To be sure, they defined who was competent somewhat differently from centrist political parties, at least theoretically. However, in practice, it is not sure that they recruited their competent people from social backgrounds very different from those privileged in liberal discourse. In any case, the reality turned out to be insufficiently different for their mass base, and this base has been abandoning them as a result.[5]

The neoliberal offensive has been made possible by this widespread popular disillusionment with the Old Left. It has garbed itself with an essentially false rhetoric about globalization. The rhetoric is false in that the economic reality is not at all new (certainly the pressure on capitalist firms to be competitive in the world market is not new), but this alleged newness has been used as the justification for abandoning the historic liberal concession of the welfare state. It is precisely for this reason that neoliberalism cannot be considered in fact a new version of liberalism. It has adopted the name, but it is in fact a version of conservatism, and conservatism is, after all, different from liberalism. Historic liberalism has not been able to survive the collapse of the Old Left, which, far from being its mortal enemy, was its most important social underpinning, in that the Old Left had for a long time been playing the crucial role of containing the democratic pressures of the dangerous classes by purveying the hope (and the illusion) of inevitable progress. To be sure, the Old Left argued that this would be in large part via its own efforts, but this argument in effect endorsed policies and practices that were merely a variant on the incrementalist liberal theme.

What brought the Old Left down was the demonstration that it had not been able in reality to stanch the polarization of the world-system, especially at the world level. The neoliberal offensive has taken advantage of this to argue that its program would be able to do this. This is an incredible claim because, in point of fact, its program has been accentuating with striking rapidity the economic, social, and demographic polarization of the world-system. Furthermore, this recent offensive has actually renewed the process of polarization internal to the wealthier states, a process that the welfare state had been able to hold at bay for a relatively long time, and most notably in the period 1945–70. The correlate of increased polarization has been the increased immigration from South (including the old so-called East) to North, despite the ever-strengthened legislative and administrative barriers to legal migration.

Perhaps most importantly, the strength of democratic sentiment is greater than ever, probably more because of all of this than despite all of this. This strength can be observed in three specific demands, which can be seen operating across the globe: more education facilities, more health facilities, and a higher income base. Furthermore, what is considered the minimum acceptable threshold has been constantly increasing, never receding. This is of course deeply at odds with the program of dismantling the welfare state, and it therefore raises the potential for acute social conflict — on the one hand, in the form of relatively spontaneous worker mobilization (as has occurred in France, for example) or, on the other hand, and more violently, in the form of civil uprising (as has occurred in Albania, following the acute loss of income base in the wake of the Ponzi scheme scandal).

Whereas, from 1848 to 1968, we lived in a geoculture that was based on the liberal consensus, and the liberals were therefore able to appropriate the term "democracy" and vitiate the efficacy of its proponents, we have now entered the world of Yeats — "the center cannot hold." The issue before us is more polarized: either egaliberty or neither liberty nor equality; either a true effort to be inclusive of everyone or a retreat into a deeply partitioned world, a kind of global apartheid system. The strength of liberalism from 1848 to 1968 had forced the democrats to choose between accepting largely liberal premises or being condemned to political irrelevance. They opted for the former, which describes the historical trajectory of the Old Left. Today, however, it is for the surviving liberals to choose: either accepting largely democratic premises or being condemned to political irrelevance. We can see this by examining more closely the two great debates today between liberals and democrats: multiculturalism and *lepénisation*.

What are the issues in the multiculturalism debate? Groups that have been significantly excluded, both at national and at world levels, from political participation, economic reward, social recognition, and cultural legitimacy — most notably women and persons of color, but of course many other groups as well — have put forward demands in three different fashions: (1) They have quantified historic outcomes and said that the figures are disgraceful. (2) They have looked at the objects of study and of esteem, and the presumed "subjects of history," and said that the choices up to now have been deeply biased. (3) They have wondered whether the standards of objectivity that have been used to justify these realities are not themselves a false barometer and a leading generator of the realities.

The liberal response to these demands has been that demands for outcomes are demands for quotas, which in turn can only lead to pervasive mediocrity and new hierarchies. They have asserted that esteem and historic relevance are not decreed but deduced from objective criteria. They have said that tampering with the standards of objectivity is the slippery slope to total subjectivity and thereby total social irrationality. These are weak arguments, but they are not arguments that do not point to real problems with multiculturalism in its vaguer, less self-aware formulations.

The problem with all multicultural claims is that they are not self-limiting. First, the number of groups is not self-limiting, and indeed they are infinitely expansible. Second, the claims lead to unresolvable disputes about hierarchies of historic injustice. Third, even if adjustments are made in one generation, there is no assurance that they will last into the next. Should then readjustments be made every x-number of years? Fourth, the claims give no clue as to how to allocate scarce resources, especially nondivisible resources. Fifth, there is no guarantee that multicultural allocation will in the end be egalitarian, since the claims can in fact simply result in designating new criteria for membership in the group of competent persons who will receive privilege.

This being said, it is hard not to see how self-serving such anti-multiculturalist arguments are in the deeply inegalitarian world in which we presently live. Despite the hype and the howls of anti-PC publicists, we are far from living in a world already dominated by multicultural realities. We are barely beginning to make a small dent in historic unfairnesses. Blacks, women, and many others are still getting the short end of the stick, by and large, whatever the marginal improvements here and there. It is certainly far too soon to call for a swing back of the pendulum.

What is really more to the point is to begin a serious investigation of how we can build structures and processes that will constantly move us in the right direction, without ending us up in the culs-de-sac that the liberals correctly fear might result from doing this. It is clearly the moment for liberals, as a dying breed with however strong intellectual traditions, to use their cleverness as part of the team, instead of carping, or denouncing, from the sidelines. To take a simple example, would it not really have been more useful for someone like Alan Sokal to enter into cooperative discussion with those who have been raising real questions about the structures of knowledge, instead of deflating foolish excesses, and thereby making the discussion of the underlying issues more, rather than less, difficult?

The thing to bear in mind is the problem: the problem is exclusion, and the fact that this problem has not at all been resolved by the so-called advance of the modern world-system. If anything, it is worse today than ever. And democrats are those who put priority on fighting exclusion. If inclusion is difficult, exclusion is immoral. And liberals who seek the good society, who seek the realization of a rational world, must bear in mind Max Weber's distinction between formal and substantive rationality. Formal rationality is problem-solving but lacks a soul, and is therefore ultimately self-destructive. Substantive rationality is extraordinarily difficult to define, lends itself to much arbitrary distortion, but is ultimately what the good society is all about.

Multiculturalism is an issue that will not go away, as long as we are in an inegalitarian world, which is as long as we are in a capitalist world-economy. I think that this will be far less long than many others do, but, even in my view, it will take another fifty years or so before our present historical system has entirely collapsed.[6] The issue during these fifty years is precisely what kind of a historical system we shall build to replace the present one. And here is where the issue of *lepénisation* comes in, for a world in which racist, exclusionary movements gain an increasing role and are able to set the agenda for public political debate is a world that is likely to end up with an even worse structure than our present one, from the point of view of maximizing egaliberty.

Let us take the concrete case of the Front National (FN) in France. This is a movement that is against both competence and inclusion. It therefore violates the principles and objectives of both liberals and democrats. The question is what to do about it. Its strength derives from a diffuse anxiety among persons of relatively little power, but across different class positions, about their personal security, physical and material. These persons have a realistic basis for their fears. What the FN offers, as do all such movements, is three things: a promise of more physical security via a repressive state; a promise of more material security through a vague program combining neoliberalism and the welfare state; and, most of all, a visible scapegoat explanation for the difficulties people are experiencing. In the case of the FN, the scapegoat is first of all "migrants," a term used to mean all non-West Europeans (who are all defined as non-Whites), adding to the potion an argument about the proper role of women. The second scapegoat, carefully intruded from time to time, but less overtly to evade French antiracist laws, is clever and wealthy Jews, cosmopolitan intellectuals, and the existing political elites. In short, the scapegoats are the excluded and the competent.

For a long time, the response to the FN has been evasive. Conservatives have sought to recoup FN voters by adopting a watered-down version of the exclusionary theme. Centrist liberals, whether in the RPR, UDF, or the Socialist Party, initially tried to ignore the FN, in the hope that it would somehow go away, if ignored. Antiexclusionist mobilization was left to a handful of movements (like SOS-Racisme) and some intellectuals, as well of course to members of the communities under attack. When, in 1997, the FN for the first time won an outright majority in a local election at Vitrolles, the panic button was pushed, and a national mobilization occurred. The government, split between its true conservatives and its centrist liberals, retreated on one egregious clause in proposed antimigrant legislation and maintained the rest. In short, the policy of seeking to recoup FN voters largely prevailed.

What has been the program of the democrats? Basically, it has been to argue that all persons already in France should one way or another be "integrated" into French society by according them rights, and to oppose all repressive legislation. But the crucial subtext is that this applies only to all persons already in France, as well as perhaps to bona fide refugees. No one has dared to suggest that *all* limitation of individual movement across frontiers be eliminated, although, indeed, such lack of limitation is already in practice among the countries of the North and was historically in practice in most of the world until the twentieth century. The reason for such reticence, of course, is that even the French democrats fear that taking such a position would strengthen the hold of the FN on members of the working class.

If I pose, however, this "extreme" possibility, it is precisely because it illuminates the issue. If the issue is exclusion, why should the struggle against exclusion only be within state frontiers and not throughout the world? If the issue is competence, why should competence be defined within state frontiers and not throughout the world? And if we take the conservative, so-called neoliberal, perspective of the virtues of deregulation, then why shouldn't the movements of people also be subject to deregulation? Neither in France, nor elsewhere, is it likely that racist, exclusionary movements will be checked if the issues are not posed clearly and up front.

Let us return to the relationship of liberals and democrats. The one, I have said, has put forward the defense of competence. The other, I have said, has put forward the urgent priority of combating exclusion. It would be easy to say, Why not do both? But it is not easy to give equal emphasis to both. Competence, almost by definition, involves exclusion. If there is competence, then there is incompetence. Inclusion involves equal weight to everyone's participation. At the level of government and all political decision making, the two themes come, almost inevitably, into conflict. The *frères* become *ennemis*.

The liberals have had their day in the sun. Today, we are threatened by the return of those who want neither competence nor inclusion, in short the worst of all worlds. If we are to build a barrier to their rise, and to construct a new historical system, it can only be on the basis of inclusion. It is time for the liberals to defer to the democrats. If they do this, they can still play a salutary role. The liberals can continue to remind democrats of the risks of foolish and hasty majorities, but they can only do so within the context of the recognition of the fundamental priority of the majority in collective decisions. The liberals can of course, in addition, constantly call for eliminating from the realm of collective decisions all those matters that should be best left to individual choice and variation, and they are legion. This kind of libertarianism would be very salutary in a democratic world. And of course, in placing inclusion before competence, we are talking primarily of the political arena. We are not suggesting that competence is irrelevant in the workplace or in the world of knowledge.

There is an old joke about the relationship of the wealthy person to the intellectual. It goes this way. The wealthy person says to the intellectual: If you're so smart, why aren't you rich? Answer: If you're so rich, why aren't you smart? Let us vary this joke slightly. The liberal says to the democrat: If you represent the majority, why don't you govern competently? Answer: If you're so competent, why can't you get the majority to agree with your proposals?

Chapter 7

Integration to What? Marginalization from What?

Both "integration" and "marginalization" are words that are currently widely used in public discussion of contemporary social structures. They are concepts central to the social science enterprise as well, insofar as both refer implicitly to the concept of "society." The problem with the discussion within social science is that, although the concept of society is basic to our analyses, it is at the same time an extraordinarily vague term, and this confuses the discussion about integration and marginalization.

The concept of society is, I suppose, millennial, in the sense that it has probably been true for at least ten thousand years, if not longer, that humans have been aware of two things about the world in which they live. They interact on a regular basis with others, usually persons located in propinquity. And this "group" has rules of which they all take account, and which in fact fashion in many ways their consciousness of the world. The membership of such groups, however, is always less than the totality of human beings on the earth, and hence the members always distinguish between "we" and "the others."

The classic myths that humans have tended to create about their own "societies" is that the gods somehow created their particular one, usually created it especially, in some remote era, and that the current members are descended from this favored original group. Aside from the self-serving character of such myths, they also imply consanguineal continuity.

Of course, we know that consanguineal continuity is quite literally a myth, in the sense that no group has ever operated this way perfectly. And we know that this is particularly true of the modern world.

Keynote address at the nineteenth Nordic Sociology Congress, entitled "Integration and Marginalization," June 13–15, Copenhagen.

Hence, since persons from outside the groups are constantly seeking to enter them or are being pulled into them in one way or another, we talk of integration. And since other people are constantly seeking to withdraw from the groups or are being pushed out of them, we speak of marginalization.

The basic intellectual problem is that the modern world-system has created considerable confusion about what we can identify as our "society" and therefore about what we can mean by integration into and marginalization from such societies. It is quite clear that, in practice, we have been using the word "society" for at least two centuries now to mean the group that is located within the boundaries of a sovereign state, or sometimes what we think ought to be the boundaries of some sovereign state, existing or to be created. Now, whatever is the ancestry of such state-bounded groups, they bear little resemblance to continuing consanguineal groups.

Indeed, one of the principles of most sovereign states in the last two centuries has been that they are composed of "citizens," of *demos* and not of *ethnos,* and therefore represent a category that is more juridical than cultural in character. Furthermore, the category "citizens" is not at all self-evident in its geographical contours; that is, it is not perfectly congruent with persons resident at any particular point of time in a given sovereign state. Some inside the state are not citizens, and some outside the state are. In addition, while states have quite varying rules about the acquisition (and loss) of citizenship, they all have some rules, as well as rules governing the entry of noncitizens into their territory (immigration) and the legal rights of resident noncitizens. Furthermore, migration (inward and outward) is not an exceptional phenomenon in the modern world-system, but rather a continuing (and relatively massive) phenomenon.

Let us begin at the beginning. The modern world-system was constructed during the long sixteenth century, and its original geographical bounds included a large part of the European continent and parts of the Americas. Within this geographic zone, an axial division of labor grew up that took the form of a capitalist world-economy. An institutional framework to sustain this kind of historical system grew up alongside it. One such institutional element, a quite essential one, was the creation of so-called sovereign states, which were located within an interstate system. Of course, this was a process and not an event. Historians describe this process when they discuss state-building within Europe beginning with the New Monarchies of the late fifteenth century, the rise of diplomacy and its rules beginning with the Italian city-states in the Renaissance, the establishment of colonial regimes in the Americas and elsewhere, the collapse of the Hapsburg world-empire in 1557, and the Thirty Years' War culminating in the Treaty of Westphalia with its new foundations for state integration and interstate order.

This process of state-construction was not, however, a process separate from the development of historical capitalism, but rather an integral part of the story. Capitalists were well served by the establishment of such sovereign states, obtaining from them a multiplicity of services: to guarantee their property rights, to provide them with protection rent,[1] to create the quasi-monopolies they needed to make significant profits, to advance their interests over those of rival entrepreneurs located in other countries, and to provide sufficient order to guarantee their security.[2] Of course, these states were not equal in strength, and it was precisely this inequality that enabled the stronger states to serve well their entrepreneurs. But there was no land area within the division of labor that was not under the jurisdiction of some state, and therefore there were no individuals who were not subject to some primary state authority.

The period going from the sixteenth to the eighteenth centuries marked the institutionalization of this system. During this period, the original claim to the exercise of sovereignty was put forward in the name of a so-called absolute monarch, although subsequently in some states the ruler was under pressure to share the exercise of these sovereign powers with a legislature or a magistrature. We are still however before the era of passports and visas, or of migration controls, or of significant voting privileges for more than a very small minority of the populations. The mass of the population were "subjects," and a distinction between subjects who had some kind of descent rights and those who did not was seldom invoked and not very meaningful. In the seventeenth century, the juridical and social difference in day-to-day life between say a Breton migrant to Paris and a Rhineland migrant to Leyden (one crossing a not very visible international frontier and the other not) was hard to discern.

The French Revolution transformed this situation, by transforming subjects into citizens. There would be no turning back, either for France or for the capitalist world-system as a whole. The states had become theoretically, and to some degree in practice, responsible to a large group of persons with constituted political claims. During the nineteenth and twentieth centuries, implementation of these political claims may have been slow and quite uneven in reality, but there was a clear triumph of the rhetoric. And rhetoric matters. But once there were citizens, there were noncitizens as well.

The transformation of subjects into citizens was the consequence of pressures both from above and below. Popular demands for participation in governance, what might be called the demand for democratization, expressed itself constantly and in whatever ways it could. It served as an underlying force that found expression in populism and in revolutionary upsurges. The claimants were regularly suppressed, but the concept survived in a larval form, always there with a potential to grow, even if often weak as an immediate presence.

The long-run response to these demands of the so-called dangerous classes was the political program of liberalism, the triumphant ideology of the capitalist world-system in the nineteenth century. The liberals proposed a program of rational reform, of measured concessions, of gradual institutional change. The nineteenth-century program of liberalism had three main components: suffrage, redistribution, and nationalism.[3] Suffrage involved giving the vote to larger and larger segments of those resident in the state. By the twentieth century, universal suffrage of adult males and females (with exceptions for specified categories like felons and the insane) came to be the norm. Redistribution involved state-decreed and state-enforced minimal levels of wages and state-administered social security and welfare benefits, the so-called welfare state, a program that also became the norm, at least in the wealthier countries, by the mid–twentieth century. The third element in the program, nationalism, involved the creation of a sense of patriotic attachment to one's own state, systematically transmitted primarily by two institutions: primary schools (once again virtually universal by the mid–twentieth century) and the armed services (participation in which came to be the norm in most countries, even in peacetime, at least for men). Collective nationalist rituals also became quite frequent everywhere.

If we look at each of these three major political institutions — suffrage, the welfare state, and nationalist rituals/sentiments — we see immediately the relevance of the distinction citizen/noncitizen, at least as it operated up to twenty years ago or so. Only citizens had votes. It was unthinkable that noncitizens would be allowed to vote, however long they might have been resident in a country. State-administered welfare benefits usually, although not in every case, made distinctions between citizens and noncitizens. And of course, nationalist rituals/sentiments were the domain of citizens, from which noncitizens were socially excluded, as a consequence of which the latter became morally suspect, especially in times of interstate tension.

It is not only that these three institutions were developed as institutions of the separate states, albeit in parallel manner, but that citizens were thereby privileged to be central to the process of constructing and strengthening their own states. Since the states were involved in an interstate competition for the "wealth of nations," and since the privileges of the citizens seemed to depend on the achievement of the states, citizenship was considered to be an exceptional privilege, certainly at least in all those states that were in the upper quartile of the hierarchy of GNP. Furthermore, these states all presented themselves to their citizens as somehow quite special, and this seemed plausible to those who benefited from citizenship.

Citizenship thus became something very valuable, and consequently not something one was very willing to share with others. Citizenship in one's state might be doled out to a few eager applicants, but in general it was an advantage to be hoarded. This was all the more true insofar as the citizens believed that they had struggled internally (and externally) to acquire this privilege and that it had not been a mere gift to them. They felt they merited the citizenship morally. Thus the fact that citizenship as a concept constituted a demand from the bottom up made it all the more efficacious as a mechanism by which the dangerous classes were tamed from the top down. All the state rituals combined to reinforce the belief that the "nation" was the only society to which one belonged or, if not the only one, the most important one by far.

Citizenship effaced, or at least obscured, all other sorts of conflicts — class conflicts; conflicts between groups or strata defined in terms of race, ethnicity, gender, religion, language, or any other social criterion other than "nation/society." Citizenship brought *national* conflict to the forefront. Citizenship was intended to be unifying within the state, and it did in practice serve this purpose well, all the more so since citizenship conferred privilege, or at least seemed to do so. The concept of citizen has been in general a quite stabilizing element in the modern world-system. It did reduce *intra*state disorder, and it cannot be argued that it increased significantly *inter*state disorder above the level that would probably have existed in its absence. It has not only been a stabilizing concept; it has been a central one. One has but to look at the juridical scaffolding of modern states to realize how much of the legislation and administration of states depends on the category of citizen.

Nonetheless, the concept of citizen has created difficulties, for one of the socioeconomic underpinnings of the capitalist world-economy is the imperative of continuing physical flows of the labor force, or migration. Migration is first of all an economic necessity. The constant shifts in the location of economic activities, combined with the uneven distribution of demographic norms, means that, inevitably, there are disparities in local supplies and demands for specific kinds of workers. Whenever this happens, the interests of some workers and some employers are clearly served by some kind of labor migration, and it therefore tends to occur, with greater or lesser promptness depending on the legal constraints (as well as the practical possibilities of evading these constraints). The disparity of local supplies and demands of the labor force cannot be calculated simply in absolute totals of the labor force. Different groups of workers tend to price themselves at different levels for similar kinds of work. This is what we mean by "historical wages." Hence, it is perfectly possible that, in a given local area, there are persons seeking wage work who will refuse to accept certain types of low-paid wage work, and employers will turn to potential or actual immigrants to fill the needs.

So, despite the fact that citizenship is a cherished good, which gives rise to "protectionist" sentiment, migration is a constantly recurring phenomenon in the modern world. This has been true since the beginnings of the modern world-system. I am not sure that migration, however defined, is really quantitatively greater today than in previous centuries as a percentage of the total population, despite the improvement in transport facilities, but it is certainly a more politically noticed and politically controversial phenomenon.

It is the concept of citizen that has changed the meaning of the term "migrant." A person who leaves a rural area or a small town and moves to a large city fifty kilometers away may be going through a social transformation as great as one who moves to a large city five thousand kilometers away. Or, if this is no longer true in many countries in the late twentieth century, it was probably more or less true everywhere until at least 1950. The difference is that the five-thousand-kilometer migrant is quite likely to traverse a state frontier, whereas the fifty-kilometer migrant is unlikely to do so. Hence, the former is legally defined as a migrant (ergo not a citizen), whereas the latter is not.

A significant proportion of migrants tend to stay in the locale (or at least the state) into which they have migrated. They tend to have children who are born in the new locale and who, quite often, are culturally the products of their birthplace and not that of their parents' birthplace. When we discuss the issue of integration, it is the integration of such long-term migrants, and their children, of which we are usually speaking. Receiving countries have different rules about the citizenship of persons born in the country, from the *jus soli* of the United States and Canada to the *jus sanguinis* of Japan and in a modified form Germany, with a continuum of possibilities in between.

Integration is a cultural concept, not a legal one. The concept of integration assumes that there is some cultural norm into the acceptance of which one has to be integrated. For some states, which are largely mono-lingual and mono-religious, such a norm may seem relatively obvious and not too intrusive, although even in such states one can always find "minorities" who deviate from these normative patterns. For other states, which have more "variegated" populations, dominant norms exist nonetheless, but they seem more overbearing and pernicious. Take the United States. At the time of the founding of the republic, the cultural norm of citizenship was to be an English-speaking Protestant of one of four varieties (Episcopalian, Presbyterian, Methodist, and Congregationalist). Of course, this definition corresponded to the upper stratum but included parts of the middle and lower strata as well. This definition was slowly extended to include other varieties of Protestants. Roman Catholics and Jews were fully included in the cultural definition only as recently as the 1950s, at which point politicians began to speak of the "Judeo-Christian heritage." African-Americans have never really been included, whereas Latinos and Asian-Americans seem to be in a holding pattern, awaiting their future admission. Muslims, now for the first time a significant minority, are still excluded.

The U.S. example shows the flexibility that is possible in defining the cultural normative pattern of any particular state. The quasi-official ideological interpretation of this flexibility within the United States is that it shows the capacity of the U.S. political system to incorporate outsiders into the category of citizen, and thereby to "integrate" them into the nation. No doubt it does show this. But it also shows that at no point have all migrants been integrated. One might wonder whether there is not something inherent in the process such that at no point would it ever be true that all outsiders will be incorporated. Emile Durkheim once suggested that, whenever deviance disappears de facto, the social system redefines its norms so as to re-create statistical deviance. Perhaps the same thing is true in relation to the concept of citizen. When all residents are de facto integrated, does the "nation" redefine itself so as to re-create "marginals"?

Such an outrageous idea assumes that there is social utility to the creation of marginals, and social scientists have in fact often suggested this in one way or another: the value of a scapegoat on whom to thrust our collective sins; the existence of an understratum to create permanent fear among the dangerous classes that they might be made even worse off than they are, and that they therefore should restrain their level of demands; the strengthening of in-group loyalty by providing visible, and undesirable, contrasting strata. These are all plausible suggestions; they are, however, also quite general and generic.

I noted earlier that this pattern remained more or less the same from about 1800 to the 1970s, intimating that matters have changed somewhat since then. I believe this is true. The world revolution of 1968 marked a turning-point in the history of our modern world-system in many ways. What has not been noticed is that one of its consequences was to put into question, for the first time since the French Revolution, the concept of citizenship. It was not merely the fact that 1968 was "internationalist" in spirit. After all, we had internationalist movements already throughout the nineteenth and twentieth centuries: on the one hand, the various workers' internationals, and, on the other hand, all kinds of peace movements. As we know, such internationalist movements were not very efficacious in constraining the outburst of nationalist sentiment among their members or audience when tension in the interstate system rose sharply. The most notable instance, regularly noted, was the response of the socialist parties to the outbreak of the First World War.[4] The reason is well explained by A. Kriegel and J. J. Becker in their book on the French socialist debates in the weeks preceding the outbreak of war in 1914:

> It appears thus that a certain socialism is nothing but a modern form of Jacobinism, and, faced with one's country in danger, the voice of the "great ancestors" outweighed that of socialist theories, whose relevance to the immediate situation was difficult to perceive. In the immense patriotic whirlwind in which the country was enveloped, war was once again

seen as capable of achieving old aspirations: instead of human fraternity through peace, it was human fraternity through war, through victory.[5]

The internationalist orientation of workers' and peace movements was deeply constrained by the fact that each had created their organizations at the national level. But even more important, they had created their organizations at the national level because they considered that their objectives could best, perhaps only, be realized at the national level. That is, they acted primarily as citizens, joined together in a political effort to influence, even transform, their states. It was their presumption that, by changing their states, they would contribute to creating the international solidarity of which they were partisan. Nonetheless, the political activity was first of all, and most often exclusively, national.

What was different about the world revolution of 1968 was that it was just the opposite, an expression of disillusionment in the possibilities of state-level reformism. Indeed, the participants went further. They argued in effect that the orientation to national reformism was itself a prime means of sustaining a world-system they wanted to reject. The revolutionaries were not against popular action but against citizen action, even when it claimed to be "revolutionary." It was this stance that perhaps aroused the greatest dismay among those distressed by the 1968 uprisings, especially among the Old Left.

This attitude of the 1968 revolutionaries arose out of two analyses they made of the history of the modern world-system. The first was that the historic two-step strategy of the world's antisystemic movements — first achieve state power, then transform the world — was in their view a historic failure. The revolutionaries of 1968 said in effect that the antisystemic movements born in the nineteenth and twentieth centuries — the Social-Democrats, the Communists, and the national liberation movements — all had in fact already come to state power, more or less, in the period following the Second World War. But, having done so, they hadn't changed the world.

This first observation was rendered still more critical by the second element of the analysis. Insofar as the antisystemic movements had achieved power, it was indeed true that they had effectuated certain reforms that seemed to be progressive, if not revolutionary. But, but... these reforms were said to have systematically favored a particular and small segment of the lower strata — those of the dominant ethnic group in each country, males primarily, those who were more educated (Shall we say more "integrated"?) into the national culture. There were many others left out, forgotten, "marginalized," who hadn't benefited really even from the limited reforms that had been instituted: the women, the "minorities," and all sorts of nonmainstream groups.

What happened after 1968 is that the "forgotten peoples" began to organize both as social movements and as intellectual movements and set forth their claims not merely against the dominant strata but against the concept of the citizen. One of the most important themes of the post-1968 movements was that they were not merely opposed to racism and sexism. After all, there had long been movements who fought against racism and sexism. But the post-1968 movements added something new. They insisted not merely that racism and sexism were matters of individual prejudice and discrimination but that they took on "institutional" forms as well. What these movements seemed to be talking about was not overt juridical discrimination but the covert forms that were hidden within the concept of "citizen," insofar as citizen was meant to indicate the combination of competence and inherited rights.

Of course, any struggle against *covert* denial of rights is plagued by the problem of plausibility, evidence, and ultimately proof. What the movements pointed to was outcome. They argued that, in point of fact, there continued to exist gross differentials in the hierarchical position of multiple groups, and this outcome could only be, it was argued, the outcome of institutional marginalization. As an argument in social science, the assertion that institutional marginalization was systematic and fundamental to the contemporary world-system has basically only two possible responses.

One is the conservative response: to deny the premises. The differential in outcomes in group hierarchization may be patently observable, but it does not follow that the cause is institutional marginalization. It can be argued that other factors explain the differential outcome, factors having to do with cultural differentials among the groups. This line of reasoning faces a simple logical problem. Even if we discover so-called cultural differentials among the groups being measured, how in turn do we explain these differentials — by other cultural differentials? Ultimately, we must return either to a social-structural explanation, which was the case of those who put forward the hypothesis of institutional racism/sexism, or alternatively to a sociobiological one, which quickly glides into classical racism-sexism.

If we wish to reject the conservative stance and accept the social-structural explanation, then the issue shifts from accounting for the differentials to reducing them, presuming that this is seen as a moral good. And indeed, this has been one of the central, if not the central, political debate of the last twenty years. Let us review the various positions put forth in this debate. The simplest position — simplest because it accords best with the traditional arguments of liberal ideology — has been that institutional racism and sexism can be overcome by making overt what was covert. And, many added, since it takes time for the process to work, it can be speeded up by *temporary* systematic assistance to those against whom institutional marginalization had historically operated. This was the essential case for the original program of this kind, the U.S. program called "affirmative action."

In effect, affirmative action programs are intended to "integrate" those who in theory should long since have been integrated. They are programs to carry out the original intent of the concept of citizenship, which, it was being argued, had somehow been subverted by forces antithetical to the full realization of democracy, or citizenship. Affirmative action programs tended to assume the good faith of the "system," but the bad faith of individual participants. They therefore seldom, if ever, posed the prior question of whether there was anything systemic in the fact that theoretical citizenship had never been fully realized, even for the categories of persons to whom it supposedly applied.

Affirmative action programs — which, even with great efforts (political and financial), had accomplished limited results — had three drawbacks. In the first place, there was considerable covert resistance to them, and this resistance found many outlets. For example, transgroup school integration was extremely difficult, as long as de facto housing segregation existed. But to challenge de facto housing segregation meant both to intrude in an area generally considered to be part of individual choice and to tackle the issue of class-based de facto housing segregation (since class and race/ethnicity categories were highly correlated).

In the second place, affirmative action only took into account in some sense those who theoretically had citizen rights. But the definition of these categories was in itself part of the issue. Should the children of migrants (Turks in Germany, Koreans in Japan, and so on) be excluded from the rights enjoyed by the children of nonmigrants? Should migrants themselves be excluded? This led to many demands for the extension of citizenship rights to juridical noncitizens — both by the easing of the mechanisms of acquiring citizenship and even by the formal extension of some rights historically accorded only to citizens to noncitizens (for example, the right to vote, at least in so-called local elections).

In the third place, the logic of affirmative action led to the expansion of the kinds of groups making claims, as well as to the subdivision of groups making claims. And inevitably, this led to a de facto quota system that seemed to have no end. Nor was it clear when this temporary adjustment could or would make place for a so-called reformed or fully implemented citizenship to operate without reference to subgroups of citizens. This led inevitably to the charge of "reverse racism" — that is, to the charge that the previously marginalized groups were now in fact being juridically favored, and particularly at the expense of other low-ranking groups who had been historically more integrated (say, members of the working classes who were male and of the dominant ethnic group). Affirmative action thereupon became not merely difficult to administer and of uncertain benefits but politically very difficult to sustain. This was true not merely within the states as political structures but within the universities as structures of knowledge as well.

There was of course another path to pursue if one wished to overcome the limitations of traditional concepts of citizenship, limitations in terms of the unequal outcomes. Instead of pursuing further "integration" into the structures of marginalized groups, one could pursue the path of the equality of groups. Whereas affirmative action found legitimation in the liberal concept of the perfect equality of all citizens, the concept of group equality found legitimacy in the liberal concept of the self-determination of nations. To be sure, the latter concept had been intended to apply only to the relations of states to each other, and hence to the rights of "colonies" to become sovereign states, but it was only a slight stretch of the concept to apply it to groups within states.

This was the path of group "identity," which, as we know, has found strong support within women's groups, within groups based on race or ethnicity, within groups based on sexuality, and indeed within an expanding number of other groups. The path of group identity has involved the rejection of the concept of integration entirely. Why, said its proponents, should marginalized groups want to integrate into dominant groups? The very concept of integration involves, they argued, the assumption of biological or at least biocultural hierarchy. It assumes that the group into which one is being called to integrate is, in some way, superior to the group that has been marginalized. On the contrary, said the proponents of group identity, our historical identity is at least as valid as, if not outrightly superior to, the identity into which we are being called to integrate.

The path of groups proclaiming the validity of their identity, and hence the need to reinforce group consciousness of their identity, is the path generically of "cultural nationalism." This is essentially a segregationist path, but (it turns out) not one necessarily antithetical to state integration. One can argue for it in the name of a state integration based not on individual citizens but on collective citizens, so to speak.

The difficulties with this path lie in the definition of the groups that could be the collective citizens. This is not necessarily insoluble. Switzerland historically has acknowledged, in certain ways, collective linguistic citizens. Some persons in Quebec have argued for the recognition of two historic "nations" within the Canadian state. Belgium has gone down this path. Without arguing the specific political situations of each of these cases, it is apparent that, whenever one puts forth the idea of collective citizens, one political dilemma is that there are always unresolved, and perhaps unresolvable, nodal points of noninclusion (so-called allophones in Canada) or overlap (Brussels in Belgium).

But this is the not the greatest difficulty of cultural nationalism. After all, one can in many cases arrive at political compromises. The greatest problem, as in the case of affirmative action, is the definition of the groups themselves, and for themselves. For, as we know, however we define cultural groups, they contain subgroups or crosscutting groups. The discussion within women's movements about the neglect of the interests of women of color (at a national level) or of Third World women (at a world level) by White women has led to divisions parallel to those provoked by the discussion within states of the neglect of the interests of women by men.

Once again, there are ways to handle this politically. They all take the form, more or less, of proposing a "rainbow" coalition, that is, a coalition of all marginalized groups within the state to pursue transformations of interests common to them. But rainbow coalitions too run into two problems: debates about comparative victimship and decisions about which groups are to be considered marginalized for the purposes of inclusion in the coalition. And they run into the same reaction as affirmative action: the charge of exclusion. If there can be separate schools for Blacks or for women, in order to foster consciousness, may there also be separate schools for Whites or for men? Essentialism is a double-edged sword.

It is no wonder that, given the fact that each proposed solution has run into difficulties, marginalized groups have been deeply divided about their strategy and have been oscillating in their tactics. One might ask the question whether the difficulties do not lie in the fact that, at the bottom, the entire debate about integration and marginalization, even for the post-1968 groups, despite their skeptical rhetoric, has been based on the assumptions of the concept of citizenship, and that the concept of citizenship is, in its essence, always simultaneously inclusionary and exclusionary.

The concept of citizen makes no sense unless some are excluded from it. And the some who are to be excluded must be, in the last analysis, an arbitrarily selected group. There is no perfect rationale for the boundaries of the categories of exclusion. Furthermore, the concept of citizen is bound up with the fundamental structure of the capitalist world-economy. It derives from the construction of a states-system that is hierarchical and polarizing, which means that citizenship (at least in the wealthier and more powerful states) is inevitably defined as a privilege that it is not in its members' interest to share. It is bound up with the need to hold in check the dangerous classes, and they can best be held in check both by including some and by excluding others.

In short, I am arguing that the entire discussion about integration and marginalization has led us into a cul-de-sac, out of which there is no exit. Better not to enter it and instead to begin to conceive how we can go beyond the concept of citizen. Of course, this means going beyond the structures of our modern world-system. But, since I believe that our modern world-system is in a terminal crisis (a case I do not have the time to develop now),[6] we should perhaps at least consider the kind of historical system we wish to construct and whether it would be possible to dispense with the concept of citizen; and if so, to replace it with what?

Chapter 8

Social Change?
Change Is Eternal. Nothing Ever Changes

I have included in my title the opening sentences of *The Modern World-System:* "Change is eternal. Nothing ever changes." It is a theme that seems to me to be central to our modern intellectual endeavor. That change is eternal is the defining belief of the modern world. That nothing ever changes is the recurrent wail of all those who have been disabused of the so-called progress of modern times. But it is also a recurrent theme of the universalizing scientific ethos. In any case, both statements are intended to be assertions about empirical reality. And of course both often, even usually, reflect normative preferences.

The empirical evidence is very incomplete and ultimately unconvincing. For one thing, the kind of evidence one can offer and the conclusions one can draw from the evidence seem to depend on the time periods measured. Measurement over short periods of time in some ways best captures the enormity of social change. Who does not think that the world looks different in 1996 from 1966? and even more from 1936? not to speak of 1906? One need only look at Portugal — its political system, its economic activities, its cultural norms. And yet of course in many ways Portugal has changed very little. Its cultural specificities are still recognizable. Its social hierarchies are only marginally different. Its geopolitical alliances still reflect the same fundamental strategic concerns. Its relative rank in the world's economic networks has remained remarkably constant in the twentieth century. And of course the Portuguese still speak Portuguese — not a small matter. So which is it: Is change eternal, or does nothing ever change?

Suppose we take a longer time period, say five hundred years — the duration of the modern world-system. In some ways the changes seem

---

Address at the opening session of the III Portuguese Congress of Sociology, Lisbon, February 7, 1996. The theme of the congress was "Practices and Processes of Social Change."

even more striking. In this period, we have seen the emergence of a worldwide capitalist system, and along with it extraordinary technological changes. Airplanes circle the globe today, and many of us, while sitting in our homes, can instantly contact persons at the other end of the globe via the Internet and download texts and graphics. In January 1996, astronomers announced that they are able to "see" so much farther than ever before that they have quintupled the estimated size of the universe. We are now talking of there being billions of galaxies, each with billions of stars, covering a distance of I cannot begin to imagine how many light-years. And at the same time these astronomers have just uncovered planets similar to the earth around two of these stars, the first such planets they have found, ones they assert to have the climatic conditions that could support complex biological structures, in short, possible life. How many more will we soon discover? Five hundred years ago Bartolemeu Dias was thought remarkable to have reached by sail the Indian Ocean, but even he never dreamed of such exotic possibilities as are now before us. Yet at the same time, we are being told by many persons, including many social scientists, that we have reached the end of modernity, that the modern world is in terminal crisis, and that we may soon find ourselves in a world that resembles the fourteenth century more than the twentieth. The more pessimistic among us foresee the possibility that the infrastructure of the world-economy, in which we have invested five centuries of work and capital, may go the way of the Roman aqueducts.

Suppose we now lengthen our horizons even more, to a period of some ten thousand years. This takes us back to a moment in time when neither Portugal nor any other contemporary politicocultural entity existed, to a moment in time that is almost beyond our ability to reconstruct historically, to a moment in time before agriculture was a significant human activity. There are those who look back on the multiple hunting and gathering bands that flourished then as structures in which humans worked many fewer hours per day and per year to maintain themselves than they do today, whose social relations were infinitely more egalitarian, and that operated in an environment that was far less polluted and dangerous. For some analysts, the so-called progress of the past ten thousand years may therefore rather be said to constitute one long regression. And, for some furthermore, the expectation and hope are that this long cycle is near an end and that we may be returning to the "healthier" conditions of yesteryear.

How may we appraise such contrasting views? And how may we deal with the issues under debate, scientifically and philosophically? These seem to me the key questions facing social scientists in general, and indeed all the bearers and creators of knowledge. They are not questions, however, that will be resolved by one more empirical study, even a very ambitious one. Nonetheless, one may say that it is very difficult to formulate intelligently empirical studies on any concrete issue, without creating for ourselves the solid underpinning of an intellectual framework that enables us to place our analyses intelligently within this larger framework. For too long, for two centuries now, we have declined to do this on the grounds that this larger framework was a lure of "philosophical speculation," not to be taken seriously by "rational scientists." This was an error that we can no longer afford to indulge.

The social sciences, as we know them today, are a child of the Enlightenment. Indeed, in some ways, they are the finest product of the Enlightenment: they represent the belief that human societies are intelligible structures whose operation we can understand. From this premise, it has been thought to follow that humans can affect their own world crucially by using their capacities to achieve rationally the good society. Of course, social science has accepted, virtually without questioning it, the further Enlightenment premise that the world is evolving inevitably toward the good society, that is to say, that progress is our natural heritage.

If one believes in the certainty of progress, and in its rationality, then the study of social change cannot be thought of as merely one particular domain of social science. Rather, all of social science is necessarily the study of social change. There is no other subject. And in that case, it is clearly true that "change is eternal," albeit in a specified direction. Indeed, the whole theme is quite teleological: from barbarism to civilization, from animal behavior to godlike behavior, from ignorance to knowledge.

If then we are called upon to discuss the practices and processes of social change, we fit ourselves into a very clear and simple mold. It becomes virtually a technocratic exercise. We are required to analyze the immediate changes that we perceive and then to judge whether they are more or less rational, or, if you prefer, functional. Essentially, we are explaining how it is that they are as they are. And we then can, if we wish, prescribe what can be done to adjust the arrangements, such that we advance collectively more rapidly toward the good society. We are thereby thought to be useful, or policy-oriented, or practical. We can of course vary the parameters of time and space we use in such exercises, applying our knowledge to the case of very small groups over very short periods of time or to much larger groups (say sovereign states) over medium-length periods of time, as, for example, when we ask what we can do to "develop the national economy."

Social scientists of all kinds have been engaged in these sorts of analyses for at least a century, overtly or covertly. When I add covertly, I mean that many social scientists would not define their activities as being so immediately tied to the exercise of public rationality. They might define it rather as the pursuit of more perfect knowledge in the abstract. But even when they do this, they know that the knowledge that they produce is being used by others to help achieve the more perfect society. And they are aware that the economic underpinnings of their scientific research are conditioned on their ability to show social benefit from the work, at least in some longer run.

The same Enlightenment assumptions, however, can lead us in a different, even opposite, direction. The presumed rationality of the social world, just like the presumed rationality of the physical world, implies that lawlike propositions may be formulated that describe it fully and that such propositions hold true across time and space. That is to say, it implies the possibility of universals that can be stated exactly and elegantly and concludes that the object of our scientific activity is precisely to formulate and test the validity of such universals. This is of course nothing but the adaptation of Newtonian science to the study of social realities. And it is therefore no accident that, already in the early nineteenth century, some authors used the label of "social physics" to describe such activity.

This search for lawlike propositions is, in fact, totally compatible with the policy-oriented practical research that is centered on the achievement of the teleological objective of the good society. No one need feel uncomfortable pursuing the two objectives at the same time. Still, there is one small hitch in this double pursuit, one that has to do with social change. If the patterns of human interaction follow universal laws that hold true across time and space, then it cannot be true that "change is eternal." Quite the opposite, in fact: it follows that "nothing ever changes," or at least nothing fundamental ever changes. At which point, not only is it not true that all of social science is the study of social change, but precisely the inverse. The study of social change becomes defined as simply the study of the deviations from equilibria. In this case, even if one starts out, like Herbert Spencer, by offering the study of social change 50 percent of the space — the study of social dynamics as a pendant to the study of social statics — one will rapidly arrive at a practice wherein social change as a topic is the vermiform appendix of social science, an antiquated leftover from an early penchant for social reform. We can see that this did in fact happen by looking at many of our elementary textbooks for students, which reserve for their very last chapter the topic of "social change," a belated acknowledgment that there exist some minor problems with the static description of the social structure.

Today, the Enlightenment view of the world is under much attack, and from many sides. Few persons would admit to accepting it without qualifications. They would seem naive. Nonetheless, the view remains deeply rooted in the practice and the theorizing of social science. And it will take more than bombastic denunciations by postmodernists to uproot it. Social scientists will not be ready to accept a basic reorientation of their view of social change without being first convinced that they will not thereby lose the raison d'être of social science. What I should like therefore to present is a rationale for a social science that has an alternative logic to one based on a belief in progress. I believe we no longer need to be prisoners of a *Methodenstreit* between idiographic and nomothetic forms of knowledge. I believe that the presumed fundamental split between the "two cultures" — science versus philosophy/literature — is a lure and a deception and must be overcome. I believe that neither statement about social change — change is eternal; nothing ever changes — can be accepted as valid as stated. I believe, in short, that we need to find another and better language with which to describe social reality.

Let me start by discussing the most traditional concept of sociology, that of society. We are said to live within, to be part of, societies. There are supposed to be many societies, but (as the term is used) each of us is supposedly a member of only one of them, and at most a visitor in any other. But what are the boundaries of such societies? This is a question that has been in many ways strenuously and deliberately ignored by social scientists. Not, however, by politicians. For the origin of our current concept of "society" lies not too very far in the past. It came into use in the fifty-year period following the French Revolution, when it became common practice in the European world to assert (or at least assume) that social life in the modern world was divided into three different spheres — the state, the market, and the civil society. The boundaries of the state were defined juridically. And implicitly, never explicitly, the boundaries of the other two spheres were assumed to share those of the state, if for no other reason than that the state asserted that this was true. France, or Great Britain, or Portugal was each assumed to have a national state, a national market or national economy, and a national society. These were a priori assertions, for which evidence was rarely offered.

Although these three constructs existed in the same boundaries, it was nonetheless insisted that they were distinct from each other — distinct both in the sense of being autonomous, each supposedly following its own set of rules, and in the sense that each was operating in ways that might put it at odds with the other entity. Thus, for example, the state might possibly not be representative of the "society." This is what the French meant when they distinguished *le pays légal* from *le pays réel*. Indeed, the social sciences were constructed originally around this distinction. To each of these hypothetical entities corresponded a "discipline." Economists studied the market; political scientists the state; and sociologists the civil society.

This partitioning of social reality was, to be sure, an immediate derivation from Enlightenment philosophy. It incarnated the belief that human social structures had "evolved" and that the defining feature of higher social structures, that is modern social structures, is their "differentiation" into autonomous spheres. This is quite recognizably the dogma of liberal ideology, the dominant ideology of the past two centuries, which has served as the geoculture of the modern world-system. The proof, incidentally, that postmodernism is less a break with modernism and more plausibly merely the latest version of modernism is the fact that the postmodernists have not at all escaped from this schematic model. When they inveigh about the oppression of objective structures and preach the virtues of "culture" embodying subjective agency, they are essentially invoking the primacy of the sphere of civil society over those of the state and the market. But in the process they are accepting the thesis that the differentiation into three autonomous spheres is real and a primordial analytic element.

I do not believe myself that these three arenas of action are in fact autonomous and that they follow separate principles. Quite the opposite! I believe that they are so thoroughly intertwined with each other that action in any of the arenas is always pursued as an option in which the overall effect is the determining consideration, and that it obscures rather than clarifies analysis of the real world to attempt to separate the description of the sequential chains of action. In this sense, I do not believe that the modern world is any different from previous periods of world history. That is to say, I do not believe that "differentiation" is a distinguishing feature of modernity. Nor do I believe that we live within multiple, distinctive "societies" within the modern world, that each state contains one and only one "society," and that each of us is a member essentially of only one such "society."

Let me explain why. It seems to me that the appropriate units of analysis for social reality are what I call "historical systems." What I mean by a historical system is implied by the name itself. It is a system insofar as it is built around an ongoing division of labor that permits it to sustain and reproduce itself. The boundaries of the system are an empirical question, to be resolved by determining the boundaries of the effective division of labor. To be sure, every social system necessarily has various kinds of institutions that in effect govern or constrain social action such that the basic principles of the system are realized, to the degree possible, and persons and groups in the social system are socialized into behavior that is consonant with the system, once again to the degree possible. We may designate various of these institutions as being economic, political, and sociocultural, if we wish, but such designations are in fact inaccurate, since all the institutions act in ways that are simultaneously political, economic, and sociocultural, and could not be effective if they did not.

But, at the same time, every system is necessarily historical. That is to say, the system came into existence at some moment in time as a result of processes we can analyze; it evolved over time by processes we can analyze; and it came (or will come) to an end because (like all systems) there comes a moment when it has or will have exhausted the ways in which it can contain its contradictions, and it thereby goes out of existence as a system.

You will notice immediately what this implies about social change. To the degree that we are talking of a system, we are saying that "nothing ever changes." If the structures do not remain essentially the same, in what sense are we talking about a system? But, to the extent that we insist that the system is "historical," we are saying that "change is eternal." The concept of history involves a diachronic process. It is what Heraclitus meant when he said that we cannot step into the same water twice. It is what some natural scientists mean today when they talk of the "arrow of time." Hence, it follows that both statements about social change are true, *within the framework of a given historical system.*

There are various kinds of historical systems. The capitalist world-economy in which we are presently living is one of them. The Roman Empire was another. The Maya structures in Central America comprised another. And there have been countless tiny historical systems. How to decide when any one of these came into existence and when it then ceased to exist is a difficult and contentious empirical question; but theoretically there is no problem at all. By definition, the label of historical system is assigned to entities that have a division of labor with integrated production structures, a set of organizing principles and institutions, and a definable life span. Our task as social scientists is to analyze such historical systems, that is, to demonstrate the nature of their division of labor, to uncover their organizing principles, to describe the functioning of their institutions, and to account for the systems' historical trajectory, including both their genesis and their demise. Of course, each of us does not have to do the whole thing. Like any other scientific activity, this is a task that can be divided up and shared. But unless we are clear about the framework of our analysis (the historical system), our work will not be very insightful or fruitful. What I have just said applies to any particular historical system. And each of us may devote energy to the analysis of one or another particular historical system. In the past, most persons who called themselves sociologists restricted their concern to an analysis of the modern world-system, but there is no sound intellectual reason for this.

There is, however, a further task for social science. If there have been multiple historical systems in the history of the world, we may wonder what their relation to each other is. Are they ontologically linked to each other, and if so in what way? This is the question of what Krzysztof Pomian calls chronosophy. The Enlightenment view of the world had a particular answer to that question. It saw the relation of what I am calling historical systems, the ones to the others, as sequential and cumulative: over time, the successive systems became more complex and more rational, culminating in "modernity." Is this the only way to describe their relationship? I do not think so. In fact, I think this is distinctly the wrong way to describe their relationship. The basic question of social change repeats itself at this level. We have to ask whether change or repetition is the norm not only about the internal life of each historical system but also about the composite history of human life on this planet. And here too I am going to argue that neither statement — change is eternal; nothing ever changes — is satisfactory.

Before, however, we discuss the composite history of human life on this planet, let us return to the issue of social change within any given historical system. And let us do this by looking at the historical system of which we are a part, and which I define as a capitalist world-economy. There are three quite separate intellectual questions that ought not to be confounded one with the other. The first is the question of genesis. How is it that this historical system came into existence, at the time and place that it did and in the way that it did? The second is the question of systemic structure. What are the rules by which this particular historical system, or perhaps more generally, this type of historical system, functions? What are the institutions through which these rules are implemented? Who are the social actors in conflict with each other? What are the secular trends of the system? The third is the question of demise. What are the contradictions of the historical system, and at what point do they become intractable, leading to a bifurcation in the system, entailing the demise of the system, and the emergence of one (or more) replacement system(s)? Not only are the three questions separate, but the methodology (the modes of possible inquiry) that may be used to respond to these queries are not at all the same.

I wish to emphasize the importance I attach to not confounding the three questions. Most analyses of social change center around only the second set of issues, the functioning of the historical system. The analysts quite often assume a functionalist teleology; that is to say, they presume that its genesis is adequately explained, once they can demonstrate that the kind of system they are describing works well, and they can argue that the system is "superior" in its mode of functioning to prior systems. In this sense, the genesis assumes a quasi-inevitable character, situated in the logic of history and tied to setting in motion the particular kind of system. As for demise, this is explained in the case of defunct systems not by the inherent contradictions in the system (for every system has contradictions) but by the asserted inferiority of its mode of functioning, which inevitably gave way to presumably superior modes of functioning. And, it should be noted, this question is seldom posed at all for the current historical system, so obvious to us seems its superiority. You can observe this kind of reasoning in the endless number of books that seek to explain the emergence of the modern Western world as the end point of a logical evolutionary process, books whose argumentation normally involves a searching in the depths of history for the seeds that have led to the present — the glorious present.

There is an alternative way of discussing this same history. Let us illustrate this by discussing the modern world-system. We may take the period of its genesis as being somewhere about A.D. 1450, and its locus western Europe. At that moment of time in that region, there occurred the more or less simultaneous great movements we call the Renaissance, the Gutenberg revolution, the *Descobrimentos,* and the Protestant Reformation. Now this moment in time came in the wake of a somber period in this same region, in which there was the Black Death, the abandonment of villages (the *Wüstungen*), and the so-called crisis of feudalism (or the crisis of seigniorial revenues). How might we go about explaining the end of the feudal system and its replacement by another system, more or less in the same geographic zone?[1]

First we need to explain why the previously existing system could no longer make the adjustments necessary to continue operating according to its rules. I believe that, in this case, it is explained by a simultaneous collapse in the three key institutions that sustained the feudal system: the seigniors, the states, and the Church. The drastic demographic collapse meant that there were fewer persons to till the land, that revenues fell, that rents fell, that commerce contracted, and that consequently serfdom as an institution declined or disappeared. In general, peasants were able to exact far better economic terms from large landowners. As a result, the power and the revenues of the seigniors declined significantly. The states in turn collapsed both because of the drop in their own revenues and because the seigniors turned on each other in order to salvage their personal situations in difficult times (which, by decimating the nobility, further weakened them vis-à-vis the peasantry). And the Church was attacked from within, both because of its weakened economic situation and because the collapse of the seigniors led to a generalized decline in authority.

When a historical system falls apart in this way, what normally happens is that it becomes subject to a renewal of the ruling strata, most frequently by conquest from without. Had this been the fate of western

Europe in the fifteenth century, we would have taken no greater notice of this transformation than we have taken of the historical replacement of the Ming dynasty in China by the Manchus (which essentially was precisely what I have described, a renewal of the ruling strata by conquest from without). This did not, however, happen in western Europe. Instead, as we know, the feudal system was in fact replaced by something radically different, the capitalist system.

The first thing we must note is, far from being inevitable, this was a surprising and unanticipatable development. And the second thing to note is that it was not necessarily a happy solution. In any case, how did this occur, or why? I would suggest that it occurred primarily because the normal external renewal of ruling strata was accidentally and unusually not possible. The most plausible conquering stratum, the Mongols, had themselves just collapsed for reasons quite external to what was happening in western Europe, and there happened to be no other conquering force immediately available. The Ottomans came along a little too late, and by the time they tried to conquer Europe, the new European system was already strong enough (but just) to keep them from advancing beyond the Balkans.

But why then was feudalism replaced by capitalism? Here we have to remember that capitalist entrepreneurial strata had long existed in western Europe as in many others parts of the globe; indeed, such groups had existed for centuries, if not millennia. There had, however, been in all previous historical systems very strong forces that limited their ability to have free rein and to make their motivations the defining characteristics of the system. This was very clearly true of Christian Europe, where the powerful institutions of the Catholic Church maintained a constant battle against "usury." In Christian Europe, as elsewhere in the world, capitalism was an illegitimate concept, and its practitioners were tolerated in only relatively small corners of the social universe. Capitalist forces did not suddenly become stronger or more legitimate in the eyes of most people. In any case, it had never been primarily the degree of strength of capitalist forces that had been the decisive factor but the strength of the social opposition to capitalism. Suddenly, the institutions that sustained this social opposition had become quite weak. And the inability to reestablish them or create similar structures by renewing the ruling strata via external conquest gave a momentary (and probably unprecedented) opening to such capitalist forces, which swiftly entered the breach and consolidated themselves. We must think of this occurrence as extraordinary, unexpected, and surely undetermined (a concept to which we shall return).

Nonetheless it happened. In terms of social change, this was a once only event, which we certainly cannot put under the heading of "nothing ever changes." The change in this instance was fundamental. Instead of calling this fundamental change "the rise of the West," as is usually and self-servingly done, I would designate it myself as "the moral collapse of the West." Since, however, capitalism, once given its head, is indeed a very dynamic system, it rapidly took hold and eventually swept the entire planet into its orbit. This is how I perceive the genesis of the modern world-system in which we are living. It is wondrously aleatory.

We thereupon come to the second question about a historical system: What are the rules by which it works? What is the nature of its institutions? What are its central conflicts? I shall not take time to deal with this here in detail about the modern world-system.[2] I shall merely briefly summarize the essential elements. What defines a system, this system, as capitalist? It seems to me that the *differentia specifica* is not the accumulation of capital but the priority given to the *endless* accumulation of capital. That is to say, it is a system whose institutions are geared to rewarding over the middle run all those who give primacy to the accumulation of capital and punish in the middle run all those who attempt to implement other priorities. The set of institutions that were established to make this possible include the elaboration of commodity chains linking together geographically disparate production activities operating to optimize profit ratios in the system as a whole, the network of modern state structures linked together in an interstate system, the creation of income-pooling households as the basic units of social reproduction, and eventually an integrated geoculture legitimating the structures and seeking to contain the discontents of the exploited classes.

Can we speak of social change within this system? Yes and no. As with any system, the social processes fluctuate constantly, in ways we can explicate. As a result the system has cyclical rhythms that can be observed and measured. Since such rhythms by definition always involve two phases, we can, if we want, suggest that there is a change each time the curve rounds the bend. But in fact we are here dealing with processes that are essentially repetitive in broad outline and that thereby define the contours of the system. Nothing, however, ever repeats itself exactly. And even more important, the mechanisms of "returning to equilibrium" involve constant changes in systemic parameters that can themselves be charted and that thereupon describe secular trends of the system over time. An example in the case of the modern world-system is the process of proletarianization, which has followed a slow secular upward trend for five centuries. Such trends provide constant quantitative increments that are measurable, but (old question) we still need to ask at what point such quantitative increments add up to a qualitative change. The answer must surely be: not as long as the system continues to function by the same basic rules. But of course sooner or later this ceases to be true, and at that point we can say that such secular trends have prepared the third phase, that of demise.

What we have described as secular trends are essentially vectors moving the system away from its basic equilibrium. All trends, if quantified as percentages, move toward an asymptote. When they approach it, it is no longer possible to increase the percentage significantly, and therefore the process no longer is able to fulfill the function of restoring thereby the equilibria. As the system moves further and further from equilibrium, the fluctuations become ever wilder, and eventually a bifurcation occurs. You will notice that I am here applying the model of Prigogine and others who see in these nonlinear processes the explanation of noncumulative, nondetermined radical transformations. The concept that the processes of the universe are explicable and ultimately orderly without being determined is the most interesting contribution to knowledge of the natural sciences in the last decades and represents a radical revision of the dominant scientific views that had previously prevailed in the modern world. It is also, may I say, the most hopeful reaffirmation of the possibility of creativity in the universe, including of course human creativity.

I believe that we are involved right now in a transformational period of the kind I have been describing in our modern world-system.[3] One can argue that there are a series of developments that have undermined the basic structures of the capitalist world-economy and therefore have created a crisis situation. The first is the deruralization of the world. To be sure, this has been regularly hailed as a triumph of modernity. We no longer need so many people to provide basic subsistence. We can move beyond what Marx scorned as the "idiocy of rural life," a value judgment that is widely shared beyond the confines of Marxists. But seen from the vantage point of the endless accumulation of capital, this development means the end of a previously seemingly inexhaustible reservoir of persons, a portion of whom could periodically be brought into market-oriented production at extremely low levels of remuneration (to restore global profit levels by balancing the greater incomes of their predecessors whose syndical action had resulted in raising their historic level of wages). This shifting pool of workers at the bottom who are paid marginal sums has been a major element in worldwide profit levels for five centuries. But no particular group of workers remained in such a category for too long, and the pool had to be regularly renewed. The deruralization of the world makes this virtually impossible. This is a good example of a trend reaching an asymptote.

The second such trend is the escalating social costs of permitting enterprises to externalize their costs. Externalizing costs (that is, making the collective world society pay in effect for a significant part of a firm's costs of production) has been a second major element in maintaining high profit levels and therefore ensuring the endless accumulation of capital. As long as the cumulative costs seemed low enough, no attention was paid. But suddenly they are too high, and the result is the worldwide concern with ecology. The fact is that too many trees have been cut down. The costs of repairing the ecological damage are enormous. Who will pay them? Even if the repair costs are spread among all persons (however unfair this might be), the problem would recur immediately unless governments insisted that firms internalize all costs. But if they did this, profit margins would catapult downward.

The third trend is the consequence of the democratization of the world-system, itself a result of the geoculture that legitimated this pressure as an essential element of political stabilization. It has now come to the point that these popular demands have become very expensive. Meeting what are the current social expectations of a large portion of humanity for adequate educational and health expenditures is beginning to take a major bite out of the total of world surplus-value. Such expenditures are in fact a form of social wage, returning to the producing classes a significant share of the surplus-value. This had been largely mediated via the state structures, as social welfare programs. We are witnessing today a major political battle about the size of the bill. Either the bill is cut (but is this compatible with political stability?) or once again the profit margins will be cut, and in no small amounts.

Finally, there is the collapse of the Old Left, of what I call the traditional antisystemic movements. This is in fact not a plus for the capitalist system, but its greatest danger. De facto, the traditional movements served as a guarantee for the existing system, in that they assured the world's dangerous classes that the future was theirs, that a more egalitarian world was on the horizon (if not for them, then for their children), and thereby these movements legitimated both optimism and patience. In the last twenty years, popular faith in these movements (in all their varieties) has disintegrated, which means that their ability to canalize angers has disappeared with them. Since all these movements had in fact preached the virtues of strengthening the state structures (in order to transform the system), faith in such reformist states has also declined radically. This is the last thing that defenders of the present system really want, despite their anti-state rhetoric. Accumulators of capital in fact count on the state both to guarantee economic monopolies and to repress "anarchistic" tendencies of the dangerous classes. We are seeing today a decline in the strength of state structures everywhere in the world, which means rising insecurity and the rise of ad hoc defensive structures. Analytically, this is the road back to feudalism.

In such a scenario, what can we say about social change? We can say that we are once again seeing the demise of a historical system, parallel to the demise of Europe's feudal system five to six hundred years ago. What will therefore happen? The answer is we cannot know for sure. We are in a systemic bifurcation, which means that very small actions by groups here and there may shift the vectors and the institutional forms in radically different directions. Structurally, can we say that we are in the midst of fundamental change? We cannot even say that. We can assert that it is unlikely that the present historical system will last too much longer (perhaps fifty years at most). But what will replace it? It could be another structure that is basically similar, or it could be a structure that is radically different. It could be a single structure over all of the same geographic area. Or it could be multiple structures in different zones of the globe. As analysts, we will not be sure until it is over. As participants in the real world, we can of course do whatever we think wise to achieve the good society.

What I have offered here is a model with which to approach the analysis of a particular historical system in terms of social change, illustrating the issues by an analysis of the modern world-system. When a historical system is in genesis or demise (the demise of one is always the genesis of one or more others), we may designate it as social change if the category of historical system that existed is replaced by a different category of historical system. This is what occurred in western Europe when feudalism was replaced by capitalism. But it is not social change if it is replaced by the same kind of historical system. This is what happened when the Ming Chinese world-empire was replaced by the Manchu world-empire. They were different in many ways, but not in their essential form. We are going through such a process of systemic transformation right now in the modern worldwide world-system, and we do not know yet whether this involves a fundamental social change or not.

This alternative model of analyzing the concept of social change allows us to see that, when we are analyzing an ongoing functioning historical system, the language of social change can be very deceptive. The details keep evolving, but the qualities that define the system remain the same. If we are concerned with fundamental social change, we have to try to discern and distinguish the secular trends from the cyclical rhythms, and estimate how long the secular trends can continue to cumulate quantitatively without endangering the underlying equilibria.

Furthermore, when we turn our attention from the analysis of particular historical systems to the collective history of humanity on the earth, there is no reason whatsoever to *assume* a linear trend. Thus far, in the known history of humanity, any such calculations give quite ambiguous results and justify a great skepticism about any theory of progress. Perhaps, with much greater depth of vision, social scientists in the year A.D. 20,000 may be able to argue that global secular trends have always existed, despite all the cyclical rhythms that the constant shifting from one set of historical systems to other sets seemed to belie. Perhaps. In the meantime, it seems far safer to me to take the intellectual and moral stance that progress may be possible, but it is by no means inevitable. My own reading of the past five hundred years leads me to doubt that our modern world-system is an instance of substantial moral progress and to believe that it is more probably an instance of moral regression. That does not render me innately pessimistic about the future, just sober.

We are faced today, as we have been faced at other points of the demise of historical systems, with historic choices in which our individual and collective inputs will make a real difference in terms of the outcome. Today's moment of choice is, however, in one way different than previous such moments. It is the first one in which the entire globe is implicated, since the historical system in which we live is the first one that encompasses the entire globe. Historic choices are moral choices, but they can be illuminated by the rational analyses of social scientists, which thus becomes the definition of our intellectual and moral responsibility. I am moderately optimistic that we shall rise to the challenge.

II

The World of Knowledge

Chapter 9

Social Science and Contemporary Society
The Vanishing Guarantees of Rationality

What is "politics" for the productive class becomes "rationality" for the intellectual class. What is strange is that some Marxists believe "rationality" to be superior to "politics," ideological abstraction superior to economic concreteness.

— ANTONIO GRAMSCI, *Prison Notebooks*

It is not only that intellectuals transformed politics into rationality but that this proclamation of the virtue of rationality constituted an expression of optimism on their part and served to fuel the optimism of everyone else. Their credo was: as we proceed toward a truer understanding of the real world, we proceed thereby to a better governance of the real society, ergo toward a greater fulfillment of human potential. Social science as a mode of constructing knowledge was not merely built on this premise; it offered itself as the surest method of realizing the rational quest.

It was not always thus. Once, social thought was dominated by a pervasive mundane pessimism. The social world was seen as unequal and imperfect and would always, it was believed, remain so. Augustine's bleak view that we are all irremediably marked by original sin dominated much of the history of Christian Europe. No doubt, by world standards, this was an unusually harsh chronosophy. However, even other more stoic visions, indeed even the more Dionysian visions, offered few guarantees for the future. The Buddhist quest for nirvana seemed a very long

Inaugural address, International Colloquium of the Italian Association of Sociology, Palermo, October 26–28, 1995. The theme of the meeting was "The University and the Social Sciences: New Paths to Public Rationality."

and difficult path, to be achieved by very few, about the same number who might achieve the Christian quest for sainthood.

If the modern world has so long celebrated itself, commended itself on the "modernity" of its *Weltanschauung,* it is because it proclaimed a chronosophy that was this-worldly, universal, and optimistic. The social world, however bad, could be made better, and made better for everyone. The faith in the possibility of social betterment has been a bedrock of modernity. It was not argued, it should be emphasized, that the individual would necessarily become morally better. Individual overcoming of sinfulness, an ancient religious quest, remained subject to the judgment (and grace) of God. Its validation and its reward were otherworldly. The modern world has been resolutely this-worldly. Whatever it promised was to be validated here and now, or here and shortly. Its quest was in fact resolutely materialist in that it promised economic improvement, ultimately once again for everyone. Its nonmaterial promises, ensconced in the concept of liberty, were all ultimately translatable into material benefits, and supposed liberties that were not translatable in this way were usually denounced as false liberties.

Finally, we must notice how collectivist the promise of modernity has been. The philosophers and the social scientists of the modern world have talked so incessantly about the centrality of the individual in this modern world that we have failed to observe the degree to which the modern world produced the first genuinely collectivist geoculture in history, in that it produced the first genuinely workaday egalitarian social vision. We have all been promised that our historical system will one day achieve a social order in which everyone will enjoy adequate, ergo roughly equal, material comforts, and in which no one will have privileges that others do not have. Of course, I am talking only of promises, not of realities. Still, no philosopher in medieval Europe or T'ang China or in the Abbassid Caliphate predicted that one day everyone on earth would be materially well off and that privilege would disappear. All previous philosophies assumed the inevitability of hierarchies and, by this fact, rejected earthly collectivism.

If, therefore, we are to understand the current dilemmas of our historical system, the capitalist world-economy, and if we are to understand why, in my view, the concept of rationality is tasting so sour in our mouths, I believe we must start from the awareness of the degree to which modernity has been justified on materialist and collectivist premises. For, of course, it was totally self-contradictory to do this. The raison d'être of the capitalist world-economy, its motor force, has been the ceaseless accumulation of capital. And the ceaseless accumulation of capital is totally incompatible with these materialist, collectivist promises, because it is based on the appropriation of surplus-value by some from others. Capitalism represents material reward for some, but in order that it be so, it can never be material reward for everyone.

We know, as social scientists, that one of the most fruitful routes of analyzing social reality is to focus on a central descriptive anomaly and ask why it exists — what explains it and what are its consequences. That is what I propose to do here. I shall discuss why the philosophers of the modern world have made unfulfillable promises to its participants, why these promises were for a long time trusted but are no longer trusted, and what are the consequences of this disillusionment. And lastly I shall try to assess the implications of all of this for us as social scientists, that is, as proponents (if not always practitioners) of human rationality.

Modernity and Rationality

It is a commonplace of social science to observe the link between the rise of a capitalist world-system and the development of science and technology. But why have the two been historically linked? To this question, both Marx and Weber (and indeed most others) have answered that capitalists had to be "rational" if they were to achieve their prime objective, which is maximizing profit. To the extent that capitalists concentrate all their energies on this objective before others, they will do what they can to reduce costs of production and produce the kind of product that will attract buyers, and this means applying rational methods not only to the processes of production but also to the administration of their enterprise. Hence, they find technological advances of every kind extremely useful to them and lend their weight to encouraging the underlying development of science.

No doubt this is true, but it seems to me to explain rather little. We may assume that persons wishing to engage in profit-making enterprises and persons capable of scientific advances have existed, in not too different a proportion, in all major zones of human life, and for thousands of years at least. The whole monumental corpus of Joseph Needham, *Science and Civilization in China*, demonstrates the extensive achievements of scientific effort in the Chinese culture-zone. And we know in great detail how intensive and commercialized was Chinese economic activity.

This is of course then the classic question, Why the West? I do not propose to discuss this question one more time. Many have done so, and I have done so myself.[1] I would simply note here that it seems to me quite obvious that the crucial difference is that, in the modern world-system, there existed clear rewards for technological advance, and that what accounts for this difference is not the attitude of entrepreneurs, who had always had obvious motives for rewarding inventors and innovators, but rather the attitude of political leaders, whose motives were always far more mixed and whose periodic hostility to technological change had constituted the major inhibition in other places and times for the kind of scientific revolution that western Europe launched in the seventeenth century.

I draw the very clear conclusion that you must have capitalism first in order to make technological innovation central, rather than the other way around. This is important because it is a clue to the realities of power relationships. Modern science is the child of capitalism and has been dependent upon it. Scientists received social sanction and support because they offered the prospect of concrete improvements in the real world — wonderful machinery that would foster productivity and reduce the constraints that time and space seemed to impose, and greater comfort for everyone. Science worked.

A whole worldview was created to surround this scientific activity. Scientists were said to be, adjured to be, "disinterested." Scientists were said to be, adjured to be, "empirical." Scientists were said to be, adjured to be, in search of "universal" truths. Scientists were said to be, adjured to be, the discoverers of the "simple." They were called upon to analyze complex realities and establish the simple, the simplest, underlying rules governing them. And finally, perhaps most important of all, scientists were said to be, adjured to be, uncoverers of efficient causes and not of final causes. Furthermore, all these descriptions and adjunctions were said to form a package; they had to be taken together.

The scientific ethos was of course mythical insofar as it pretended to describe fully and truly what scientists actually did. We have but to refer to Steven Shapin's lovely study, *A Social History of Truth*,[2] to realize how central social prestige and extrascientific authority were in establishing the credentials and scientific credibility of the Royal Society of London in the seventeenth century. It was, as he notes, the credibility of gentlemen, based on trust, civility, honor, and integrity. Nonetheless, science, empirical science, indeed Newtonian mechanics — as it was theorized — became the model of intellectual activity to which analysts of the social world would repair, the model they would by and large aspire to copy thereafter.[3] And it was this gentlemanly scientific ethos that the modern world would come to insist was the only possible meaning of rationality, and that became and has remained the leitmotiv of its intellectual class.

What, however, does rationality mean? There is a major discussion of this issue, well known to all sociologists. It is the discussion found in Weber's *Economy and Society.*[4] Weber has two pairs of definitions of rationality. The first is found in his typology of four types of social action. Two of these four types are deemed rational: the "instrumentally rational (*zweckrational*)" and the "value-rational (*wertrational*)." The second is found in his discussion of economic action, in which he distinguishes between "formal" and "substantive" rationality. The two antinomies are almost the same, but not quite, not at least (it seems to me) in their connotations.

Allow me to quote at some length from Weber in order to discuss this question. Weber's definition of instrumentally rational social action is action that is "determined by expectations as to the behavior of objects in the environment and of other human beings; these expectations are used as 'conditions' or 'means' for the attainment of the actor's own rationally pursued and calculated ends" (1:24). His definition of value-rational social action is action that is "determined by belief in the value for its own sake of some ethical, aesthetic, religious, or other form of behavior, independently of its prospect of success" (1:24–25).

Weber then proceeds to elaborate these definitions with more concrete examples:

> Examples of pure value-rational orientation would be the actions of persons who, regardless of possible cost to themselves, act to put into practice their convictions of what seems to them to be required by duty, honor, the pursuit of beauty, a religious call, personal loyalty, or the importance of some "cause" no matter in what it consists. In our terminology, value-rational action always involves "commands" or "demands" which, in the actor's opinion, are binding on him. It is only in cases where human action is motivated by the fulfillment of such unconditional demands that it will be called value-rational. This is the case in widely varying degrees, but for the most part only to a relatively slight

extent. Nevertheless, it will be shown that the occurrence of this mode of action is important enough to justify its formulation as a distinct type; though it may be remarked that there is no intention here of attempting to formulate in any sense an exhaustive classification of types of action.

Action is instrumentally rational (*zweckrational*) when the end, the means, and the secondary results are all rationally taken into account and weighed. This involves rational consideration of alternative means to the end, of the relations of the end to the secondary consequences, and finally of the relative importance of different possible ends. Determination of action either in affectual or in traditional terms is thus incompatible with this type. Choice between alternative and conflicting ends and results may well be determined in a value-rational manner. In that case, action is instrumentally rational only in respect to the choice of means. On the other hand, the actor may, instead of deciding between alternative and conflicting ends in terms of a rational orientation to a system of values, simply take them as given subjective wants and arrange them in a scale of consciously assessed relative urgency. He may then orient his action to this scale in such a way that they are satisfied as far as possible in order of urgency, as formulated in the principle of "marginal utility." Value-rational action may thus have various different relations to the instrumentally rational action. From the latter point of view, however, value-rationality is always irrational. Indeed, the more the value to which action is oriented is elevated to the status of an absolute value, the more "irrational" in this sense the corresponding action is. For, the more unconditionally the actor devotes himself to this value for its own sake, to pure sentiment or beauty, to absolute goodness or devotion to duty, the less is he influenced by considerations of the consequences of his action. The orientation of action wholly to the rational achievement of ends without relation to fundamental values is, to be sure, essentially only a limiting case. (1:25–26)

Now let us turn to Weber's other distinction, which I again quote in full:

The term "formal rationality of economic action" will be used to designate the extent of quantitative calculation or accounting which is technically possible and which is actually applied. The "substantive rationality," on the other hand, is the degree to which the provisioning of given groups of persons (no matter how delimited) with goods is shaped by economically oriented social action under some criterion (past, present, or potential) of ultimate values (*wertende Postulate*), regardless of the nature of these ends. These may be of a great variety.

1. The terminology suggested above is thought of merely as a means of securing greater consistency in the use of the word "rational" in this

field. It is actually only a more precise form of the meanings which are continually recurring in the discussion of "rationalization" and of the economic calculus in money and in kind.

2. A system of economic activity will be called "formally" rational according to the degree in which the provision for needs, which is essential to every rational economy, is capable of being expressed in numerical, calculable terms, and is so expressed. In the first instance, it is quite independent of the technical form these calculations take, particularly whether estimates are expressed in money or in kind. The concept is thus unambiguous, at least in the sense that expression in money term yields the highest degree of formal calculability. Naturally, even this is true only relatively, so long as other things are equal.

3. The concept of "substantive rationality," on the other hand, is full of ambiguities. It conveys only one element common to all "substantive" analyses: namely, that they do not restrict themselves to note the purely formal and (relatively) unambiguous fact that action is based on "goal-oriented" rational calculation with the technically most adequate available methods, but apply certain criteria of ultimate ends, whether they be ethical, political, utilitarian, hedonistic, feudal (*ständisch*), egalitarian, or whatever, and measure the results of the economic action, however formally "rational" in the sense of correct calculation they may be, against these scales of "value-rationality" or "substantive goal rationality." There is an infinite number of possible value scales for this type of rationality, of which the socialist and communist standards constitute only one group. The latter, although by no means unambiguous in themselves, always involve elements of social justice and equality. Others are criteria of status distinctions, or of the capacity for power, especially of the war capacity, of a political unit; all these and many others are of potential "substantive" significance. These points of view are, however, significant only as bases from which to judge the *outcome* of economic action. In addition and quite independently, it is possible to judge from an ethical, ascetic, or aesthetic point of view the *spirit* of economic activity (*Wirtschaftsgesinnung*) as well as the *instruments* of economic activity. All of these approaches may consider the "purely formal" rationality of calculation in monetary terms as of quite secondary importance or even as fundamentally inimical to their respective ultimate ends, even before anything has been said about the consequences of the specifically modern calculating attitude. There is no question in this discussion of attempting value judgments in this field, but only of determining and delimiting what is to be called "formal." In this context the concept "substantive" is itself in a certain sense "formal"; that is, it is an abstract generic concept. (1:85–86)

When I say that the connotations of the two pairs of distinctions are not quite the same, I admit this is a highly subjective interpretation. It seems to me that in distinguishing instrumentally rational social action from value-rational social action, Weber suggests considerable reserve toward the latter. He talks of "unconditional demands." He reminds us that from the point of view of instrumentally rational social action, "value-rationality is always irrational." However, when he distinguishes formal and substantive rationality, he seems to tilt the tone the other way. Substantively rational analyses "do not restrict themselves to note the purely formal and (relatively) unambiguous fact that action is based on 'goal-oriented' rational calculation," but measure it against some value scale.

We could discuss this inconsistency as an issue in the ambivalence of Weber's position on the role of the intellectual in the modern world. But that is not my interest here. I believe rather that the ambivalence or ambiguity of the distinction is built into our modern world's geoculture. It comes back to the quote from Gramsci that I used as an epigraph to this discussion. When Gramsci says that what the productive class calls political the intellectual class renames rational, he is pointing precisely to this fundamental ambiguity. By calling the "political" the "rational," are we not implying that issues of substantive rationality should be put in the background so that issues of formal rationality will be the only ones that remain under discussion? And if so, is this not because issues of formal rationality in fact involve unadmitted but quite clear commitments to value-rational social action of a particular kind, the kind that takes conflicting ends, in Weber's words, "as given subjective wants and arrange[s] them in a scale of consciously assessed relative urgency"? As Weber points out, this is what the principle of marginal utility is about. To decide, however, what is marginally useful, one must design a scale. He who designs the scale determines the outcome.

Rationality and the Dangerous Classes

To talk of rationality is to obscure the political, the value-rational choices, and to tilt the process against the demands of substantive rationality. From the sixteenth to the eighteenth centuries, the intellectual classes could still believe that, in pressing the claims of rationality, their primary enemy was medieval clerical obscurantism. Their slogan was the one shouted loud and clear by Voltaire, "Ecrasez l'infâme." The French Revolution changed all that because it transformed and clarified the terms of the world cultural debate. The French Revolution, I have long argued,[5] did less to change France than it did to change the world-system. It was the direct cause of establishing a viable and durable geoculture within the world-system, one of whose consequences (and not the least) was that it led to the institutionalization of something called the social sciences. We come therefore to the heart of what we are discussing.

The French Revolution and its Napoleonic aftermath spread two beliefs that became pervasive in the world-system and that have dominated mentalities ever since, notwithstanding the ferocious opposition of some very powerful forces. These beliefs are (1) that political change is continuous and normal, that is, the norm, and (2) that sovereignty resides in the "people." Neither of these beliefs was widespread before 1789, and both have flourished since, persisting to this day despite their many ambiguities and mishaps. The problem with these two beliefs is that they are available as arguments to everyone, and not only to those who have power, authority, and/or social prestige. They can indeed be used by the "dangerous classes," a concept that came into existence precisely in the early nineteenth century to describe persons and groups who had neither power, nor authority, nor social prestige, but were making political claims nonetheless. These were the growing urban proletariat of western Europe, the displaced peasants, the artisans threatened by expanded machine production, and the marginal migrants from cultural zones other than the one into which they had migrated.

The problems of social adjustment of such groups and the consequent social turmoil are familiar ones to sociologists and other social historians, ones we have long treated in our literature. But what has this to do with the concept of rationality? Everything, in fact! The political problem posed by the dangerous classes was not, as we know, a minor one. At the very moment that the capitalist world-economy was getting into full swing in terms of expanded productivity and major reductions in the impediments imposed by time and space to the rapid accumulation of capital (a phenomenon we have labeled incorrectly the industrial "revolution," as though it had just started then), and just as the capitalist world-economy was expanding to cover the entire territory of the globe (a phenomenon we have misleadingly called the onset of imperialism, as though it were special to this era), just at this time the dangerous classes were beginning to pose a most serious threat to the political stability of the world-system (a phenomenon we no longer like to call the class struggle, but it was one). We can assume that privileged strata are reasonably intelligent and alert in defense of their interests and will normally seek to meet emerging challenges with sophisticated tools. The tools this time were three: social ideologies, social sciences, and social movements. Each merits discussion, though I shall concentrate my attention on the second.

If political change is considered the norm and if sovereignty is widely believed to reside in the people, the question becomes how one rides the tiger, or, to state this more academically, how one manages the social pressures so as to minimize turmoil, disruption, and in fact change itself. This is where ideologies come in. Ideologies are political programs to manage change. The three principal ideologies of the nineteenth and twentieth centuries represent the three possible ways one can manage change so as to minimize it: one can slow it down as much as possible; one can search for the exactly right pace; and one can speed it up. We have invented various labels for these three programs. One is right, center, and left. The second (a bit more expressive) is conservatism, liberalism, and radicalism/socialism. We know them well.

The conservative program appealed to the value of long-existing institutions — the family, the community, the Church, the monarchy — as founts of human wisdom and therefore as guides to political judgment as well as to codes of personal behavior. Any proposed changes in the ways counseled by these "traditional" structures required exceptional justification and should, it was argued, be approached with great prudence. The radicals, on the contrary, believed basically in Rousseau's general will, incarnating the sovereignty of the people, as the fount of political judgment. Political judgments should, they argued, reflect such general will and do so as rapidly as possible. The middle road, that of the liberals, was one that based its case on doubts about the eternal merits of existing traditional institutions, too subject to the imperatives of maintaining existing privilege, but equally on doubts about the validity of expressions of the general will, too subject to the vagaries of impulsive, short-term advantages for the majority. They counseled remitting judgments to the experts, who would carefully assess the rationality of existing institutions and the rationality of proposed new institutions and would come up with measured and appropriate reforms, that is, with political changes at precisely the right pace.

I shall not here retrace the political history of nineteenth-century Europe or of the twentieth-century world. I will rather summarize this history in a few sentences. The liberal *via media* prevailed politically. Its beliefs became the geoculture of the world-system. It established the forms of the state structures in the dominant states of the world-system and the model toward which other states were, indeed still are, required to aspire. Most consequentially of all, liberalism tamed both conservatism and radicalism, transforming them (at least between 1848 and 1968) from ideological alternatives into minor variants, avatars, of liberalism. Through their threefold political program of universal suffrage, the welfare state, and the creation of national identity (combined with externally oriented racism), nineteenth-century liberals effectively ended the menace of the dangerous classes in Europe. Twentieth-century liberals attempted a similar program to tame the dangerous classes of the Third World and seemed for a long time to be succeeding there as well.[6]

The strategy of liberalism as a political ideology was to *manage* change, and this required that it be done by the right persons and in the right way. Thus, first, the liberals had to ensure that this management be in the hands of *competent* persons. Since they believed that competency could be guaranteed neither through selection by heritage (the conservative bias) nor through selection by popularity (the radical bias), they turned to the only remaining possibility, selection by merit, which of course meant turning to the intellectual class or at least that part of it that was ready to concentrate on "practical" matters. The second requirement was that these competent persons act not on the basis of acquired prejudices but rather on the basis of prior information about the probable consequences of proposed reforms. In order so to act, they needed knowledge about how the social order really functioned, and this meant that they needed research, and researchers. Social science was absolutely crucial to the liberal enterprise.

The link between liberal ideology and the social science enterprise has been essential and not merely existential. I am not saying simply that most social scientists were adherents of liberal reformism. This is true, but minor. What I am saying is that liberalism and social science were based on the same premise — the certainty of human perfectibility based on the ability to manipulate social relations, provided that this be done scientifically (that is, rationally). It is not merely that they shared this premise but that neither could have existed without it, and that both built it into their institutional structures. The existential alliance was the natural consequence of the essential identity. To be sure, I am not denying that there were social scientists who were conservatives or radicals; of course there were many such. But almost none of them strayed very far from the central premise that rationality was the key to what we sought to do, and that it was its own justification.

What social scientists did not do, by and large, was face up to the consequences of the distinction between formal and substantive rationality, and therefore to a clear reflexive awareness of their social role. However, as long as the social world functioned reasonably well in terms of liberal ideology, that is, as long as optimism prevailed about the reality of steady, even if uneven, progress, then these issues could be relegated to the periphery of the intellectual arena. I believe this was true even in the dark days when the monsters of fascism achieved so much power. Their strength shook up this facile faith in progress but never really undid it.

Rationality and Its Discontents

I have chosen the title of this section with an allusion, of course, to Sigmund Freud's important work *Civilization and Its Discontents.*[7] This work is an important sociological statement, even if the essential explanation Freud offers is stated in terms of psychoanalytic theory. The underlying problem is stated simply by Freud:

> Life as we find it is too hard for us; it entails too much pain, too many disappointments, impossible tasks. We cannot do without palliative remedies. We cannot dispense with auxiliary constructions, as Theodor Fontane said. There are perhaps three of these means: powerful diversions of interest, which lead us to care little about our misery; substitutive gratifications, which lessen it; and intoxicating substances, which make us insensitive to it. Something of this kind is indispensable. (25)

But why is it so hard for humans to be happy? Freud finds three sources of human suffering:

> namely, the superior force of nature, the disposition to decay of our bodies, and the inadequacy of our methods of regulating human relations in the family, the community and the state. In regard to the first two, our judgment cannot hesitate: it forces us to recognize these sources of

suffering and to submit to the inevitable. We shall never completely sub-
due nature; our body, too, is an organism, itself a part of nature, and
will always contain the seeds of dissolution, with its limited powers of
adaptation and achievement. The effect of this recognition is in no way
disheartening; on the contrary, it points out the direction for our efforts.
If we cannot abolish all suffering, yet a great deal of it we can, and can
mitigate more; the experience of several thousand years has convinced us
of this. To the third, the social source of our distresses, we take up a different attitude. We prefer not to regard it as one at all; we cannot see why
the systems we have ourselves created should not rather ensure protection
and well-being for us all. (43–44)

Having said this, Freud then speaks historically. Writing in the 1920s,
he reflects upon the attitude taken toward the social sources of our
distresses and notes that an element of disappointment has entered
the scene:

> In the last generations man has made extraordinary strides in knowledge
> of the natural sciences and technical applications of them, and has es-
> tablished his dominion over nature in a way never before imagined. The
> details of this forward progress are universally known: it is unnecessary
> to enumerate them. Mankind is proud of its exploits and has a right
> to be. But men are beginning to perceive that all this newly won power
> over space and time, this conquest of the forces of nature, this fulfillment
> of age-old longings, has not increased the amount of pleasure they can
> obtain in life, has not made them any happier. (46)

Let us see what Freud is telling us. People try to undo the social
sources of their unhappiness because it seems the only truly tractable
source, the only one they could, they believe, totally eliminate. Freud
does not tell us if this perception is correct, only that it is the understandable perception. I have said that liberalism offered the dangerous
classes the hope that, at last, it would now be possible to eliminate the
social sources of unhappiness. It is no wonder that this assertion had
such a positive response. It is no wonder that conservatives and radicals
had to rally around liberal themes. Furthermore, liberals said that they
could guarantee this success, via the spread of rationality. They pointed
to the clear successes of rationality in the natural sciences and said it
would work as well in the social sciences. It was we, the social scientists,
who made this guarantee.

Freud also said that humans protect themselves against pain in three
ways: diversion, substitute gratifications, and intoxication. We should at

the very least ask ourselves if the guarantees of rationality, the promises of a progress that was said to be certain, were not in reality a form of intoxication — the opium of the masses said Marx, the opium of the intellectual class itself retorted Raymond Aron. Perhaps both Marx and Aron were right. And finally Freud suggested that perhaps, in his day, there were the beginnings of disappointment with the palliative. After all, intoxicants use themselves up. Addicts require larger and larger doses to have the same effect. The side effects become too great. Some persons die of this; others kick the habit.

Freud saw this beginning in his era. I see this having happened to a far larger extent in the 1970s and 1980s. As a result, the survivors are kicking the habit in a very big way. To understand this, we have to re-turn to the question of the tools with which those with power met the challenge of the dangerous classes. I said there were three such tools: social ideologies, social science, and social movements. You may per-haps have wondered how I dared suggest that social movements were a tool of those in power, since by social movements we normally mean structures that oppose those in power, even sometimes seek to overthrow completely the basic structures that sustain those in power.

This standard definition of social movements is of course basically correct. The antisystemic movements that came into existence in the nineteenth century in their two principal forms — labor/socialist move-ments and nationalist movements — did oppose those in power and in many cases did seek to overthrow completely the basic structures that sustained those in power. Nonetheless, over time, these movements be-came one of the key mechanisms by which the structures of power were in fact sustained. How did such a paradoxical result come about? The answer is not conspiracy: in general, those in power did not plan it thus and did not corrupt the leadership of these movements. No doubt such conspiracies occasionally occurred, but they were not the basic mechanism; they were not even a very important mechanism. The true explanation, as most sociologists normally contend about everything, is structural.

Popular opposition to those in power has repeatedly taken the form of disruption, everywhere and throughout the history of the world. There have been riots, strikes, rebellions. Almost all of these have been spontaneous in the sense of there being some immediate situational provocation but no prior organizational base. As a result, such disrup-tions may have resulted in amelioration of the immediate problem but did not result in any continued social transformation. Occasionally, such opposition took the form of religious movements, or more precisely of dissident religious views that resulted in the creation of sects or orders or other ongoing organizational structures. The long history of the world's major religious communities has been one of the eventual absorption of such dissident movements into marginal but stable structured roles within the larger religious communities, whereupon they tended to lose most of their steam as expressions of political opposition.

In the post-1789 atmosphere of the nineteenth century, especially in Europe, oppositional movements took on more secular garb. The world-system revolution of 1848 was a major turning-point. It became clear in the defeat that popular forces suffered that conspiratorial sects were not going to be very efficacious. What ensued was a major social innovation. For the first time, antisystemic forces made the decision that social transformation, if it were to come about, had to be planned and therefore organized. The victory of the Marxists over the Anarchists within the socialist/labor movements and the victory of political over cultural nationalists within the various nationalist movements were victories of those who stood for the bureaucratization of revolution, that is, the creation of ongoing organizations that would prepare the ground in multiple ways for the gaining of political power.

What I am calling the bureaucratization of revolution had powerful arguments in its favor. They were essentially three. One, those in power would make significant concessions only if they were forced to do so by the threat of worse. Two, those who were socially and politically weak could become an effective political force only by assembling their forces within disciplined organizations. Three, the key political institutions were the state structures, which were daily becoming stronger, and no significant transfer of power could come about unless it was mediated by a change in the nature and personnel of the state structures. It seems to me hard to argue with any of the three postulates, and it is hard to see that, as of 1848, antisystemic movements had any alternative to the bureaucratization of revolution.

Nonetheless, it was a medicine with fatal side effects. On the one hand, the medicine worked. In the 100 to 125 years thereafter, the political strength of these movements grew steadily, and the political concessions offered to these movements grew accordingly. They achieved many, even most, of their short-run objectives. On the other hand, at the end of this process, for argument's sake let us say as of 1968, the situation seemed very unsatisfactory from the perspective of popular forces. The inequalities in the world-system seemed very far from having been liquidated. Indeed, many of them seemed to be worse than ever. While formal participation in political decision making seemed to have increased notably for the mass of the population, only a small percentage of them felt that they had any real power. As Freud said, they were disappointed.

Why should this have been so? There is a downside to the bureaucratization of revolution. One of them was documented a very long time ago by an Italian social scientist, Roberto Michels, when he spelled out the ways in which the process of bureaucratization of revolution transforms the leadership of the movements and in effect corrupts and defangs them. This finding is now considered a commonplace sociological truism. What Michels's analysis omitted was the impact of the bureaucratization of revolution on the followers. This seems to me even more important.

I believe this is where Freud's discussion of intoxification comes in. Basically, the antisystemic movements intoxicated their members and followers. They organized them, mobilized their energies, disciplined their lives, and structured their thinking processes. The intoxicant was hope, hope in the rational future that beckoned before them, hope in the new world that these movements would construct when they came to power. Nor was this just simple hope; rather, it was inevitable hope. History, that is God, was on the side of the oppressed — not in the afterlife, but here and now, in the world in which they lived or at least the one in which their children would live. One can see why, from the point of view of those in power, the social movements could be described as a tool with which to manage change. As long as popular angers were channeled via social movements, these angers could be limited. The bureaucratized movements became the *interlocuteurs valables* of the defenders of privilege. These movements guaranteed in effect the restraint of their followers against certain kinds of concessions, including the social mobility of the leadership and its children. By the twentieth century, it could be said that the only thing that effectively stood in the way of real revolutions were the revolutionary movements themselves. This is not to say that these movements did not bring about important reforms. They did. What they did not do was transform the system. By postponing to the Greek calends such transformation, they became the guarantors of systemic stability.

The world revolution of 1968 was when these popular masses began to kick the habit. The popular antisystemic message was for the first time turned against the leadership of the major antisystemic movements in the world themselves — the social-democratic movements in the Western world, Communist movements in the bloc from the Oder to the Yalu, national liberation movements in Asia and Africa, populist movements in Latin America. Kicking the habit is never an easy task. It took twenty years for the revolution of 1968 to reach its climax in 1989[8] and for popular disillusionment with antisystemic forces to overcome the legacy of loyalty engendered by past indoctrination, but eventually it succeeded in breaking the umbilical cord. The process was aided and abetted by the reality of the fact, which became clear in the 1970s and 1980s, that the social improvements of the 1945–70 period had been a passing chimera, that the capitalist world-economy could never offer a real prospect of universal prosperity that would overcome the ever-growing gap between core and periphery.[9]

The result of this disillusionment has been the turn against the state, so visible worldwide in the 1990s. It is being touted as the turn to neoliberalism. But it is in reality the turn against liberalism and its promise of salvation via social reformism that would be implemented by the states. It is being touted as the return to individualism. It is in reality the resurgence of collectivism. It is being touted as the return to optimism. It is in reality a turn to a deep pessimism. Freud's essay once again offers us help in understanding what has happened:

> Human life in communities only becomes possible when a number of men unite together in strength superior to any single individual and remain united against all single individuals. The strength of this united party is then opposed as "Right" against the strength of any individual, which is condemned as "brute force." The substitution of the power of a united number for the power of a single man is the decisive step toward civilization. The essence of it lies in the circumstance that the members of the community have restricted their possibilities of gratification, whereas the individual recognized no such restriction. The first requisite of culture, therefore, is justice — that is, the assurance that a law once made will not be broken in favor of any individual. This implies nothing about the ethical value of any such law. The further course of cultural development seems to tend toward ensuring that the law shall no longer represent the will of any small body — caste, tribe, section of the population — which may behave like a predatory individual toward other

such groups perhaps containing larger numbers. The end result would be a state of law to which all — that is, all who are capable of uniting — have contributed by making some sacrifice of their own desires, and which leaves none — again with the same exception — at the mercy of brute force.

The liberty of the individual is not a benefit of culture. It was greatest before any culture, though indeed it had little value at that time, because the individual was hardly in a position to defend it. Liberty has undergone restrictions through the evolution of civilization, and justice demands that these restrictions should apply to all. The desire for freedom that makes itself felt in a human community may be a revolt against some existing injustice and so may prove favorable to a further development of civilization and remain compatible with it. But it may also have its origin in the primitive roots of the personality, still unfettered by civilizing influences, and so become a source of antagonism to culture. Thus the cry for freedom is directed either against particular demands of culture or else against culture itself. (59–60)

Social Science and Substantive Rationality

Today, the guarantees that rationality once seemed to offer — guarantees to those in power, but guarantees as well, other guarantees, to those who were oppressed — all seem to have vanished. We are faced with the "cry for freedom." It is a cry for freedom from the relentless subordination to formal rationality that masks a substantive irrationality. The cry for freedom is growing so strong that our essential choice, as Freud said, is whether it is to be directed primarily only against particular demands of culture or more fundamentally against culture itself. We are coming into a black period, when the horrors of Bosnia and Los Angeles will be magnified and occur everywhere. We are being placed before our responsibilities as the intellectual class. And the last thing that will be helpful is to deny the political by designating a particular politics the rational and refusing thereby to discuss its merits directly.

Social science was born as the intellectual pendant of liberal ideology. If it remains this, it will die as liberalism dies. Social science built itself upon the premise of social optimism. Can it find something to say in an era that will be marked by social pessimism? I believe that we social scientists must totally transform ourselves or we shall become socially irrelevant and relegated to some minor corner of some minor academy, condemned to while away our time in meaningless rituals as the last monks of a forgotten god. I believe that the key element in our survival is to return the concept of substantive rationality to the center of our intellectual concerns.

When the rupture between science and philosophy became definitive at the end of the eighteenth and beginning of the nineteenth centuries, social science proclaimed itself science and not philosophy. The justification of this deplorable split of knowledge into two hostile camps was that science was deemed to be empirical in its search for truth whereas philosophy was metaphysical, that is, speculative. This was an absurd distinction, since all empirical knowledge has metaphysical foundations that are inescapable, and no metaphysics is worth considering unless it can be demonstrated to speak to this-worldly realities, which means that it must have empirical markers. In the effort to jump out of the frying pan of imposed, revealed truth, the intellectual class jumped into the fire of the mysticism of formal rationality. We all did it, even the Marxists, as Gramsci reminded us.

Today, we are tempted to jump back in the other direction, and we are being burned again. Disillusionment has given birth to howling intellectual critics. They are making very powerful critiques about the irrationality of the scientific enterprise. Much of what they say is very salutary, but it is going far too far and threatens to end in a kind of nihilistic solipsism that will get us nowhere, and will shortly begin to bore even its most ardent adepts. Nonetheless, we cannot ward off their critiques by exposing their weaknesses. If that is the path we follow, we shall all crash together. Social science must instead re-create itself.

It must recognize that science is not and cannot be disinterested, since scientists are socially rooted and can no more escape their minds than their bodies. It must recognize that empiricism is not innocent, but always presumes some a priori commitments. It must recognize that our truths are not universal truths and that if there exist universal truths they are complex, contradictory, and plural. It must recognize that science is not the search for the simple, but the search for the most plausible interpretation of the complex. It must recognize that the reason we are interested in efficient causes is as markers on the road to understanding final causes. It must finally accept that rationality involves the choice of a moral politics and that the role of the intellectual class is to illuminate the historical choices that we collectively have.

We have wandered down false paths for two hundred years. We have misled others, but most of all we have misled ourselves. We are in the process of writing ourselves outside the real game of the struggle to achieve human freedom and collective welfare. We must turn ourselves around, if we are to have any hope of helping everyone else (or indeed anyone else) to turn the world around. We must most of all lower our arrogance decibels. We must do all these things because social science really does have something to offer the world. What it has to offer is the possibility of applying human intelligence to human problems, and thereby to achieving human potential, which may be less than perfection but is certainly more than humans have achieved heretofore.

Chapter 10

Differentiation and Reconstruction in the Social Sciences

Differentiation is one of the basic concepts in the sociological armory. It refers to a presumed process whereby tasks that were at one point seen as singular or to be done by a single person and/or group are divided such that they are seen as multiple and done by more than one actor. It is a morphological concept and thus can be applied to any field of activity. It is the process that results in a division of labor.

On the one hand, it has been argued that one of the marked features of the modern world has been the extent of its differentiation. A division of labor is said to be by definition more efficient, and therefore to lead to increased collective productivity. Obviously, the more differentiation there is, the more specialized the roles that are played by actors, and therefore the more room there is for individuation, ultimately resulting in greater (worldwide) heterogeneity.

On the other hand, it has been argued that, in the modern world, we are moving from *Gemeinschaft* to *Gesellschaft*, that we are therefore increasingly speaking a common conceptual language and increasingly operating by a single set of presumably rational values, that everything is becoming more integrated, ultimately resulting in greater (worldwide) homogeneity.

So we are said to have two processes, both fundamental, moving in directly opposite directions. Nor is it totally clear from these assertions what substantive value we are to put on homogeneity and heterogeneity. Which is to be preferred, for what ends, and why? It is not obvious that either heterogeneity or homogeneity is inherently more efficient. Nor are we even agreed on the empirical evidence as to the direction in which we have been moving. There are many analysts who have argued

Presentation at the International Sociological Association Research Council, Montreal, August 6, 1997.

that the modern world has been one of increasing convergence (and hence implicitly harmony), whereas other analysts have insisted that the modern world has been one of increasing polarization (and hence implicitly deep conflict). In this debate, both sides seem to be asserting that homogeneity would be better, but one side sees it occurring and the other does not. There are, however, also many analysts who have been arguing that individuals are freer from social control than ever before, whereas other analysts have been arguing that social control has never been greater (whether in the form of Orwell's *1984* or Marcuse's "repressive tolerance"). In this debate, both sides seem to be asserting that not homogeneity but heterogeneity would be better, but one side sees it occurring and the other does not.

When we turn to the analysis of the structures of knowledge, we find a situation that is not too different from the analysis of the political economy of the world-system. We have assertions of greater heterogeneity. Today, knowledge is divided into a multiplicity of disciplines, and each discipline has an ever-lengthening list of fields of interest, so-called specializations. Yet our knowledge structures seem to transcend many differences of space and time, and a defining characteristic of modern structures of knowledge has been the prominence, in fact the dominance, of the claim to the existence of universal knowledge, a claim that admits of no possible theoretical variation in what constitutes truth. Here too, we find no real consensus about whether homogeneity or heterogeneity is the preferred outcome. Indeed, the intensity of the contemporary so-called science wars and culture wars is clear testimony to the depth of division within the scholarly world on this valuation.

Let us look at the International Sociological Association. It itself is the product of a several-centuries-long process of differentiation. When Machiavelli or Spinoza or even Montesquieu wrote their books, they did not call themselves sociologists; indeed, there was no such concept as "sociologist." More, there was not even yet a clear distinction between such broader categories as "philosopher" and "scientist." This latter distinction, fundamental to the university system we have created in the last two hundred years, was initially an invention based on the Cartesian antinomy of humans and nature, one that became fully crystallized only in the late eighteenth century. The additional conceptual category of social science, as a third scholarly domain in between science and philosophy, or in university jargon between the faculty of natural sciences and what in some languages is called the faculty of humanities, emerged only in the nineteenth century. And separate university departments that distinguished among various social sciences came into existence only between the 1880s and 1945, an institutionalization that was fully consummated in many parts of the world only in the 1950s and 1960s.

As late as the 1950s, national meetings of sociologists, as well as the meetings of the ISA, were still intellectually unified events of a small number of scholars. To further its work, the ISA created first a single all-encompassing research committee, then several committees with specific names. Today we have fifty such research committees, and many other applicants knocking at the doors. The story is replicated within most of our national associations, at least the larger ones. There is every reason to believe that the pressure for creating these specialized structures will continue and may even accelerate. And I should not at all be surprised to see these research committee structures, or specialized groupings, themselves fractionate in turn. Is this evidence of healthy division of labor or of cancerous growth? We know from biology that the line between the two models is thin, and the medical researchers for their part are not yet able to explain exactly what turns one into the other. Can we?

There is a further problem. If, as we subdivided, the subgroupings were all, so to speak, isolationist, keeping to themselves, we might have an atmosphere that could be accused of being intellectually stunting, but it would at least be organizationally quite viable. But this is not at all the case. The more divided we become, the more imperialist each subunit seems to become. Once upon a time, economists were in one corner, sociologists in another, and historians in a third. They saw themselves as constituting separate, quite different, disciplines, with clearly defined and distinctive objects of study, and indeed of modes of studying them. But today economists seek to explain how families function, sociologists explain historical transformations, and historians explain entrepreneurial strategies. I offer a simple test. Take the titles of papers listed in the programs of a half-dozen international social science congresses of different organizations. Shuffle the titles, and ask a group of social scientists to identify at which congress these papers were offered. I haven't done this, but my guess is that a 50 percent correct response would be very high. So we have incredible so-called overlap, which is sometimes dressed up as the spread of "interdisciplinarity." Is this an instance of efficiency or of inefficiency? I think the same test using the papers offered at different research committees of ISA at its congress would show a similar difficulty in identification of the committee at which they were being offered, perhaps not quite as great as the first test identifying the so-called discipline. Nonetheless, there will clearly be titles that could have been given at a half-dozen, if not a dozen, different research committees.

What is the source of this homogeneity amid heterogeneity? One simple, structural answer is size. The number of researchers in the world today has grown enormously in the last five hundred years, and geometrically in the last fifty years. This has in turn two organizational expressions. First, each individual researcher is still required to prove his or her originality. Each must therefore find a niche, or an approach, or a reserved corner, or something. And there just do not seem to be enough of these to go around. So poaching has become a widespread strategy of survival. However, one can never admit that one is poaching, because that would prove lack of originality. So everyone insists that his or her particular variant is significantly different from everyone else's variant. Second, as the number of researchers grows, the size of their meetings grows and tends to become less manageable and less conducive to intellectual exchange. Hence, there is a search for groups that are smaller in size. One can achieve this in turn in two ways. One is by elite selection. And the second is by democratic subdivision. Both have been occurring. The ISA research committees have sought to be an instance of the latter, but as they grow in size, they may discover within them new pressures for elite selection, leading to the creation of elite smaller groups outside the research committees.

You will note that, thus far, I have not explained subdivision by the overall accumulation of knowledge. This is a common explanation. It is said that knowledge has become too large for any single person to handle (presumably unlike in earlier times), and hence requires specialization. The expansion of cumulated knowledge has of course occurred. I wish, however, to register a certain skepticism that the increase is as great as many assert. It is too facile and self-serving an explanation and is self-contradictory. If the existing knowledge in field x is so great that it requires specialization into x_1 and x_2, who is able to know this, since no one presumably can handle all of x? Or if some exceptionally endowed person can know this, are we saying that the subdivisions are to be those decreed valid by this exceptionally endowed person? Clearly, this is not how it works. People divide into the specializations and then, only then, tend to assert, without any real evidence, that it was necessary because of the growth of knowledge overall.

Given the thin intellectual justification for much of our so-called specialization, there have been multiple responses. One is the defensive one: the attempt to erect cumbersome theoretical and methodological justifications for the autonomy of the specialty (whether it be sociology as a whole or some subfield). A second is to go in the opposite direction and undertake a search for "transversal" themes. Yes, say some, there may well be different zones of inquiry (say health, education, religion, and so on), but there are common ways of analyzing these fields (say rational choice or conflict theory). The transversal themes seek to be universalizing, hence homogenizing. But in organizational terms, far from reducing the variety of names of subfields, they tend instead largely to expand the number of specialized units and the overlap. The third response is the call for something more than transversal themes, to call for synthesis. The proponents of synthesis often denigrate the reality and/or the importance of the specializations, and not only within the disciplines, but among the social sciences, and even within the world of knowledge as a whole. But, as in the case of the transversal themes, whatever the intellectual intent, the organizational consequence is often merely the creation of one more specialization. F. Scott Fitzgerald quipped, already in the 1920s in *The Great Gatsby*, about that narrowest of all specialists, the well-rounded man.

Shall we then just throw up our hands? We dare not, both for organizational and for intellectual reasons. Organizationally, the drive for subdivision is getting out of hand. The Research Council of ISA, like similar bodies in other international and national organizations, is beset by requests for new groups, which quite often seem to "overlap" with existing groups. The new groups always insist that they are different, to which existing groups often respond that the theme of the already existing group encompasses the interests of the new applicants. Organizationally, we are having turf battles, and it taxes the sagacity and diplomatic skills of those making the decisions. As time goes by, this can only get worse. We could of course fall back on laissez-faire: any group of a specified number of persons shall be authorized to form a research committee and they may give it any title they choose. Or we could create a morphology, like the table of chemical elements, edicting that only groups filling one of the empty boxes would be acceptable. In practice, we try to follow an intellectually ill-defined middle ground between these two possible practices, but that in turn has given rise to charges of bureaucratic arbitrariness. Even if unfair, such charges create organizational dissensus.

The fundamental issue is, however, not organizational but intellectual. Are we on the right organizational path in terms of the possible, or probable, intellectual consequences? The question is as old as the concept of education. No one doubts that each of us studies only a corner of the intellectual universe. And no one doubts that each of us finds utility in reading and/or talking to others who are studying the same corner or nearby corners. However, two things are to be noted immediately. First, corners resemble each other as loci of research effort. It is not more or less difficult to study the macro or the micro. To study the cosmology of the universe from the "big bang" to now is as small, or as large, a corner as to study the patterns of conversational exchange on a police emergency phone. That is to say, the macro-micro distinction has no impact whatsoever on the amount of time and energy, and prior training, it requires to study well one's particular corner. Macro is not bigger than micro as a research project; it is bigger only in the spatiotemporal definition of the boundaries of the corner under study. Second, there is no simple schema that defines how we may delimit a corner of the intellectual universe. Or rather, there are innumerable such schemas, and none has attained clear intellectual hegemony over the others.

But third, and perhaps most important, these schemas close out intellectual issues just as much as they open them up. It is not that some schemas are nefarious and others virtuous. In a sense, all scholarly activity is a process of establishing schemas, and thereby closing out alternatives is in some sense the objective of all knowledge. We seek to demonstrate that things work like this and not like that. We seek to demonstrate that this way of attaining knowledge is better than that way of attaining knowledge. We seek to demonstrate that this kind of knowledge is better than that kind of knowledge. We all do this. And when others perceive our relative and momentary success, they say we have developed a paradigm.

When we find ourselves amid competing paradigms, proponents of the stronger one tend to argue that it is the only possible one, and proponents of the weaker ones assert that they are being oppressed. The latter frequently make use of the argument of the relativism of paradigms — all paradigms are equally valid. Aside from the fact that this is an argument from weakness, it is also one no one really believes, least of all those who make the argument. Do postmodernists really believe that positivism is simply another point of view in a world of endless perspectives? If so, they haven't made that very clear.

I myself believe that there are multiple possible paradigms, but that some are more valid, that is more useful, than others. But the validity and utility of given paradigms are not eternal, and therefore dominant paradigms can never rest on past laurels. They should always take intellectual challenges seriously, and they need to spend time reexamining basic premises, in the light of serious criticisms. Of course, the key word is "serious," and most defenders of the status quo will assert that the critics are not serious. But in many cases, it is evident that the assertion that the critics are not serious is itself not serious. We know this simply by looking at the past history of scholarship. Accepted wisdom has so frequently been subsequently overthrown and regarded as wildly fallacious that it scarcely needs to be illustrated. And yet if we look at the writings in the moments just before a set of accepted truths became a set of rejected falsities, we shall almost always find the defenders of the faith passionate in the intellectual defense of these truths that were in fact on the verge of collapse — indeed more than passionate, violent and deeply intolerant. This history should give us pause.

The question then before us is whether or not there is anything special about the current moment with regard to the persistent issue of competing paradigms as they are reflected in the structures of knowledge. I believe there is. I believe we can see what is special only if we move not only beyond our subfields, but beyond sociology, and indeed beyond social science. I believe we are living a moment in which the Cartesian schema that has undergirded our entire university system, and therefore our entire edifice of specialization, is being challenged seriously for the first time since the late eighteenth century. I believe that this challenge will in fact lead to considerable institutional restructuring in the next fifty years. And I believe that it is relatively urgent for all of us to take a look at the basic epistemological questions that are under debate — that is, to look up from each of our specialized concerns to this common concern of all scholars. To be sure, we normally don't want to spend time on such epistemological questions, regarding them as the purview of simply one more group of specialists. But that is true only when there is not much argument and when we operate, so to speak, normally. But the argument today about undebated premises has become acute and important, and in that sense we are not in normal times.

The most fundamental and original challenge to the basic culture underlying the work of most sociologists, and to be sure of most other social scientists as well (indeed of all scholars), is a challenge that has been largely ignored by sociologists, or at least treated as though it were a minor, marginal revision to accepted premises of thought. It is the challenge to the validity of Baconian-Newtonian concepts of what constitutes science. Since at least the seventeenth century, the Newtonian model has been the consecrated model of science, at least until the 1970s, when, for the first time, a major challenge gained sufficient organizational strength within the natural scientific community to make the model an open question, a question internal to science.

I shall ignore for the moment the questions of the sociology of science, how it is that, at this point of time, such a challenge is being posed. And I shall ignore for the moment the multiple challenges to the validity of science as an enterprise, because in my view they represent nothing new. They are a continuation of the "romantic" rejection of science that followed in the wake of the so-called divorce between science and philosophy, the affirmation of the particular and of agency. It is not that these challenges, in their current forms, are not strong and even significant, but that they are attacking a model that is cracking from within. If we are to reevaluate what place we should give science in the structures of knowledge, we need first to be very aware in what direction the natural sciences have been heading.

We are all familiar with the Newtonian model. Let us nonetheless review its principal elements. It asserts that there is a real material universe. It asserts that everything that exists in this universe is governed by universal natural laws and that science is the activity of uncovering what these universal natural laws are. It asserts that the only reliable, or useful, way we can know what are these laws is through empirical investigation, and specifically that assertions of knowledge by authorities (clerical or lay) that are not validated empirically have no standing as knowledge. It asserts that empirical investigation involves measurement and that the more precise the measurements the better the quality of the data. It asserts that measuring instruments can be devised, can always be improved, and that there is no intrinsic reason why we cannot one day arrive at measurements that are quasi-perfect in their precision.

Nor is this all. It asserts that the most adequate statement of natural laws is the statement that is simplest and covers the largest number of natural phenomena. Ultimately, we should be able to state all knowledge in a single equation. It asserts that the trajectories of most natural phenomena are linear and that such trajectories always tend to return to equilibria. It asserts (and this is the most difficult to understand in prima facie terms) that all laws are mathematically "reversible," which means that time is irrelevant to the understanding of natural processes. Therefore, provided we know a law and know so-called initial conditions, we can predict or postdict what will be or was the location and measurement of any process in the future or the past. Finally, it asserts that any process that seems to behave in any other way does not really do so. What we are observing is the consequence of our ignorance of how the process really works, and when we have devised better measuring instruments, we shall arrive at knowledge of a process conforming to these tenets.

Now let us take a very recent summation by Ilya Prigogine of the alternate set of assumptions that sometimes is called the science of complexity.[1] He asserts two basic things. Science is in transition to a new form of rationality based on complexity, one that moves beyond the rationality of determinism and therefore of a future that has already been decided. And the fact that the future is not given is a source of basic hope.

In place of the omnipresence of repetition, stability, and equilibrium, which was the vision of classical science, the science of complexity sees instability, evolution, and fluctuation everywhere, not merely in the social arena but in the most fundamental processes of the natural arena. Prigogine calls this moving from a geometrical universe to a narrative universe, in which the problem of time is the central problem. Hence nature and humans are not separate, even less strangers to each other. This is not, however, because humans operate in terms of the descriptions of classical science about nature, but precisely for the opposite reason, that nature operates in terms of the descriptions we have usually used about humans.

He draws from this not a rejection of science but the necessity for science to enunciate a more universal message. It is not that equilibria do not exist, but that they are exceptional and temporary phenomena. All structures move away from equilibrium over time. "The subjective emerges from everything, while being a part of this everything" (68). The arrow of time is the common element of the universe. While time makes everything grow old in the same direction, it also differentiates everything. Evolution is multiple. Probability is not a lesser form of truth, the *pis aller* because we are ignorant. It is the only scientific truth there is. Probability derives from the fact that there are always new statistical solutions of dynamic equations. Interactions within systems are continual, and this communication constitutes the irreversibility of the process, creating ever more numerous correlations. Matter, not merely humans, has memory.

Alongside therefore the experience of repetition, humans have a second experience, that of creativity. These two experiences are not incompatible, nor a matter of choice. We have both experiences, and both experiences are part of reality. Science, in its more universal form, has to be the search for "the narrow passage" between the determined and the arbitrary.

The implications for social science seem to me obvious. The distinction between nomothetic and idiographic epistemologies, the great *Methodenstreit*, is erased. Or rather, this reading of science renders a nomothetic view untenable (as well it might, since the nomothetic view was based on Newtonian premises), but it also renders an idiographic view untenable, since precisely the features that the idiographic epistemology singled out as its justification are now to reside in scientific activity itself, even into the very sanctuary of physics. It raises questions about what we mean by order and therefore by rationality, without suggesting that we live in an anarchic and meaningless universe. It raises questions about the very objective of precision and about the presumed correlation between precision and validity (or even reliability). It raises questions about whether anything can or ever could be value-neutral, while holding to the principle that communication really exists and therefore some statements are more valid than others.

It is as though we were tearing down the building in which we all have lived for some four hundred years now, while at the very same time trying to build new pillars that will hold up some kind of roof over our heads, metaphorically one more open to the light than the old one. No wonder Prigogine argues that science is at its very beginnings. Social science, which is the effort to study the most complex systems of all, becomes not merely the queen of the sciences, but the most difficult of the sciences. It also becomes, however, the arena from which the epistemological truths of science (even the natural sciences) will now be drawn.

Are we ready for such a central role? Far from it, I would say. For many of us are just burrowing inward instead of exploding outward. The "crisis" of continual splicing off into new specializations that are ever more overlapping with other transversal splices may not be a sign of loss of function or viability but rather a sign of the crumbling of the old structures under the weight of the epicycles we have been constructing because we have not been ready to recognize the end of the Newtonian era. Can we also tear down the old structure of social science while simultaneously constructing new pillars for some kind of roof? And will this roof be limited to just social science or rather encompass a reunited single world of knowledge that knows no division between humans and nature, no divorce between philosophy and science, no separation of the search for the true and the search for the good? Can we unthink social science while reconstructing the structures of knowledge?

I do not know. Indeed, the science of complexity tells us that no one can know. But we can try. Insofar as we give ourselves such an intellectual task, what does this imply for our organizational structures? At the very least, that we should interpret organizational and bureaucratic boundaries with great flexibility and that we should encourage intelligent collaboration all over the place. Perhaps one day when we have opened up enough, and reconstructed the world of knowledge enough, we can close down again for a while and talk of "disciplines" and of specializations. But this is not the moment. Opening ourselves up, singly and collectively, is a not an option; it is the minimum strategy for intellectual survival and relevance.

Chapter 11

Eurocentrism and Its Avatars

The Dilemmas of Social Science

Social science has been Eurocentric throughout its institutional history, which means since there have been departments teaching social science within university systems. This is not in the least surprising. Social science is a product of the modern world-system, and Eurocentrism is constitutive of the geoculture of the modern world. Furthermore, as an institutional structure, social science originated largely in Europe. We shall be using "Europe" here more as a cultural than as a cartographical expression; in this sense, in the discussion about the last two centuries, we are referring primarily and jointly to western Europe and North America. The social science disciplines were in fact overwhelmingly located, at least up to 1945, in just five countries — France, Great Britain, Germany, Italy, and the United States. Even today, despite the global spread of social science as an activity, the large majority of social scientists worldwide remain Europeans. Social science emerged in response to European problems, at a point in history when Europe dominated the whole world-system. It was virtually inevitable that its choice of subject matter, its theorizing, its methodology, and its epistemology all reflected the constraints of the crucible within which it was formulated.

However, in the period since 1945, the decolonization of Asia and Africa, plus the sharply accentuated political consciousness of the non-European world everywhere, has affected the world of knowledge just as much as it has affected the politics of the world-system. One major such difference, today and indeed for some thirty years now at least, is that the "Eurocentrism" of social science has been under attack, severe attack. The attack is of course fundamentally justified, and there is no question that if social science is to make any progress in the twenty-first

Keynote address at the International Sociological Association's East Asian regional colloquium, "The Future of Sociology in East Asia," November 22–23, 1996, Seoul, Korea.

century, it must overcome the Eurocentric heritage that has distorted its analyses and its capacity to deal with the problems of the contemporary world. If, however, we are to do this, we must take a careful look at what constitutes Eurocentrism, for, as we shall see, it is a hydra-headed monster and has many avatars. It will not be easy to slaughter the dragon swiftly. Indeed, if we are not careful, in the guise of trying to fight it, we may in fact criticize Eurocentrism using Eurocentric premises and thereby reinforce its hold on the community of scholars.

There are at least five different ways in which social science has been said to be Eurocentric. These do not constitute a logically tight set of categories, since they overlap in unclear ways. Still, it might be useful to review the allegations under each heading. It has been argued that social science expresses its Eurocentrism in (1) its historiography, (2) the parochiality of its universalism, (3) its assumptions about (Western) civilization, (4) its Orientalism, and (5) its attempts to impose the theory of progress.

Historiography. This is the explanation of European dominance of the modern world by virtue of specific European historical achievements. The historiography is probably fundamental to the other explanations, but it is also the most obviously naive variant and the one whose validity is most easily put in question. Europeans in the last two centuries have unquestionably sat on top of the world. Collectively, they have controlled the wealthiest and militarily most powerful countries. They have enjoyed the most advanced technology and were the primary creators of this advanced technology. These facts seem largely uncontested and are indeed hard to contest plausibly. The issue is what explains this differential in power and standard of living with the rest of the world. One kind of answer is that Europeans have done something meritorious and different from peoples in other parts of the world. This is what is meant by scholars who speak of the "European miracle."[1] Europeans have launched the industrial revolution or sustained growth, or they have launched modernity, or capitalism, or bureaucratization, or individual liberty. Of course, we shall need then to define these terms rather carefully and discover whether it was really Europeans who launched whatever each of these novelties is supposed to be, and if so exactly when.

But even if we agree on the definition and the timing, and therefore so to speak on the reality of the phenomenon, we have actually explained very little. For we must then explain why it is that Europeans, and not others, launched the specified phenomenon, and why they did so at a certain moment of history. In seeking such explanations, the instinct of most scholars has been to push us back in history to presumed antecedents. If Europeans in the eighteenth or sixteenth century did *x*, it is said to be probably because their ancestors (or attributed ancestors, for the ancestry may be less biological than cultural, or assertedly cultural) did, or were, *y* in the eleventh century, or in the fifth century B.C., or even further back. We can all think of the multiple explanations that, once having established or at least asserted some phenomenon that has occurred in the sixteenth to nineteenth centuries, proceed to push us back to various earlier points in European ancestry for the truly determinant variable.

There is a premise here that is not really hidden, but was for a long time undebated. The premise is that whatever is the novelty for which Europe is held responsible in the sixteenth to nineteenth centuries, this novelty is a good thing, one of which Europe should be proud, one of which the rest of the world should be envious, or at least appreciative. This novelty is perceived as an achievement, and numerous book titles bear testimony to this kind of evaluation.

There seems to me little question that the actual historiography of world social science has expressed such a perception of reality to a very large degree. This perception can be challenged of course on various grounds, and this has been done increasingly in recent decades. One can challenge the accuracy of the picture of what happened within Europe and in the world as a whole in the sixteenth to nineteenth centuries. One can certainly challenge the plausibility of the presumed cultural antecedents of what happened in this period. One can implant the story of the sixteenth to nineteenth centuries in a longer duration, from several centuries longer to tens of thousands of years. If one does that, one is usually arguing that the European "achievements" of the sixteenth to the nineteenth centuries thereby seem less remarkable, or more like a cyclical variant, or less like achievements that can be credited primarily to Europe. Finally, one can accept that the novelties were real, but argue that they were less a positive than a negative accomplishment.

This kind of revisionist historiography is often persuasive in detail and certainly tends to be cumulative. At a certain point, the debunking, or deconstructing, may become pervasive, and perhaps a countertheory takes hold. This is, for example, what seems to be happening (or has already happened) with the historiography of the French Revolution, where the so-called social interpretation that had dominated the literature for at least a century and a half was challenged and then to some degree toppled in the last thirty years. We are probably entering into such a so-called paradigmatic shift right now in the basic historiography of modernity.

Whenever such a shift happens, however, we ought to take a deep breath, step back, and evaluate whether the alternative hypotheses are indeed more plausible, and most of all whether they really break with the crucial underlying premises of the formerly dominant hypotheses. This is the question I wish to raise in relation to the historiography of European presumed achievements in the modern world. It is under assault. What is being proposed as a replacement? And how different is this replacement? Before, however, we can tackle this large question, we must review some of the other critiques of Eurocentrism.

Universalism. Universalism is the view that there exist scientific truths that are valid across all of time and space. European thought of the last few centuries has been strongly universalist for the most part. This was the era of the cultural triumph of science as a knowledge activity. Science displaced philosophy as the prestige mode of knowledge and the arbiter of social discourse. The science of which we are talking is Newtonian-Cartesian science. Its premises were that the world was governed by determinist laws taking the form of linear equilibria processes and that, by stating such laws as universal reversible equations, we only needed knowledge in addition of some set of initial conditions to permit us to predict the state of the system at any future or past time.

What this meant for social knowledge seemed clear. Social scientists might discover the universal processes that explain human behavior, and whatever hypotheses they could verify were thought to hold across time and space, or should be stated in ways such that they hold true across time and space. The persona of the scholar was irrelevant, since scholars were operating as value-neutral analysts. And the locus of the empirical evidence could be essentially ignored, provided the data were handled correctly, since the processes were thought to be constant. The consequences were not too different, however, in the case of those scholars whose approach was more historical and idiographic, as long as one assumed the existence of an underlying model of historical development. All stage theories (whether of Comte or Spencer or Marx, to choose only a few names from a long list) were primarily theorizations of what has been called the Whig interpretation of history, the presumption that the present is the best time ever and that the past led inevitably to the present. And even very empiricist historical writing, however much it proclaimed abhorrence of theorizing, tended nonetheless to reflect subconsciously an underlying stage theory.

Whether in the ahistorical time-reversible form of the nomothetic social scientists or the diachronic stage theory form of the historians, European social science was resolutely universalist in asserting that whatever it was that happened in Europe in the sixteenth to nineteenth centuries represented a pattern that was applicable everywhere, either because it was a progressive achievement of mankind that was irreversible or because it represented the fulfillment of humanity's basic needs via the removal of artificial obstacles to this realization. What you saw now in Europe was not only good but the face of the future everywhere.

Universalizing theories have always come under attack on the grounds that the particular situation in a particular time and place did not seem to fit the model. There have also always been scholars who argued that universal generalizations were intrinsically impossible. But in the last thirty years a third kind of attack has been made against the universalizing theories of modern social science. It has been argued that these allegedly universal theories are not in fact universal, but rather a presentation of the Western historical pattern as though it were universal. Joseph Needham quite some time ago designated as the "fundamental error of Eurocentrism . . . the tacit postulate that modern science and technology, which in fact took root in Renaissance Europe, is universal and that it follows that all that is European is."[2]

Social science thus has been accused of being Eurocentric insofar as it was particularistic. More than Eurocentric, it was said to be highly parochial. This hurt to the quick, since modern social science prided itself specifically on having risen above the parochial. To the degree that this charge seemed reasonable, it was far more telling than merely asserting that the universal propositions had not yet been formulated in a way that could account for every case.

Civilization. Civilization refers to a set of social characteristics that are contrasted with primitiveness or barbarism. Modern Europe considered itself to be more than merely one "civilization" among several; it considered itself to be (uniquely or at least especially) "civilized." What characterized this state of being civilized is not something on which there has been an obvious consensus, even among Europeans. For some, civilization was encompassed in "modernity," that is, in the advance of technology and the rise of productivity as well as the cultural belief in the existence of historic development and progress. For others, civilization meant the increased autonomy of the "individual" vis-à-vis all other social actors — the family, the community, the state, the religious institutions. For others, civilization meant nonbrutal behavior in everyday life, social manners in the broadest sense. And for still others, civilization meant the decline or narrowing of the scope of legitimate violence and the broadening of the definition of cruelty. And of course, for many, civilization involved several or all of these traits in combination.

When French colonizers in the nineteenth century spoke of *la mission civilisatrice*, they meant that, by means of colonial conquest, France (or more generally Europe) would impose upon non-European peoples the values and norms that were encompassed by these definitions of civilization. When, in the 1990s, various groups in Western countries spoke of the "right to interfere" in political situations in various parts of the world, but almost always in non-Western parts of the world, it was in the name of such values of civilization that they were asserting such a right.

This set of values, however we prefer to designate them — civilized values, secular-humanist values, modern values — permeates social science, as one might expect, since social science is a product of the same historical system that has elevated these values to the pinnacle of a hierarchy. Social scientists have incorporated such values in their definitions of the problems (the social problems, the intellectual problems) they consider worth pursuing. They have incorporated these values into the concepts they have invented with which to analyze the problems and into the indicators they utilize to measure the concepts. Social scientists no doubt have insisted, for the most part, that they were seeking to be value-free, insofar as they claimed they were not intentionally misreading or distorting the data because of their sociopolitical preferences. But to be value-free in this sense does not at all mean that values, in the sense of decisions about the historical significance of observed phenomena, are absent. This is of course the central argument of Heinrich Rickert (1913) about the logical specificity of what he calls the "cultural sciences."[3] They are unable to ignore "values" in the sense of assessing social significance.

To be sure, the Western and social scientific presumptions about "civilization" were not entirely impervious to the concept of the multiplicity of "civilizations." Whenever one posed the question of the origin of civilized values, how it was that they have appeared originally (or so it was argued) in the modern Western world, the answer almost inevitably was that they were the products of long-standing and unique trends in the past of the Western world — alternatively described as the heritage of antiquity and/or of the Christian Middle Ages, the heritage of the Hebrew world, or the combined heritage of the two, the latter sometimes renamed and respecified as the Judeo-Christian heritage.

Many objections can and have been made to the set of successive presumptions. Whether the modern world, or the modern European world, is civilized in the very way the word is used in European discourse has been challenged. There is the notable quip of Mahatma Gandhi, who, when asked, "Mr. Gandhi, what do you think of Western civilization?" responded, "It would be a good idea." In addition, the assertion that the values of ancient Greece and Rome or of ancient Israel were more conducive to laying the base for these so-called modern values than were the values of other ancient civilizations has also been contested. And finally whether modern Europe can plausibly claim either Greece and Rome on the one hand or ancient Israel on the other as its civilizational foreground is not at all self-evident. Indeed, there has long been a debate between those who have seen Greece or Israel as alternative cultural origins. Each side of this debate has denied the plausibility of the alternative. This debate itself casts doubt on the plausibility of the derivation.

In any case, who would argue that Japan can claim ancient Indic civilizations as its forerunner on the grounds that they were the place of origin of Buddhism, which has become a central part of Japan's cultural history? Is the contemporary United States closer culturally to ancient Greece, Rome, or Israel than Japan is to Indic civilization? One could after all make the case that Christianity, far from representing continuity, marked a decisive break with Greece, Rome, and Israel. Indeed Christians, up to the Renaissance, made precisely this argument. And is not the break with antiquity still today part of the doctrine of Christian churches?

However, today, the sphere in which the argument about values has come to the fore is the political sphere. Prime Minister Mahathir of Malaysia has been very specific in arguing that Asian countries can and should "modernize" without accepting some or all of the values of European civilization. And his views have been widely echoed by other Asian political leaders. The "values" debate has also become central within European countries themselves, especially (but not only) within the United States, as a debate about "multiculturalism." This version of the current debate has indeed had a major impact on institutionalized social science, with the blossoming of structures within the university grouping scholars who deny the premise of the singularity of something called civilization.

Orientalism. Orientalism refers to a stylized and abstracted statement of the characteristics of non-Western civilizations. It is the obverse of the concept "civilization" and has become a major theme in public discussion since the writings of Anouar Abdel-Malek and Edward Said.[4] Orientalism was not too long ago a badge of honor.[5] Orientalism is a mode of knowledge that claims roots in the European Middle Ages, when some intellectual Christian monks set themselves the task of understanding better non-Christian religions, by learning their languages and reading carefully their religious texts. Of course, they based themselves on the premise of the truth of Christian faith and the desirability of converting the pagans, but nonetheless they took these texts seriously as expressions, however perverted, of human culture.

When Orientalism was secularized in the nineteenth century, the form of the activity was not very different. Orientalists continued to learn the languages and decipher the texts. In the process, they continued to depend upon a binary view of the social world. In partial place of the Christian/pagan distinction, they placed the Western/Oriental, or modern/nonmodern, distinction. In the social sciences, there emerged a long line of famous polarities: military and industrial societies, Gemeinschaft and Gesellschaft, mechanical and organic solidarity, traditional and rational-legal legitimation, statics and dynamics. Though these polarities were not usually directly related to the literature on Orientalism, we should not forget that one of the earliest of these polarities was Henry Maine's status and contract, and it was explicitly based on a comparison of Hindu and English legal systems.

Orientalists saw themselves as persons who diligently expressed their sympathetic appreciation of a non-Western civilization by devoting their lives to erudite study of texts in order to understand (*verstehen*) the culture. The culture that they understood in this fashion was of course a construct, a social construct by someone coming from a different culture. It is the validity of these constructs that has come under attack, at three different levels: it is said that the concepts do not fit the empirical reality; that they abstract too much and thus erase empirical variety; and that they are extrapolations of European prejudices.

The attack against Orientalism was however more than an attack on poor scholarship. It was also a critique of the political consequences of such social science concepts. Orientalism was said to legitimate the dominant power position of Europe, indeed to play a primary role in the ideological carapace of Europe's imperial role within the framework of the modern world-system. The attack on Orientalism has become tied to the general attack on reification and allied to the multiple efforts to deconstruct social science narratives. Indeed, it has been argued that both some non-Western attempts to create a counterdiscourse of "Occidentalism" and, for example, "all elite discourses of antitraditionalism in modern China, from the May Fourth movement to the 1989 Tienanmen student demonstration, have been extensively orientalized,"[6] therein sustaining rather than undermining Orientalism.

Progress. Progress, its reality, its inevitability, was a basic theme of the European Enlightenment. Some would trace it back through all of Western philosophy.[7] In any case, it became the consensus viewpoint of nineteenth-century Europe (and indeed remained so for most of the twentieth century as well). Social science, as it was constructed, was deeply imprinted with the theory of progress.

Progress became the underlying explanation of the history of the world and the rationale of almost all stage theories. Even more, it became the motor of all of applied social science. We were said to study social science in order better to understand the social world, because then we could more wisely and more surely accelerate progress everywhere (or at least help remove impediments in its path). The metaphors of evolution or of development were not merely attempts to describe; they were also incentives to prescribe. Social science became the adviser to (handmaiden of?) policy-makers from Bentham's panopticon to the Verein für Sozialpolitik, to the Beveridge Report and endless other governmental commissions, to UNESCO's postwar series on racism, to the successive researches of James Coleman on the U.S. educational system. After the Second World War, the "development of underdeveloped countries" was a rubric that justified the involvement of social scientists of all political persuasions in the social and political reorganization of the non-Western world.

Progress was not merely assumed or analyzed; it was imposed as well.

This is perhaps not so different from the attitudes we discussed under the heading of "civilization." What needs to be underlined here is that, at the time when civilization began to be a category that had lost its innocence and attracted suspicions (primarily after 1945), progress as a category survived and was more than adequate to replace civilization, smelling somewhat prettier. The idea of progress seemed to serve as the last redoubt of Eurocentrism, the fallback position.

The idea of progress of course has always had conservative critics, although the vigor of their resistance could be said to have declined dramatically in the 1850–1950 period. But since at least 1968 the critics of the idea of progress have burst forth anew, with renewed vigor among the conservatives and with newly discovered faith on the left. There are however many different ways one can attack the idea of progress. One can suggest that what has been called progress is a false progress but that a true progress exists, arguing that Europe's version was a delusion or an attempt to delude. Or one can suggest that there can be no such thing as progress, because of "original sin" or the eternal cycle of humanity. Or one can suggest that Europe has indeed known progress but that it is now trying to keep the fruits of progress from the rest of the world, as some non-Western critics of the ecology movement have argued.

What is clear, however, is that for many the idea of progress has become labeled as a European idea, and hence has come under the attack on Eurocentrism. But this attack is often rendered quite contradictory by the efforts of other non-Westerners to appropriate progress for part or all of the non-Western world, pushing Europe out of the picture, but not progress.

The multiple forms of Eurocentrism and the multiple forms of the critique of Eurocentrism do not necessarily add up to a coherent picture. What we might do is try to assess the central debate. Institutionalized social science started as an activity in Europe, as we have noted. It has been charged with painting a false picture of social reality by misreading, grossly exaggerating, and/or distorting the historical role of Europe, particularly its historical role in the modern world.

The critics fundamentally make, however, three different (and somewhat contradictory) kinds of claims. The first is that whatever it is that Europe did, other civilizations were also in the process of doing it, up to the moment that Europe used its geopolitical power to interrupt the process in other parts of the world. The second is that whatever

Europe did is nothing more than a continuation of what others had already been doing for a long time, with the Europeans temporarily coming to the foreground. The third is that whatever Europe did has been analyzed incorrectly and subjected to inappropriate extrapolations, which have had dangerous consequences for both science and the political world. The first two arguments, widely offered, seem to me to suffer from what I would term "anti-Eurocentric Eurocentrism." The third argument seems to me to be undoubtedly correct and deserves our full attention. What kind of curious animal could "anti-Eurocentric Eurocentrism" be? Let us take each of these arguments in turn.

There have been throughout the twentieth century persons who have argued that, within the framework of say Chinese or Indian or Arab-Muslim "civilization," there existed both the cultural foundations and the sociohistorical pattern of development that would have led to the emergence of full-fledged modern capitalism or that were indeed in the process of leading in that direction. In the case of Japan, the argument is often even stronger, asserting that modern capitalism did develop there, separately but temporally coincident with its development in Europe. The heart of most of these arguments is a stage theory of development (frequently its Marxist variant), from which it logically follows that different parts of the world were all on parallel roads to modernity or capitalism. This form of argument presumes both the distinctiveness and social autonomy of the various civilizational regions of the world on the one hand and their common subordination to an overarching pattern on the other.

Since almost all the various arguments of this kind are specific to a given cultural zone and its historical development, it would be a massive exercise to discuss the historical plausibility of the case of each civilizational zone under discussion. I do not propose to do so here. What I would point out is one logical limitation to this line of argument whatever the region under discussion, and one general intellectual consequence. The logical limitation is very obvious. Even if it is true that various other parts of the world were going down the road to modernity/capitalism, perhaps were even far along this road, this still leaves us with the problem of accounting for the fact that it was the West, or Europe, that reached there first and was consequently able to "conquer the world." At this point, we are back to the question as originally posed, Why modernity/capitalism in the West?

Of course today there are some who are denying that Europe in a deep sense did conquer the world, basing their argument on the grounds that there has always been resistance, but this seems to me to be stretching our reading of reality. There was after all real colonial conquest that covered a large portion of the globe. There are after all real military indicators of European strength. No doubt there were always multiple forms of resistance, both active and passive, but if the resistance were truly so formidable, there would be nothing for us to discuss today. If we insist too much on non-European agency as a theme, we end up whitewashing all of Europe's sins, or at least most of them. This seems to me not what the critics were intending.

In any case, however temporary we deem Europe's domination to be, we still need to explain it. Most of the critics pursuing this line of argument are more interested in explaining how Europe interrupted an indigenous process in their part of the world than in explaining how it was that Europe was able to do this. Even more to the point, by attempting to diminish Europe's credit for this deed, this presumed achievement, they reinforce the theme that it was an achievement. The theory makes Europe into an "evil hero" — no doubt evil, but also no doubt a hero in the dramatic sense of the term, for it was Europe that made the final spurt in the race and crossed the finish line first. And worse still, there is the implication, not too far beneath the surface, that, given half a chance, Chinese or Indians or Arabs not only could have, but would have, done the same — that is, launch modernity/capitalism, conquer the world, exploit resources and people, and play themselves the role of evil hero.

This view of modern history seems to be very Eurocentric in its anti-Eurocentrism because it accepts the significance (that is, the value) of the European "achievement" in precisely the terms that Europe has defined it and merely asserts that others could have done it too, or were doing it too. For some possibly accidental reason, Europe got a temporary edge on the others and interfered with their development forcibly. The assertion that we others could have been Europeans too seems to me a very feeble way of opposing Eurocentrism and actually reinforces the worst consequences of Eurocentric thought for social knowledge.

The second line of opposition to Eurocentric analyses is that which denies that there is anything really new in what Europe did. This line of argument starts by pointing out that, as of the late Middle Ages, and indeed for a long time before that, western Europe was a marginal (peripheral) area of the Eurasian continent whose historical role and cultural achievements were below the level of various other parts of the world (such as the Arab world or China). This is undoubtedly true, at least as a first-level generalization. A quick jump is then made to situating modern Europe within the construction of an *ecumene* or world structure that has been in creation for several thousand years.[8] This is not implausible, but the systemic meaningfulness of this *ecumene* has yet to be established, in my view. We then come to the third element in the sequence. It is said to follow from the prior marginality of western Europe and the millennial construction of a Eurasian world *ecumene* that whatever happened in western Europe was nothing special and simply one more variant in the historical construction of a singular system.

This latter argument seems to me conceptually and historically very wrong. I do not intend however to reargue this case.[9] I wish merely to underline the ways in which this is anti-Eurocentric Eurocentrism. Logically, it requires arguing that capitalism is nothing new, and indeed some of those who argue the continuity of the development of the Eurasian *ecumene* have explicitly taken this position. Unlike the position of those who are arguing that a given other civilization was also en route to capitalism when Europe interfered with this process, the argument here is that we were all of us doing this together, and that there was no real development toward capitalism in modern times because the whole world (or at least the whole Eurasian *ecumene*) had been capitalist in some sense for several thousand years.

Let me point out first of all that this is the classic position of the liberal economists. This is not really different from Adam Smith arguing that there exists a "propensity [in human nature] to truck, barter, and exchange one thing for another."[10] It eliminates essential differences between different historical systems. If the Chinese, the Egyptians, and the western Europeans have all been doing the same thing historically, in what sense are they different civilizations or different historical systems?[11] In eliminating credit to Europe, is there any credit left to anyone except to pan-humanity?

But again worst of all, by appropriating what modern Europe did for the balance sheet of the Eurasian *ecumene,* we are accepting the essential ideological argument of Eurocentrism, that modernity (or capitalism) is miraculous and wonderful, and are merely adding that everyone has always been doing it in one way or another. By denying European credit, we deny European blame. What is so terrible about Europe's "conquest of the world" if it is nothing but the latest part of the ongoing march of the *ecumene?* Far from being a form of argument that is critical of Europe, it implies applause that Europe, having been a "marginal" part of the *ecumene,* at last learned the wisdom of the others (and elders) and applied it successfully.

And the unspoken clincher follows inevitably. If the Eurasian *ecumene* has been following a single thread for thousands of years, and the capitalist world-system is nothing new, then what possible argument is there that would indicate that this thread will not continue forever, or at least for an indefinitely long time? If capitalism did not begin in the sixteenth (or the eighteenth) century, it is surely not about to end in the twenty-first. Personally, I simply do not believe this, and I have made the case in several recent writings.[12] My main point here, however, is that this line of argument is in no way anti-Eurocentric, since it accepts the basic set of values that have been put forward by Europe in its period of world dominance and thereby in fact denies and/or undermines competing value systems that were, or are, in honor in other parts of the world.

I think we have to find sounder bases for being against Eurocentrism in social science, and sounder ways of pursuing this objective. For the third form of criticism — that whatever Europe did has been analyzed incorrectly and subjected to inappropriate extrapolations, which have had dangerous consequences for both science and the political world — is indeed true. I think we have to start with questioning the assumption that what Europe did was a positive achievement. I think we have to engage ourselves in making a careful balance sheet of what has been accomplished by capitalist civilization during its historical life and assess whether the pluses are indeed greater than the minuses. This is something I tried once, and I encourage others to do the same.[13] My own balance sheet is negative overall, and therefore I do not consider the capitalist system to have been evidence of human progress. Rather, I consider it to have been the consequence of a breakdown in the historic barriers against this particular version of an exploitative system. I consider that the fact that China, India, the Arab world, and other regions did not go forward to capitalism evidence that they were better immunized against the toxin, and to their historic credit. To turn their credit into something that they must explain away is to me the quintessential form of Eurocentrism.

Let me be clear. I believe that, in all major historical systems (civilizations), there has always been a certain degree of commodification and hence of commercialization. As a consequence, there have always been persons who sought profits in the market. But there is a world of difference between a historical system in which there exist some entrepreneurs or merchants or "capitalists" and one in which the capitalist ethos and practice are dominant. Prior to the modern world-system, what happened in each of these other historical systems is that whenever capitalist strata got too wealthy or too successful or too intrusive on existing institutions, other institutional groups (cultural, religious, military, political) attacked them, utilizing both their substantial power and their value systems to assert the need to restrain and contain the profit-oriented strata. As a result, these strata were frustrated in their attempts to impose their practices on the historical system as a priority. They were often crudely and rudely stripped of accumulated capital, and in any case made to give obeisance to values and practices that inhibited them. This is what I mean by the antitoxins that contained the virus.

What happened in the Western world is that, for a specific set of reasons that were momentary (or conjunctural, or accidental), the antitoxins were less available or less efficacious, and the virus spread rapidly, and then proved itself invulnerable to later attempts at reversing its effects. The European world-economy of the sixteenth century became irremediably capitalist. And once capitalism consolidated itself in this historical system, once this system was governed by the priority of the ceaseless accumulation of capital, it acquired a kind of strength vis-à-vis other historical systems that enabled it to expand geographically until it absorbed physically the entire globe, the first historical system ever to achieve this kind of total expansion.

The fact that capitalism had this kind of breakthrough in the European arena, and then expanded to cover the globe, does not however mean that this was inevitable or desirable or in any sense progressive. In my view, it was none of these. And an anti-Eurocentric point of view must start by asserting this.

I would prefer therefore to reconsider what is not universalist in the universalist doctrines that have emerged from the historical system that is capitalist, our modern world-system. The modern world-system has developed structures of knowledge that are significantly different from previous structures of knowledge. It is often said that what is different is the development of scientific thought. But it seems clear that this is not true, however splendid modern scientific advances are. Scientific thought long antedates the modern world and is present in all major civilizational zones. This has been magisterially demonstrated for China in the corpus of work that Joseph Needham launched.[14]

What is specific to the structures of knowledge in the modern world-system rather is the concept of the "two cultures." No other historical system has instituted a fundamental divorce between science and philosophy/humanities, or what I think would be better characterized as the separation of the quest for the true and the quest for the good and the beautiful. Indeed, it was not all that easy to enshrine this divorce within the geoculture of the modern world-system. It took three centuries before the split was institutionalized. Today, however, it is fundamental to the geoculture and forms the basis of our university systems.

This conceptual split has enabled the modern world to put forward the bizarre concept of the value-neutral specialist, whose objective assessments of reality could form the basis not merely of engineering decisions (in the broadest sense of the term) but of sociopolitical choices as well. Shielding the scientists from collective assessment, and in effect merging them into the technocrats, did liberate scientists from the dead hand of intellectually irrelevant authority. But simultaneously, it removed the major underlying social decisions we have been taking for the last five hundred years from substantive (as opposed to technical) scientific debate. The idea that science is over here and sociopolitical decisions are over there is the core concept that sustains Eurocentrism, since the only universalist propositions that have been acceptable are those that are Eurocentric. Any argument that reinforces this separation of the two cultures thus sustains Eurocentrism. If one denies the specificity of the modern world, one has no plausible way of arguing for the reconstruction of knowledge structures, and therefore no plausible way of arriving at intelligent and substantively rational alternatives to the existing world-system.

In the last twenty years or so, the legitimacy of this divorce has been challenged for the first time in a significant way. This is the meaning of the ecology movement, for example. And this is the underlying central issue in the public attack on Eurocentrism. The challenges have resulted in so-called science wars and culture wars, which have themselves often been obscurantist and obfuscating. If we are to emerge with a reunited, and thereby non-Eurocentric, structure of knowledge, it is absolutely essential that we not be diverted into sidepaths that avoid this central issue. If we are to construct an alternative world-system to the one that is today in grievous crisis, we must treat simultaneously and inextricably the issues of the true and the good.

And if we are to do that we have to recognize that something special was indeed done by Europe in the sixteenth to eighteenth centuries that did indeed transform the world, but in a direction whose negative consequences are upon us today. We must cease trying to deprive Europe of its specificity on the deluded premise that we are thereby depriving it of an illegitimate credit. Quite the contrary. We must fully acknowledge the particularity of Europe's reconstruction of the world because only then will it be possible to transcend it and to arrive hopefully at a more inclusively universalist vision of human possibility, one that avoids none of the difficult and imbricated problems of pursuing the true and the good in tandem.

Chapter 12

The Structures of Knowledge, or How Many Ways May We Know?

The report of the Gulbenkian Commission for the Restructuring of the Social Sciences bears the title *Open the Social Sciences*.[1] The title bears witness to the sense of the commission that the social sciences have become closed off, or have closed themselves off, from a full understanding of social reality, and that the methods that the social sciences had historically developed in order to pursue this understanding may themselves today be obstacles to this very understanding. Let me try to summarize what I think the report says about the past two hundred years, and then turn to what this implies for what we should now do.

The commission saw the enterprise of the social sciences as a historical construction, institutionalized primarily in the period 1850–1945. We emphasized that this construction was therefore quite recent and that the way in which social science was constructed was neither inevitable nor unchangeable. We tried to explain what elements in the nineteenth-century world led those who constructed this edifice to make the decisions that were made concerning the distinctions that were created between a named list of "disciplines." We sought to outline the underlying logic that accounted for why the multiple disciplines adopted various epistemologies and why each chose certain practical methodologies as their preferred ones. We also tried to explain why the post-1945 world found this logic constraining and set in motion a series of changes in the academy that had the effect of undermining the distinctions among the disciplines.

The picture that we drew of the history of the social sciences was that of a U-shaped curve. Initially, from 1750 to 1850, the situation was very confused. There were many, many names being used as the appellations

Presentation at conference, "Which Sciences for Tomorrow? Dialogue on the Gulbenkian Report: *Open the Social Sciences*," Stanford University, Palo Alto, California, June 2–3, 1996.

of proto-disciplines, and none or few seemed to command wide support. Then, in the period from 1850 to 1945, this multiplicity of names was reduced to a small standard group clearly distinguished the ones from the others. In our view, there were only six such names that were very widely accepted throughout the scholarly world. But then, in the period from 1945 on, the number of legitimate names of fields of study has been once again expanding, and there is every sign that the number will continue to grow. Furthermore, whereas in 1945 there still seemed to be clear demarcations that separated one discipline from another, these distinctions have in the subsequent period been steadily eroded, so that today there is considerable de facto overlap and confusion. In short, we have in a sense returned to the situation of 1750–1850, one in which a large number of categories do not provide a useful taxonomy.

But this overlap and confusion are the least of our problems. This process of defining the categories of the social sciences has been occurring within the context of a much larger turmoil that goes beyond the social sciences and implicates the entire world of knowledge. We have been living for two hundred years in a structure of the organization of knowledge in which philosophy and science have been considered distinctive, indeed virtually antagonistic, forms of knowledge. It is salutary to remember that this was not always so. This division between the so-called two cultures is also a rather recent social construction, only a bit older than that which divided up the social sciences into a specified list of disciplines. It was in fact virtually unknown anywhere in the world before the middle of the eighteenth century.

The secularization of society, which has been a continuing feature of the development of the modern world-system, expressed itself in the world of knowledge as a two-step process. The first step was the rejection of theology as the exclusive, or even the dominant, mode of knowing. Philosophy replaced theology; that is, humans replaced God as the source of knowledge. In practice, this meant a shift of locus of the authorities who could proclaim the validity of knowledge. In place of priests who had some special access to the word of God, we honored rational men who had some special insight into natural law, or natural laws. This shift was not enough for some persons, who argued that philosophy was merely a variant of theology: both proclaimed knowledge as being ordained by authority, in the one case of priests, in the other of philosophers. These critics insisted on the necessity of evidence drawn from the study of empirical reality. Such evidence, they said, was the basis of another form of knowledge they called "science." By the eighteenth century, these protagonists of science were openly rejecting philosophy as merely deductive speculation, and proclaiming that their form of knowledge was the only rational form.

On the one hand, this rejection of philosophy seemed to argue a rejection of authorities. It was in that sense "democratic." The scientists seemed to be saying that anyone could establish knowledge, provided he (or she) used the right methods. And the validity of any knowledge that any scientists asserted could be tested by anyone else, simply by replicating the empirical observations and manipulation of data. Since this method of asserting knowledge seemed to be capable of generating practical inventions as well, it laid claim to being a particularly powerful mode of knowing. It was not long, therefore, before science achieved a dominant place in the hierarchy of knowledge production.

There was one major problem, however, in this "divorce" between philosophy and science. Theology and philosophy had both traditionally asserted that they could know *two* kinds of things: both what was true and what was good. Empirical science did not feel it had the tools to discern what was good, only what was true. The scientists handled this difficulty with some panache. They simply said they would try only to ascertain what was true and they would leave the search for the good in the hands of the philosophers (and the theologians). They did this knowingly and, to defend themselves, with some disdain. They asserted that it was more important to know what was true. Eventually some would even assert that it was impossible to know what was good, only what was true. This division between the true and the good constituted the underlying logic of the "two cultures." Philosophy (or more broadly, the humanities) was relegated to the search for the good (and the beautiful). Science insisted that it had the monopoly on the search for the true.

There was a second problem about this divorce. The path of empirical science was in fact less democratic than it seemed to claim. There rapidly arose the question of who was entitled to adjudicate between competing scientific claims to truth. The answer that the scientists gave was that only the community of scientists could do this. But since scientific knowledge was inevitably and increasingly specialized, this meant that only subsets of scientists (those in each subspecialty) were deemed part of the group that had a claim to judge the validity of scientific truth. In point of fact, these groups were no larger than the group of philosophers who had previously claimed the ability to judge each other's insights into natural law or laws.

There was a third problem about this divorce. Most persons were unwilling truly to separate the search for the true and the good. However hard scholars worked to establish a strict segregation of the two activities, it ran against the psychological grain, especially when the object of study was social reality. The desire to reunify the two searches returned clandestinely, in the work of both scientists and philosophers, even while they were busy denying its desirability, or even possibility. But because the reunification was clandestine, it impaired our collective ability to appraise it, to criticize it, and to improve it.

All three difficulties were kept in check for two hundred years, but they have returned to haunt us in the last third of the twentieth century. The resolution of these difficulties constitutes today our central intellectual task.

There have been two major attacks on the trimodal division of knowledge into the natural sciences, the humanities, and the social sciences. And neither of these attacks has come from within the social sciences. These attacks have come to be called "complexity studies" (in the case of the natural sciences) and "cultural studies" (in the case of the humanities). In reality, starting from quite different standpoints, both of these movements have taken as their target of attack the same object, the dominant mode of natural science since the seventeenth century, that is, that form of science that is that based on Newtonian mechanics.

To be sure, in the early twentieth century Newtonian physics had been challenged by quantum physics. But quantum physics still shared the fundamental premise of Newtonian physics that physical reality was determined and had temporal symmetry, that therefore these processes were linear, and that fluctuations always returned to equilibria. In this view, nature was passive, and scientists could describe its functioning in terms of eternal laws, which could eventually be asserted in the form of simple equations. When we say that science as a mode of knowing became dominant in the nineteenth century, it is this set of premises of which we are speaking. That which could not be fit into this set of premises, for example, entropy (which is the description of necessary transformations in matter over time), was and is interpreted as an example of our scientific ignorance, which could and would eventually be overcome. Entropy was seen as a negative phenomenon, a sort of death of material phenomena.

Since the late nineteenth century, but especially in the last twenty years, a large group of natural scientists has been challenging these premises. They see the future as intrinsically indeterminate. They see equilibria as exceptional and see material phenomena as moving constantly far from equilibria. They see entropy as leading to bifurcations that bring new (albeit unpredictable) orders out of chaos, and therefore the process is not one of death but of creation. They see auto-organization as the fundamental process of all matter. And they resume this in two basic slogans: not temporal symmetry, but the arrow of time; not simplicity as the ultimate product of science, but rather the explanation of complexity.

It is important to see what complexity studies is and what it is not. It is not a rejection of science as a mode of knowing. It is a rejection of a science based on a nature that is passive, in which all truth is already inscribed in the structures of the universe. What it is rather is the belief that "the possible is 'richer' than the real."[2] It is the assertion that all matter has a history, and it is its sinuous history that presents material phenomena with the successive alternatives between which each "chooses" throughout its existence. It is not the belief that it is impossible to know, that is, to understand how the real world operates. It is the assertion that this process of understanding is far more complex that science traditionally asserted that it was.

Cultural studies attacked the same determinism and universalism under attack by the scientists of complexity. But for the most part those who put forward these views neglected to distinguish between Newtonian science and the science of complexity, or in many cases to be aware of the latter. Cultural studies attacked universalism primarily on the grounds that the assertions about social reality that were made in its name were not in fact universal. It represented an attack against the views of the dominant strata in the world-system that generalized their realities into universal human realities and thereby "forgot" whole segments of humanity, not only in the substantive statements but in the very epistemology of their research.

At the same time, cultural studies represented an attack on the traditional mode of humanistic scholarship, which had asserted universal values in the realm of the good and the beautiful (the so-called canons) and analyzed texts internally as incarnating these universal appreciations. Cultural studies insists that texts are social phenomena, created in a certain context and read or appreciated in a certain context.

Classical physics had sought to eliminate certain "truths" on the grounds that these seeming anomalies merely reflected the fact that we were still ignorant of the underlying universal laws. Classical humanities had sought to eliminate certain appreciations of "the good and beautiful" on the grounds that these seeming divergences of appreciation merely reflected the fact that those who made them had not yet acquired good taste. In objecting to these traditional views in the natural sciences and the humanities, both movements — complexity studies and cultural studies — sought to "open" the field of knowledge to new possibilities that had been closed off by the nineteenth-century divorce between science and philosophy.

Where then does social science fit in this picture? In the nineteenth century, the social sciences, faced with the "two cultures," internalized their struggle as a *Methodenstreit*. There were those who leaned toward the humanities and utilized what was called an idiographic epistemology. They emphasized the particularity of all social phenomena, the limited utility of all generalizations, the need for empathetic understanding. And there were those who leaned toward the natural sciences and utilized what was called a nomothetic epistemology. They emphasized the logical parallel between human processes and all other material processes. They sought to join physics in the search for universal, simple laws that held across time and space. Social science was like someone tied to two horses galloping in opposite directions. Social science had no epistemological stance of its own and was torn apart by the struggle between the two colossi of the natural sciences and the humanities.

Today we find we are in a very different situation. On the one hand, complexity studies is emphasizing the arrow of time, a theme that has always been central to social science. It emphasizes complexity and admits that human social systems are the most complex of all systems. And it emphasizes creativity in nature, thus extending to all nature what was previously thought to be a unique feature of *Homo sapiens*.

Cultural studies is emphasizing the social context within which all texts, all communications, are made and are received. It is thus utilizing a theme that has always been central to social science. It emphasizes the nonuniformity of social reality and the necessity of appreciating the rationality of the other.

These two movements offer social science an incredible opportunity to overcome its derivative and divided character and to place the study of social reality within an integrated view of the study of all material reality. Far from being torn apart by horses galloping in opposite directions, social science, I believe, lies in the direction that both complexity studies and cultural studies are moving. In a sense, what we are seeing is the "social scientization" of all knowledge.

Of course, like all opportunities, we shall only get *fortuna* if we seize it. What is now possible is a rational restructuring of the study of social reality. It can be one that understands that the arrow of time offers the possibility of creation. It can be one that understands that the multiplicity of human patterns of behavior is precisely the field of our research, and that we may approach an understanding of what is possible only when we shed our assumptions about what is universal.

Finally, we are all offered the possibility of reintegrating the knowledge of what is true and what is good. The probabilities of our futures are constructed by us within the framework of the structures that limit us. The good is the same as the true in the long run, for the true is the choice of the optimally rational, substantively rational, alternatives that present themselves to us. The idea that there are two cultures, a fortiori that these two cultures are in contradiction to each other, is a gigantic mystification. The tripartite division of organized knowledge is an obstacle to our fuller understanding of the world. The task before us is to reconstruct our institutions in such a way that we maximize our chances of furthering collective knowledge. This is an enormous task, given the inherent conservatism of institutional authorities and the danger such a reconstruction poses to those who benefit from the inegalitarian distribution of resources and power in the world. But the fact that it is an enormous task does not mean that it is not doable. We have entered a bifurcation in the structures of knowledge, which appears in many ways to be chaotic. But of course we shall emerge from it with a new order. This order is not determined, but it is determinable. But we can only have *fortuna* if we seize it.

Chapter 13

The Rise and Future Demise of World-Systems Analysis

World-systems analysis as an explicit perspective within social science dates from the 1970s, although of course it reflects a point of view that has a long history and builds on much earlier work. It never put itself forward as a branch of sociology or of social science. It did not think of itself as the "sociology of the world," side by side with urban sociology or the sociology of small groups or political sociology. Rather it presented itself as a critique of many of the premises of existing social science, as a mode of what I have called "unthinking social science."

It is for this reason that I, for one, have always resisted using the term "world-systems theory," frequently used to describe what is being argued, especially by nonpractitioners, and have insisted on calling our work "world-systems analysis." It is much too early to theorize in any serious way, and when we get to that point it is social science and not world-systems that we should be theorizing. I regard the work of the past twenty years and of some years to come as the work of clearing the underbrush, so that we may build a more useful framework for social science.

If world-systems analysis took shape in the 1970s, it was because conditions for its emergence were ripe within the world-system. Let us review what they were. The prime factor can be summarized as the world revolution of 1968 — both the events themselves and the underlying conditions that gave rise to the events. Let us remember the shape of U.S. and world social science of the 1950s and 1960s. The biggest change in world social science in the twenty-five years after 1945 had been the discovery of the contemporary reality of the Third

Paper delivered at the Ninety-first Annual Meeting of the American Sociological Association, New York, August 16, 1996.

World. This geopolitical discovery had the effect of undermining the nineteenth-century construction of social science that had created separate theories and disciplines for the study of Europe/North America on the one hand and for that of the rest of the world on the other hand. After 1945, social science became, was forced to become, geographically integrated, so to speak. Thus it became legitimate, but only then, for persons called sociologists or historians or political scientists to do research on and in Africa or Asia or Latin America.[1]

This was the era of area studies, and area studies changed the social organization of social science, first in the United States and then in most other parts of the world.[2] In seeking to justify area studies intellectually, its advocates faced a fundamental epistemological dilemma. They wished to argue that the theories of social science applied to all areas of the world, and not merely to Europe/North America. Previously the theories of the nomothetic social sciences had been applied de facto only to what was thought of as the modern "civilized" world, and only Europe/North America was considered as belonging to such a world. In this sense, area studies proposed "universalizing universalism." At the same time, however, proponents of area studies wished to argue that this could not be done simply by applying the generalizations previously developed in Europe/North America to the Third World. Conditions in the Third World, said the area studies people, were quite different. After all, if they had not been different, why would we have needed area studies?

Arguing that conditions are the same and arguing simultaneously that they are different is not the easiest thing to do. However, area studies people came up with a clever, and plausible, solution to the apparent dilemma. They based their work on a view that had already been widespread in the social sciences, to wit, that there exist stages through which society goes (and therefore societies go), and that these stages represent evolutionary progress. Applied to the Third World, this theory was baptized "modernization theory" or developmentalism. Modernization theory argued quite simply the following: all societies go through a defined set of stages in a process ending in modernity. The operational definition of a society was a state, presently in existence as either a sovereign member of the interstate system or a colony destined one day to become a sovereign member. The names of these stages varied among the theorists, but the general idea remained the same. The point of the theorizing was to figure out how states moved from stage to stage, to enable us to indicate at what stage given states presently were, and to help all states arrive at modernity.

The epistemological advantages of the theory were great. All states were the same, insofar as they went through identical stages for identical reasons. But all states were also different, in that they presently were at different stages, and the timing of the movements of each from stage to stage was particular. The political advantages of the theory were great as well. The theory enabled all and sundry to engage in applying the theory to the practical situation by advising governments how best to act to speed up the process of moving upward along the stages. The theory also justified a considerably increased allocation of governmental funds (more or less everywhere) to social scientists, especially to those who claimed to be working on "development."

The limitations of the theory were easy to discern as well. Modernization theory purported to be based on the systematic comparison of independent cases, and this presumed a dubious and totally unproven premise, that each state operated autonomously and was substantially unaffected by factors external to its borders. The theory further presumed a general law of social development (the so-called stages), a process furthermore that was presumed to be progressive, both of which arguments were also undemonstrated. And the theory therefore predicted that those states currently at earlier stages of development could, would, and should arrive at an endpoint in which they were essentially clones of whatever was considered by the theorist the model of the most "advanced" state or states.

Politically, the implications were clear. If a state at a so-called lower stage wanted to resemble a state at a so-called advanced stage in terms of prosperity and internal political profile, it had best copy the pattern of the advanced state, and implicitly therefore had best follow the advice of that state. In a world defined by the rhetoric of the Cold War, this meant that states were adjured by some to follow the model of the United States and by others to follow the model of the USSR. Nonalignment was disqualified by objective scientific analysis.

Of course, these political implications were the object of ferocious refusal by the revolutionaries of 1968. It was an easy jump for them (and others) to deny the epistemological premises. This created the atmosphere in which there was receptivity for the kind of protest that world-systems analysis represented. It is important to remember this original intention of world-systems analysis, the protest against modernization theory, if we are to understand the directions in which it has moved since. I see four major thrusts to the work we have done collectively. None of these thrusts has been exclusively the work of persons involved in world-systems analysis per se. But in each case, those involved in world-systems analysis have played an important role in pursuing and defining the thrust.

The first thrust was *globality*. It followed from the famous concern with the unit of analysis, said to be a world-system rather than a society/state. To be sure, modernization theory had been international, in that it insisted on comparing systematically all states. But it had never been global, since it posited no emergent characteristics of a world-system, indeed never spoke of a world-system at all. World-systems analysis insisted on seeing all parts of the world-system as parts of a "world," the parts being impossible to understand or analyze separately. The characteristics of any given state at T_2 were said to be not the result of some "primordial" characteristic at T_1, but rather the outcome of processes of the system, the world-system. This is the meaning of Gunder Frank's famous formula, the "development of underdevelopment."

The second thrust was *historicity*, and it followed from the first. If the processes were systemic, then the history — the entire history — of the system (as opposed to the history of subunits, taken separately and comparatively) was the crucial element in understanding the present state of the system. To be sure, for this purpose one had to make a decision on the temporal boundaries of the systemic processes, and in practice this has been the subject of contentious debate. Nonetheless, the overall thrust was to push analysis away from exclusively contemporary data, or even from data covering only the nineteenth and twentieth centuries, in the direction of Braudel's *longue durée*.

The third thrust was *unidisciplinarity*, and it followed from the second. If there were historically emergent and historically evolving processes in the world-system, what would lead us to assume that these processes could be separated into distinguishable and segregated streams with particular (even opposed) logics? The burden of proof was surely on those who argued the distinctiveness of the economic, political, and sociocultural arenas. World-systems analysis preferred to insist on seeing "totalities."

The fourth thrust was therefore *holism*. This thrust was historico-epistemological, and it followed from all the previous ones. The arguments of world-systems analysis led its advocates to be dubious of, even opposed to, the boundary lines within the social sciences, as they had been historically constructed in the period 1850–1945. These boundaries did not seem to hold water, and thus there was talk of restructuring knowledge. Indeed, holism leads to rethinking as well the historically constructed and now-consecrated great divide between the sciences and the humanities, and perhaps unthinking it as well.

It is important to distinguish these four thrusts from currents that used seemingly similar terminology but were in no sense intended as protests against the dominant modes of social science.

Globalism was *not* "globalization." As used by most persons in the last ten years, "globalization" refers to some assertedly new, chronologically recent, process in which states are said to be *no longer* primary units of decision making, but are now, only now, finding themselves located in a structure in which something called the "world market," a somewhat mystical and surely reified entity, dictates the rules.

Historicity was *not* "social science history." As used by most persons in the last twenty-five years, "social science history" refers to the need for persons dealing with past data (so-called historians) to use that data to test social science generalizations derived from the analysis of contemporary data. Social science history is in many ways an antihistorical process and relegates empirical work (especially about the past) to the position of hierarchical subordination to so-called theoretical work. Social science history is compatible with globalization but not with globality.

Unidisciplinarity was *not* "multidisciplinarity." Multidisciplinarity accepted the legitimacy of the boundaries of the social sciences but asked the various practitioners to read and use each other's findings, in an additive fashion. It was the belief that more cooks often improve the broth. It resisted the study of totalities on the grounds that it is hard to specify the data in ways amenable to testable propositions, and therefore encouraged vague and nondisprovable argumentation.

And finally, holism was *not* a rehash of "general education." General education had accepted the basic premises of the modern divisioning of knowledge into three superdomains: the natural sciences, the humanities, and (in between the so-called two cultures) the social sciences. General education was the case for making all scholars (and indeed all educated persons) sensitive to the premises underlying each of the separate domains. Holism asks whether the superdomains are in fact different kinds of knowledge, or ought to be thought of in this way.

This debate is directly relevant to the crucial question of the relation of the quest for the true and the quest for the good.

If I have emphasized not only what the thrusts of world-systems analysis have been but also what they have not been, it is because we are running the danger of success. It is because of the strength, and not the weakness, of our efforts that our terminology is in the process of being appropriated for other, indeed opposite, purposes. This can cause serious confusion in the general scholarly public and, even worse, may lead to confusion on our own part, thus undermining our ability to pursue the tasks we have set ourselves.

I have in my title used the phrase "rise and future demise of world-systems analysis." So far, I have talked only about the rise. Wherein do I see a demise? The demise of a movement, and world-systems analysis has been essentially a movement within contemporary social science, derives from its contradictions and from the eventual exhaustion of its utility. We are not there yet, but we are clearly moving in the direction of such a demise, or if you will permit my prejudices, a bifurcation. What are the contradictions of world-systems analysis?

The first is that world-systems analysis is precisely not a theory or a mode of theorizing, but a perspective and a critique of other perspectives. It is a very powerful critique, and I personally believe the critique is devastating for a large number of the premises on which much of social science presently operates. Critiques are destructive; they intend to be. They tear down, but they do not by themselves build up. I called this earlier the process of clearing the underbrush. Once one has cleared the underbrush, however, one has only a clearing, not a new construction but only the possibility of building one.

Old theories never die, but they usually don't just fade away either. They first hide, then mutate. Thus, the work of critique of the old theories may seem never-ending. The risk is that we shall become so enamored of this task that we may lose ourselves in it and refuse the necessary risk of moving on ourselves. To the extent that we shall fail to do this, we shall become redundant and irrelevant. At which point the mutants come back, stronger than ever. The attempt in the 1990s to relegitimize modernization theory is an instance of this, albeit thus far one that has been rather weak. If I might continue the medical metaphor, the problem today of world-systems analysis is analogous to the problem of overused antibiotics. The solution is to move forward from medical therapy to preventive medicine.

There is a second problem with critiques, especially critiques that are past the moment of initial shock and vigor. Critiques are not that difficult to pseudo–co-opt. I have tried already to indicate the ways in which our terminology, or something close to it, is being used for purposes other than we had in mind, which then can have the effect of corrupting what we ourselves do. So then this becomes a question of "physician, heal thyself." But I am making more than a general admonition always to be self-critical. I am suggesting that there is a tendency to forget our own original critical stance, as we hail those who seem to be emulating us, and that this tendency poses considerable risks both to the critical task and to the putative task of reconstruction.[3] At the end of the road, we risk finding ourselves in the situation of so many intellectual movements, a name that has become a shell.

The third problem is that we have shifted over the years from criticizing the ways in which we analyze the contemporary situation in peripheral zones of the world-economy to criticizing the ways in which the history of the modern world has been written, to criticizing the theories that are supposed to explain the modern world-system, to criticizing the methodologies used in the historical social sciences, to criticizing the ways in which knowledge institutions have been constructed. We have been following the paths of our critiques and of answering those who have in turn been critical of our work. It is as though we have been going through doors to find other doors behind them, in a constant regress. Perhaps the problem is deeper than we have imagined.

Perhaps the problem is the entire thought-system of the capitalist world-economy. This has been suggested, to be sure, by the so-called postmodernists. I am sympathetic to many of their critiques (most of which, however, we have been saying more clearly, and indeed earlier). However, I find them on the whole neither sufficiently "post"-modern nor sufficiently reconstructive. They will certainly not do our job for us.

To be a movement within social science had, and has, certain distinct advantages. It enables us to group forces, to clarify our critiques, and to sustain each other in a sometimes hostile environment. On the whole, I give us good marks for how we have conducted ourselves. On the one hand, we have allowed multiple views to coexist, and thus avoided becoming a sect. On the other hand, we have not defined our program so loosely that it has lacked critical teeth, which is what would have happened if we had followed the recurrent suggestions that we rename ourselves (and therefore blend into) "the sociology of development" or "political economy" or "global sociology."

Nonetheless, being a movement has certain distinct disadvantages. I am often appalled by the two-line summaries of our perspective one can find in the books of others who have manifestly read virtually nothing of what we have written. I am equally appalled by the suavity with which our research findings are appropriated (and misappropriated) not only without credit but even more important without any integration of the underlying approach that gave rise to the research findings. This is in part inevitable, since movements tend to talk to themselves, and after a while this constrains radically their impact.

There is of course an alternative road we might follow that might overcome the limitations of being an intellectual movement. That road is that of moving into the very center of social science, not as a movement but as consensual premise. How might we do that? The facetious answer would be that we should be writing, or some of us should be writing, general textbooks for first-year students of social science. The real answer is that persons involved in world-systems analysis should be addressing, and addressing urgently, some very fundamental questions, questions that in my view can be satisfactorily addressed only if one has unthought nineteenth-century social science and structures of knowledge and thoroughly absorbed the lessons of world-systems analysis.

Allow me to list some of these fundamental questions:

- What is the nature of the distinctive arena of knowledge we may call social science, if there is one? How do we define its parameters and social role? In particular, in what ways, if any, is such a field to be distinguished from the humanities on the one side and the natural sciences on the other?

- What is the relation, theoretically, between social science and social movements? between social science and power structures?

- Are there multiple kinds of social systems (I would prefer the concept "historical systems"), and, if so, what are the defining features that distinguish them?

- Do such historical systems have a natural history or not? If so, can this history be called an evolutionary history?

- How is TimeSpace socially constructed, and what differences does this make for the conceptualizations underlying social science activity?

- What are the processes of transition from one historical system to another? What kinds of metaphors are plausible: self-organization, creativity, order out of chaos?

- What is the theoretical relation between the quest for truth and the quest for a just society?

- How can we conceive our existing historical system (world-system)? And what can we say about its rise, its structure, and its future demise, in the light of our answers to the other questions?

As you can see, the last is the question with which we started. A number of the other questions have been worrying various persons who consider themselves part of the network of scholars involved in world-systems analysis. Furthermore, of course, many other scholars, present and past, have worried about these questions, or at least some of them. The point however is to see that these questions are interrelated and can really be answered only in relation to each other, that is, from a world-systems perspective.

The other point is that world-systems analysts are, on the whole, better trained than most social scientists today to address these questions as an interrelated set. When we do begin to address them in this way, we shall no longer be acting primarily as a movement within social science, but we shall be laying claim to formulating the central questions of the enterprise. Is this hubris? Not really. As world-systems analysts, we know that intellectual activities are a matter not simply of intelligence or will but of social timing, in terms of the world-system. It is because the historical system in which we live is in terminal crisis that there exists the chance of addressing these questions in ways that can make possible substantively rational social constructions. This was not a possibility available to nineteenth-century scholars, however insightful or masterly they were. It is because the legitimacy of the hierarchies that are fundamental to the capitalist world-economy — hierarchies of class, of race, of gender — is being fundamentally challenged (both politically and intellectually) that it may be possible to construct, for the first time, a more inclusive and relatively more objective social science.

It is the times that make it possible, again for the first time, to stand on the shoulders of those nineteenth-century giants and see something beyond, provided we have the energy and the will. It is the times that permit us, without disgracing ourselves, to follow Danton's exhortation:

"De l'audace, encore de l'audace, et toujours de l'audace." These are our times, and it is the moment when social scientists will demonstrate whether or not they will be capable of constructing a social science that will speak to the worldwide social transformation through which we shall be living.

Chapter 14

Social Science and the Quest for a Just Society

Macro and micro constitute an antinomy that has long been widely used throughout the social sciences and indeed in the natural sciences as well. In the last twenty years, the antinomy global/local has also come into wide use in the social sciences. A third pair of terms, structure/agency, has also come to be widely adopted and is central to the recent literature of cultural studies. The three antinomies are not exactly the same, but in the minds of many scholars they overlap very heavily, and as shorthand phrases they are often used interchangeably.

Macro/micro is a pair that has the tone merely of preference. Some persons prefer to study macrophenomena, others microphenomena. But global/local, and even more structure/agency, are pairs that have passions attached to them. Many persons feel that only the global or only the local make sense as frameworks of analysis. The tensions surrounding structure/agency are if anything stronger. The terms are often used as moral clarion calls; they are felt by many to indicate the sole legitimate rationale for scholarly work.

Why should there be such intensity in this debate? It is not difficult to discern. We are collectively confronted with a dilemma that has been discussed by thinkers for several thousand years. Beneath these antinomies lies the debate of determinism versus free will, which has found countless avatars within theology, within philosophy, and within science. It is therefore not a minor issue, nor is it one about which, over the thousands of years, a real consensus has been reached. I believe that our inability to find a way beyond this opposition constitutes a major obstacle to our collective ability to create a form of knowledge that is adequate for what I expect will be a quite transformed world in the

Opening lecture, Social Science Study-Day 1996, SISWO (Netherlands Universities Institute for Coordination of Research in Social Sciences), Amsterdam, April 11, 1996.

coming century and millennium. I therefore propose to look at how this long-standing debate has been conducted within our community, that is, within the framework of that very recent construct "social science." I intend to argue that the way the problem has been posed heretofore has made it insoluble. I intend also to argue that we are today at a point where we may be able to overcome the social constructions of the nineteenth century in ways that will allow us to move forward constructively, and collectively, on this question.

Let me start with determinism and free will in theological discourse. The concept that everything is determined seems to derive quite directly from the concept of the omnipotence of God, central to all the monotheistic religions at least. On the one hand, if there is an omnipotent God, then everything is determined by the will of God, and to suggest otherwise would seem to be blasphemous. On the other hand, the churches of the world are in the business of regulating moral behavior. And determinism provides an easy excuse for the sinner. Has God indeed determined that we shall sin? And if so, should we try to counter the will of God? This is a conundrum that has plagued theologians from the beginning. One way out is to argue that God has bestowed upon us free will, that is, the option to sin or not to sin. It is however too easy a solution. Why would it have been necessary or desirable for God to have done this? It makes us seem like God's playthings. Furthermore, it does not provide a logically tight argument. If God has given us free will, can we exercise it in unpredictable ways? If so, is God omnipotent? And if not, can we really be said to have free will?

Let me say once again how impressed I have always been with the astuteness of Calvin's attempt to resolve this dilemma. The Calvinist argument is very simple. Our destinies are indeed not predetermined, not because God could not predetermine everything, but because if humans assert that everything is predetermined, they are thereby limiting God's ability to determine. In effect, Calvin is saying, perhaps *we* cannot change our minds, but God can, or else God is not omnipotent. Still, as you well know, Calvinists were not persons to countenance immoral behavior. How then could humans be induced to make the necessary effort to behave according to the norms that Calvinists believed they ought to observe? Remember, Calvin was part of the Reformation attempt to refute the doctrine of the Catholic Church that good deeds are rewarded by God (a view that, by derivation, justified the sale of indulgences). To get out of the box, Calvinists resorted to the concept of negative grace, which is in reality a familiar and very modern device of science, the concept of disproof. While we could not have foreknowledge of who was saved, since that would limit God's decisions, we could have foreknowledge of who was *not* saved. It was argued that God displays the prospect of damnation in the sinful behavior of humans, as sinful behavior is defined by the Church. Those who sin are surely *not* saved, because God would not permit the saved so to act.

The Calvinist solution is so astute that it was subsequently adopted by its successor expression, the revolutionary movements of the nineteenth and twentieth centuries. The analogous argument went like this. We cannot know for sure who is advancing the revolution, but we can know for sure who is *not* advancing it, those who act in ways that are sinful, that is, in ways that run counter to the decisions of the revolutionary organization. Every member is a potential sinner, even if the militant has behaved appropriately in the past. Members are thus continuously subject to the judgment of the revolutionary authorities as to whether or not they have gone against the will of God, that is, against the will of the revolutionary organization.

Nor was it only the revolutionary organizations that adopted the Calvinist solution. Essentially, modern science adopted it as well. We can never know with certainty whether a scientist has reached truth, but we can know when the scientist has sinned. It is when he has failed to follow the norms of appropriate scientific methods, as defined by the community of scientists, and therefore has ceased to be "rational," that is, when the scientist has stooped to politics, or to journalism, or to poetry, or to other such nefarious activities.

The Calvinist solution is astute, but it has one enormous drawback. It confers inordinate power on those humans — church authorities, revolutionary authorities, scientific authorities — who are the interpreters of whether or not other human actors are showing signs of negative grace. And who will guard the guardians? Is there then a remedy to this drawback? The consecrated remedy is to proclaim the virtue of human freedom. That good Calvinist, John Milton, wrote a marvelous poem extolling this remedy. It was called *Paradise Lost*. There are many readers who have said that, behind Milton's ostensible vindication of God, his real hero was Lucifer, and that Lucifer's rebellion represented humanity's attempt to rise up against the constraint of the will of an unseeable and unknowable God. But the remedy seems almost as bad as the malady. Shall we praise Lucifer? After all, in whose interests does he act?

I have come to bury Caesar, not to praise him.

Consider the Enlightenment. What was the sermon? It seems to me the essential message was anticlerical: humans were capable of rational judgment and hence had the ability to arrive at both truth and goodness directly, through their own best efforts. The Enlightenment represented the definitive rejection of religious authorities as judges of either truth or goodness. But who were substituted for them? I suppose one has to say the philosophers. Kant was anxious to take away from the theologians the right to judge either truth or goodness. He found it easy enough to do this for truth, but more difficult to do for goodness. Having decided that one cannot prove laws of morality as though they were laws of physics, he might have conceded goodness to the theologians. But no, he insisted that here too the philosophers could offer the answer, which for Kant was located in the concept of the categorical imperative.

However, in the process of secularizing knowledge, the philosophers enshrined doubt, and this proved to be their own subsequent undoing. For along came the scientists to proclaim that the philosophers were merely disguised theologians. The scientists began to challenge the right of philosophers as well as of theologians to proclaim truth, asserting very stridently that scientists were *not* philosophers. Is there anything, the scientists asked, that legitimates the speculations, the ratiocinations, of the philosophers, anything that allows us to say that they are true? The scientists asserted that they, on the contrary, possessed a firm basis for truth, that of empirical investigation leading to testable and tested hypotheses, to those provisional universals called scientific theorems. The scientists, however, unlike Kant, wiser or perhaps less courageous than Kant, wanted nothing to do with moral laws. They laid claim therefore to only one-half of the task the philosophers had inherited from the theologians. Scientists would search only for truth. As for goodness, they suggested that it was uninteresting to search for it, asserting that goodness was incapable of being an object of knowledge as science was defining knowledge.

The claims of the scientists that science represented the unique path to locate truth gained wide cultural support, and they came to be the preeminent constructors of knowledge in the course of the late eighteenth and early nineteenth centuries. However, at that very moment, there was a small happening called the French Revolution, a happening whose protagonists claimed they were acting in the furtherance of goodness. Ever since, the French Revolution has served as the source of a belief system at least as powerful as that provided by the rise to cultural predominance of science. As a result, we have spent the last two hundred years trying to reunite the search for truth and the search for goodness. Social science, as it came to be established during the nineteenth century, was precisely the heir to both searches, and in some ways offered itself as the ground on which they could be reconciled. I must however admit that social science has not been very successful in its quest since, rather than reunifying them, it has itself been torn apart by the dissonance between the two searches.

The centrifugal pressure of the "two cultures" (as we now call them) has been impressively strong. It has provided the central themes of the rhetoric of public discourse about knowledge. It has determined the structures of the universities in the course of their being rebuilt and reinvigorated in the nineteenth century. Its continuing strength explains the persistingly high degree of passion about the antinomies to which I referred. It explains the fact that social science has never achieved true autonomy as an arena of knowledge nor ever acquired the degree of public esteem and public support to which it aspires and that it believes it merits.

The gulf between the "two cultures" was the deliberate construction of Newtonian-Cartesian science. Science was very sure of itself in this struggle. This is well illustrated by two famous declarations of the Marquis de Laplace. One was his bon mot in replying to Napoleon's query about the absence of God in his physics — "Sire, I have not found any need for that hypothesis."[1] The other was his unyielding statement about how much science could know:

> The present state of the system of nature is evidently a resultant of what it was in the preceding instant, and if we conceive of an Intelligence who, for a given moment, embraces all the relations of beings in the Universe, It will be able to determine for any instant of the past or future their respective positions, motions, and generally their affections.[2]

Triumphant science was not prepared to admit any doubts or to share the stage with anyone else.

Philosophy and, more generally, what came to be called in the nineteenth century the humanities fell in public esteem and retreated to a defensive stance. Unable to deny science's capacity to explain the physical world, they abandoned that domain entirely. Instead, they insisted that there existed another quite separate domain — the human, the spiritual, the moral — that was as important as, if not more important than, the domain of science. That is why, in English at least, they assumed the label of the humanities. From this human domain they sought to exclude science, or at the very least relegate it to a very secondary role. As long as the humanities engaged in metaphysics or literature, science was quite willing to allow itself to be excluded, on the deprecatory grounds that these were nonscientific matters. But when the subject matter was the description and analysis of social reality, there was no accord, even a tacit one, between the two camps. Both cultures laid claim to this arena.

A cadre of professional specialists on the study of social reality emerged slowly and, be it said, unsurely. In many ways, the most interesting story is that of history. Of all the fields that we today call social science, history has the longest lineage. It was a concept and a term long before the nineteenth century. But the basis of the modern discipline of history was the historiographical revolution we associate with Leopold von Ranke. And the modern version of history, which Ranke and his colleagues called *Geschichte* and not *Historie*, was extraordinarily scientistic in its fundamental premises. Its practitioners asserted that social reality was knowable. They asserted that such knowledge could be objective — that is, that there were correct and incorrect statements about the past — and that historians were obliged to write history "as it really happened," which is why they gave it the name of *Geschichte*. They asserted that scholars must not intrude their biases into the analysis of the data or its interpretation. Hence they asserted that scholars must offer evidence for their statements, evidence based on empirical research, evidence subject to control and verification by the community of scholars. Indeed, they even defined what kind of data would be acceptable evidence (primary documents in archives). In all these ways they sought to circumscribe the practices of the "discipline" and eliminate from history anything that was "philosophical," that is, speculative, deductive, mythical. I have called this attitude "history in search of science."[3] But historians proved in practice to be timid scientists. They wished to stick extremely close to their data and to restrict causal statements to statements of immediate sequences — immediate particular sequences. They balked at "generalizations," which is what they called either inductions of patterns of behavior from specific instances or assertions of causal sequences in which two variables were less immediately linked in time and space. We may be generous and say they did this because they were sensitive to the thin basis the collected empirical data in the nineteenth century afforded them for sound inductions. In any case, they were haunted by the fear that to generalize was to philosophize, that is, to be antiscientific. And so they came to idolize the particular, the idiographic, even the unique, and thereupon to shun, for the most part, the label of social science, despite the fact that they were "in search of science."

Other practitioners were more audacious. The emerging disciplines of economics, sociology, and political science by and large wrapped themselves in the mantle and the mantra of "social science," appropriating the methods and the honors of triumphant science (often be it noted to the scorn and/or despair of the natural scientists). These social science disciplines considered themselves nomothetic, in search of universal laws, consciously modeling themselves on the good example of physics (as nearly as they could). They had, of course, to admit that the quality of their data and the plausibility/validity of their theorems were far beneath the level achieved by their confreres in the physical sciences, but they defiantly asserted optimism about future progress in their scientific capacities.

I should like to underline that this great *Methodenstreit*, as it was called, between idiographic history and the nomothetic trio of "real" social sciences was in many ways huff and puff, since *both* sides of this disciplinary and methodological debate fully acknowledged the superiority of science over philosophy. Indeed, science might have won the battle for the soul of the social sciences hands down were the natural scientists not rather snobbish in refusing to accept the importuning social scientists into full membership in the fraternity.

History and the nomothetic trio remained up to 1945 very much social sciences of the civilized world, by the civilized world, and about the civilized world. To deal with the colonized world of what were called primitive peoples, a separate social science discipline was constructed, anthropology, with its separate set of methods and traditions. And the remaining half of the world, that of non-Western, so-called high civilizations — that is, China, India, the Arabo-Islamic world, among others — was left to a special group of persons engaged in something that was given the name of "Oriental studies," a discipline that insisted on its humanistic character and refused to be considered part of the social sciences. It is obvious today why a cleavage between a social science of and for the civilized world and a second social science of and for the rest of the world seemed so natural to nineteenth-century European scholars, and why it seems so absurd today. I shall not dwell on this issue.[4] I wish merely to note that both the anthropologists and the Orientalist scholars, by virtue of the logic of engaging in a social science about the others/the nonmodern world/the barbarians, felt very much more comfortable on the idiographic side of the *Methodenstreit*, since the universalist implications of nomothetic social science seemed to leave no place for what they wanted to say.

In the nineteenth century, the idiographers and the nomothetists were in great competition as to who could be more objective in their work, which had a strange consequence for the macro/micro distinction. If one looks at the earliest works and major figures in each of these emerging disciplines, one notices that they wrote about very large themes, such as universal history or stages of civilization. And the titles of their books tended to be all-encompassing. This fit in very well with the turn that modern thought was taking in that century, the turn to evolution as the fundamental metaphor. These books were very "macro" in the sweep of their subject matter, and they described the evolution of mankind. They were seldom monographic. But this macro quality of the research did not seem to last very long.

In the interests of creating corporate structures, the various social science disciplines sought to control the training and career patterns of those who would enter the fraternity. They insisted on both originality and objectivity, and this turned them against macroscholarship. Originality required that each successive scholar say something new, and the easiest way to do that was to divide up the subject matter into subjects of ever smaller scope, in terms of time, of space, and of variables under consideration. The process of subdivision opened up endless possibilities of not repeating the work of earlier scholars. And by circumscribing the scope, the disciplines believed they were making it more possible for scholars to be careful in their collection and analysis of data. It was the mentality of the microscope, and it pushed scholars to using ever more powerful microscopes. It fit in well with a reductionist ethos.

This microscopization of social science reinforced the gulf between idiographic and nomothetic social science. The two camps were equally in search of objectivity but pursued diametrically opposite paths to achieving it, because they singled out opposite risks of subjectivity.

The idiographic camp had two principal fears. They saw the danger of subjectivity deriving on the one hand from inadequate contextual understanding and on the other hand from the intrusion of self-interest. Insofar as one was dependent upon primary documents, one was obliged to read them correctly, and not anachronistically or from the prism of another culture. This required considerable knowledge of the context: the empirical detail, the definition of boundaries, the use of the language (even in many cases the handwriting), and the cultural allusions in the documents. The scholars hence sought to be hermeneutic, that is, to enter into the mentality of persons and groups who were remote from them, and to try to see the world as the persons under study saw it. This required long immersion in the language and culture under observation. For the historians, it seemed easiest therefore to study their own nation/culture, in which they were already immersed. For the anthropologists, who by definition could not follow this path, it required so great an investment to know enough to study a particular group of "others" that it seemed sensible to devote one's life work to the study of one such people. And for the Orientalist scholars, doing well their philological exercises required a lifelong improvement of difficult linguistic skills. There were thus, for each field, objective pressures that led scholars to narrow the scope of their research and to attain a level of specialization at which there were at most a few other persons in the world who had a matching profile of skills.

The problem of noninvolvement was also a serious one for idiographic scholars. The historians solved it first of all by insisting that history could not be written about the present and then by ending the "past" at a point relatively distant from the present. The argument was that we are all inevitably committed politically in the present, but that as we move backward in time we may feel less involved. This was reinforced by the fact that historians made themselves dependent upon archives, and the states that provided the materials for the archives were (and are) unwilling to make the documents available about current happenings, for obvious reasons. The Orientalist scholars ensured their neutrality by avoiding real intercourse with the civilizations they studied. Theirs being primarily a philological discipline, they were immersed in reading texts, a task they could and largely did conduct in their study. As for the anthropologists, the great fear of the discipline was that some colleagues would "go native," and thereby be unable to continue to play the role of the scientific observer. The main control employed was ensuring that the anthropologist did not stay out in the "field" too long. All of these solutions emphasized remoteness as the mechanism of controlling bias. In turn validity was guaranteed by the interpretative skills of carefully trained scholars.

The nomothetic trio of economics, political science, and sociology turned these techniques on their head. They emphasized not remoteness but closeness as the road to avoiding bias; but it was a very particular kind of closeness. Objective data were defined as replicable data, that is, precisely data that were *not* the result of an "interpretation." The more quantitative the data, the easier it was to replicate them. But data from the past or from remote parts of the world lacked the infrastructural basis for the necessary guarantees of quality, of "hardness." Quite the opposite: the best data were the most recent, and collected in the countries with the best infrastructure for the recording of data. Older or remoter data were necessarily incomplete, approximate, perhaps even mythical. They might be sufficient for the purposes of journalism or travel reports but not for science. Furthermore, even newly collected data rapidly became obsolete, since the passing of time brought ever-increased quality of data collection, especially in terms of the comparability of data collected in two or more sites. So the nomothetic trio retreated into the present, even into the immediate and instantaneous present.

Furthermore, insofar as one wanted to perform sophisticated operations on quantitative data, it was optimal to reduce the number of variables and to use indicators about which one could collect good data, hard data. Thus, reliability pushed these social scientists into constantly narrowing the time and space scope of the analyses and into testing only carefully limited propositions. One might wonder then about the validity of the results. But the epistemological premises solved this problem. Insofar as one believed that there existed universal laws of human behavior, the locus of the research became irrelevant. One chose sites of data collection according to the quality of the data it was possible to obtain, not because of their superior relevance.

I draw from this the conclusion that the great methodological debates that illustrated the historical construction of the social sciences were sham debates, which distracted us from realizing the degree to which the "divorce" between philosophy and science effectively eliminated the search for the good from the realm of knowledge and circumscribed the search for truth into the form of a microscopic positivism that took on many guises. The early hopes of social scientists that they could be modern philosopher-kings proved totally vain, and social scientists settled into being the handmaidens of governmental reformism. When they did this openly, they called it applied social science. But for the most part they did this abashedly, asserting that their role was merely to do the research, and that it was up to others, the political persons, to draw from this research the conclusions that seemed to derive from this research. In short, the neutrality of the scholar became the fig leaf of their shame, in having eaten the apple of knowledge.

As long as the modern world seemed to be one long success story of technological triumph, the necessary political base to maintain a certain equilibrium in the system continued to exist. Amid the success, the world of science was carried from honor to honor within this system, as though it were responsible for the triumph. The social sciences were swept along in the tide. No one was seriously questioning the fundamental premises of knowledge. The many maladies of the system — from racism to sexism to colonialism as expressions of the manifestly growing polarization of the world, from fascist movements to socialist gulags to liberal formalisms as alternative modes of suppressing democratization — were all defined as transitory problems because they were all thought to be capable of being brought under control eventually, as so many turbulent deviations from the norm, in a world in which the trajectory always returned to the curve of linear upward-moving equilibrium. The political persons on all sides promised that goodness was coming at the end of the horizon, a prospect presumably guaranteed by the continual progress in the search for truth.

This was an illusion, the illusion bred by the separation and reification of the two cultures. Indeed the separation of the two cultures was one of the main factors pushing the trajectories far from equilibrium. Knowledge is in fact a singular enterprise, and there are no fundamental contradictions between how we may pursue it in the natural and in the human world, for they are both integral parts of a singular universe. Nor is knowledge separate from creativity or adventure or the search for the good society. To be sure, knowledge will always remain a pursuit, never a point of arrival. It is this very fact, however, that permits us to see that macro and micro, global and local, and above all, structure and agency are not unsurpassable antinomies but rather yin and yang.

There have been two remarkable intellectual developments of the last two decades that constitute an entirely new trend, signs that the world may be now in the process of overcoming the two cultures. These trends are only marginally the doing of social scientists, but they are wonderfully encouraging about the future of social science. I refer to what has been called complexity studies in the natural sciences and what has been called cultural studies in the humanities. I am not going to review the now immense literature in each of these two fields. Rather I shall try to situate each of these fields in terms of their epistemological implications for knowledge and their implications for the social sciences.

Why are complexity studies given that name? It is because they reject one of the most basic premises of the modern scientific enterprise. Newtonian science assumed that there were simple underlying formulas that explained everything. Einstein was unhappy that $e=mc^2$ explained only half the universe. He was searching for the unified field theory that would in an equally simple equation explain everything. Complexity studies argue that all such formulas can at best be partial, and at most explain the past, never the future. (We must of course be careful to distinguish between the dubious belief that truth is simple and the sound methodological injunction of Occam's razor, that we ought always to try to eliminate logical curlicues from our reasoning and include in our equations only the terms necessary to stating them clearly.)

Why is truth complex? Because reality is complex. And reality is complex for one essential reason: the arrow of time. Everything affects everything, and as time goes on, what is everything expands inexorably. In a sense, nothing is eliminated, although much fades or becomes blurred. The universe proceeds — it has a life — in its orderly disorder or its disorderly order. There are of course endless provisional orderly patterns, self-established, holding things together, creating seeming coherence. But none is perfect, because of course perfect order is death, and in any case enduring order has never existed. Perfect order is what we may mean by God, which is by definition beyond the known universe. So the atoms, the galaxies, and the biota pursue their paths, their evolution if you will, until the internal contradictions of their structures move them further and further away from whatever temporary equilibria they enjoy. These evolving structures repeatedly reach points at which their equilibria can no longer be restored, at points of bifurcation, and then new paths are found, new orders established, but we can never know in advance what these new orders will be.

The picture of the universe that derives from this model is an intrinsically nondeterministic one, since the aleatory combinations are too many, the number of small decisions too many, for us to predict where the universe will move. But it does not follow that the universe can therefore move in any direction whatsoever. It is the child of its own past, which has created the parameters within which these new paths are chosen. Statements about our present trajectories can of course be made, and can be made carefully, that is, can be stated quantitatively. But if we try to overdo the accuracy of the data, the mathematicians tell us we get unstable results.[5]

If physical scientists and mathematicians are now telling us that truth in their arena is complex, indeterminate, and dependent on an arrow of time, what does that mean for social scientists? For, it is clear that, of all systems in the universe, human social systems are the most complex structures that exist, the ones with the briefest stable equilibria, the ones with the most outside variables to take into account, the ones that are most difficult to study.

We can only do what the natural scientists can only do. We can search for interpretative patterns, of two sorts. We can search for what might be called *formal* interpretative patterns, of the kind that state, for example, that all human social systems are historical social systems, not only in the sense that they follow a historical trajectory, but in the sense that they are born or emerge at certain times and places for specific reasons, operate according to specific sets of rules for specific reasons, and come to a close or die or disintegrate at certain times and places because they are unable any longer to handle their contradictions for specific sets of reasons. Such formal interpretative patterns are of course themselves subject to a finite relevance. One day, a given particular formal pattern may no longer operate, though for the moment this day may seem remote.

We can also search, however, for what might be called *substantive* interpretative patterns, such as the description of the rules of a particular historical social system. For example, when I term the modern world-system a capitalist world-economy, I am laying claim to the existence of a particular substantive pattern. It is of course a debatable one, and it has been much debated. Furthermore, like a series of boxes within boxes, there are substantive patterns within substantive patterns, such that, even if we all agree that the world in which we live is a capitalist world-economy, we may nonetheless differ about whether it has had discernible stages, or about whether unequal exchange has been its norm, or about endless other aspects of its functioning.

What is crucial to note about complexity studies is that they have in no sense rejected scientific analysis, merely Newtonian determinism. But in turning some premises on their head, and in particular by rejecting the concept of reversibility in favor of the concept of the arrow of time, the natural sciences are taking a giant's step in the direction of the traditional terrain of social science, the explanation of reality as a constructed reality.

If we now turn to cultural studies, let us start with the same question. Why are they called cultural studies? For a group of scholars so taken with linguistic analysis, to my knowledge this question has never been posed. The first thing I note is that cultural studies are not really studies of culture but studies of cultural products. This is the consequence of their deep root in the humanities and explains in turn their deep attraction to the humanities. For the humanities, in the division of the two cultures, were attributed above all the domain of cultural products.

They were also attributed the domain of goodness, but they were very reluctant to seize hold of it. It seemed so political, so uncultural, so fleeting and unsolid, so lacking in eternal continuities. The personal path of Wordsworth from poet of the French Revolution to poet of poetry illustrates the repeated flight of the artists and the scholars of cultural products to the surer ground of "art for art's sake," an aesthetic turning inward. They comforted themselves with Keats's lines in "Ode on a Grecian Urn": "Beauty is truth, truth beauty — that is all / Ye know on earth, and all ye need to know."

To be sure, there were always those who asserted that cultural products were a product of the culture and that this could be explained in terms of the structures of the system. Indeed, cultural studies as we know it today originated in England in the 1950s with persons who were arguing this long-standing theme. They were, let us remember, in search of a workers' culture. But then cultural studies took what has been called a linguistic turn or a hermeneutic turn, but which I think of as a 1968 turn. The revolutions of 1968 were against the liberal center and put forward the argument not only that the Old Left was part of this liberal center, but also that this liberal center was as dangerous as (if not more dangerous than) the true conservatives.

In terms of the study of cultural products, it meant that the enemy became not merely those who would study cultural products according to conservative, traditional aesthetic norms (the so-called canons), but also those (the Old Left) who would analyze cultural products in terms of their presumed explanations in the political economy. An explosion followed, in which everything was deconstructed. But what is this exercise? It seems to me the core of it is to assert the absence of absolute aesthetics, to insist that we have to explain how particular cultural products were produced when they were produced and why in that form, and then to proceed to ask how they were *and are* being received by others, and for what reasons.

We are clearly involved here in a very complex activity, one in which equilibria (canons) are at best transient and one in which there can be no determinate future, since the aleatory elements are too vast. In the process, the study of cultural products has moved away from the traditional terrain of the humanities and onto the terrain of the social sciences, the explanation of reality as a constructed reality. This is of course one of the reasons why so many social scientists have been receptive to it.

The move of natural scientists toward the social sciences (complexity studies) and the move of scholars in the humanities toward the social sciences (cultural studies) have not been without opposition within the natural sciences and within the humanities. The opposition has in fact been ferocious, but it seems to me that it has been largely a rearguard operation. Nor have the proponents of complexity studies or the proponents of cultural studies defined themselves as moving into the camp of the social sciences. Nor have all (or even most) social scientists analyzed the situation in this way.

But it is time that we all call a spade a spade. We are in the process of overcoming the two cultures via the social scientization of all knowledge, by the recognition that reality is a constructed reality and that the purpose of scientific/philosophical activity is to arrive at usable, plausible interpretations of that reality, interpretations that will inevitably be transitory but nonetheless correct, or more correct, for their time, than alternative interpretations. But if reality is a constructed reality, the constructors are the actors in the real world, and not the scholars. The role of the scholars is not to construct reality but to figure out how it has been constructed, and to test the multiple social constructions of reality against each other. In a sense, this is a game of never-ending mirrors. We seek to discover the reality on the basis of which we have constructed reality. And when we find this, we seek to understand how this underlying reality has in turn been socially constructed. In this navigation amid the mirrors, there are however more correct and less correct scholarly analyses. Those scholarly analyses that are more correct are more socially useful in that they aid the world to construct a substantively more rational reality. Hence the search for truth and the search for goodness are inextricably linked the one to the other. We are all involved, and involved simultaneously, in both.

In his latest book, Ilya Prigogine says two things very simply. "The possible is richer than the real. Nature presents us in effect with the image of creation, of the unforeseeable, of novelty"; and, "Science is a dialogue with nature."[6] I should like to take these two themes as the basis of my concluding remarks.

The possible is richer than the real. Who should know this better than social scientists? Why are we so afraid of discussing the possible, of analyzing the possible, of exploring the possible? We must move not utopias, but utopistics, to the center of social science. Utopistics is the analysis of possible utopias, their limitations, and the constraints on achieving them. It is the analytic study of real historical alternatives in the present. It is the reconciliation of the search for truth and the search for goodness.

Utopistics represents a continuing responsibility of social scientists. But it represents a particularly urgent task when the range of choice is greatest. When is this? Precisely when the historical social system of which we are a part is furthest from equilibrium, when the fluctuations are greatest, when the bifurcations are nearest, when small input has great output. This is the moment in which we are now living and shall be living for the next twenty-five to fifty years.[7]

If we are to be serious about utopistics, we must stop fighting about nonissues, and foremost of these nonissues is determinism versus free will, or structure versus agency, or global versus local, or macro versus micro. It seems to me that what we can now see clearly is that these antinomies are not a matter of correctness, or even of preference, but of timing and depth of perspective. For very long and very short time-spans, and from very deep and very shallow perspectives, things seem to be determined, but for the vast intermediate zone things seem to be a matter of free will. We can always shift our viewing angle to obtain the evidence of determinism or free will that we want.

But what does it mean to say that something is determined? In the realm of theology, I can understand it. It means we believe that there is an omnipotent God and that he has determined everything. Even there, we get quickly into trouble, as I have suggested. But at least, as Aristotle would have put it, we are dealing with an efficient cause. But if I say that the possibility of reducing unemployment in Europe in the next ten years is determined, who or what is doing this determining, and how far back shall I trace it? Even if you were to convince me that this had some analytical meaning (and that would be difficult), does it have any practical relevance? But does it follow then that it is merely a matter of free will, and that, were Dutch or German or French politicians, or entrepreneurs, or trade union leaders, or someone else to do specific things, then I could assure you that unemployment would in fact be reduced? Even if they, or I, knew what these things were, or believed we knew, what would motivate us to do them now when we did not do them previously? And if there were an answer to this, does that mean that our free will is determined by something prior? And if so, what? This is an endless, pointless, sequential chain. Starting with free will, we end up with determinism, and starting with determinism, we end up with free will.

Can we not approach this another way? Let us agree that we are trying to make sense of the complexity, to "interpret" it usefully and plausibly. We could start with the simple task of locating seeming regularities. We could also try provisionally to assess the relative strength of various constraints on individual and collective action. This task we might call locating structures of the *longue durée*. I call this a simple task, but of course it is not at all an easy task. It is simple rather in the sense that it explains little, and also in the sense that it is a prior task, prior, that is, to other more complex tasks. If we don't have the structures clearly in mind, we cannot go on to analyze anything more complex, like for example so-called microhistories or texts or voting patterns.

Analyzing structures does not limit whatever agency exists. Indeed, it is only when we have mastered the structures, yes have invented "master narratives" that are plausible, relevant, and provisionally valid, that we can begin to exercise the kind of judgment that is implied by the concept of agency. Otherwise, our so-called agency is blind, and if blind it is manipulated, if not directly then indirectly. We are watching the figures in Plato's cave, and are thinking that we can affect them.

This brings me to Prigogine's second apothegm: "Science is a dialogue with nature." A dialogue has two partners. Who are they in this case? Is science a scientist or the community of scientists or some particular scientific organization(s), or is it everyman insofar as he or she is a thinking being? Is nature a living entity, some sort of pantheistic god, or God omnipotent? I do not think we know for sure who is engaged in this dialogue. The search for the partners in the dialogue is part of the dialogue itself. What we must hold constant is the possibility of knowing more and of doing better. This remains only a possibility, but not an unattainable one. And the beginning of realizing that possibility is ceasing to debate the false issues of the past erected to distract us from more fruitful paths. Science is at its very earliest moments. All knowledge is social knowledge. And social science lays claim to being the locus of self-reflection of knowledge, a claim it makes neither against philosophy nor against the natural sciences, but at one with them.

Much as I think that the next twenty-five to fifty years will be terrible ones in terms of human social relations — the period of disintegration of our existing historical social system and of transition toward an uncertain alternative — I also think that the next twenty-five to fifty years will be exceptionally exciting ones in the world of knowledge. The systemic crisis will force social reflection. I see the possibility of definitively ending the divorce between science and philosophy, and, as I have said, I see social science as the inevitable ground of a reunited world of knowledge. We cannot know what that will produce. But I can only think, as did Wordsworth about the French Revolution in *The Preludes:* "Bliss was it in that dawn to be alive. / But to be young was very Heaven!"

Chapter 15

The Heritage of Sociology, the Promise of Social Science

I wish here to discuss the subject of social knowledge and its heritage, challenges, and perspectives. I shall argue that the heritage of sociology is something I shall call "the culture of sociology," and I shall try to define what I think this is. I shall further argue that, for several decades now, there have been significant challenges precisely to that culture. These challenges essentially consist of calls to unthink the culture of sociology. Given both the persistent reassertion of the culture of sociology and the strength of these challenges, I shall try finally to argue convincingly that the only perspective we have that is plausible and rewarding is to create a new open culture, this time not of sociology but of social science, and (most importantly) one that is located within an epistemologically reunified world of knowledge.

We divide and bound knowledge in three different ways: intellectually as disciplines; organizationally as corporate structures; and culturally as communities of scholars sharing certain elementary premises. We may think of a discipline as an intellectual construct, a sort of heuristic device. It is a mode of laying claim to a so-called field of study, with its particular domain, its appropriate methods, and consequently its boundaries. It is a discipline in the sense that it seeks to discipline the intellect. A discipline defines not only what to think about and how to think about it, but also what is outside its purview. To say that a given subject is a discipline is to say not only what it is but what it is not. To assert therefore that sociology is a discipline is, among other things, to assert that it is not economics or history or anthropology. And sociology is said not to be these other names because it is considered to have a different field of study, a different set of methods, a different approach to social knowledge.

Presidential address, Fourteenth World Congress of Sociology, Montreal, July 26, 1998.

Sociology as a discipline was an invention of the late nineteenth century, alongside the other disciplines we place under the covering label of the social sciences. Sociology as a discipline was elaborated more or less during the period 1880 to 1945. The leading figures of the field in that period all sought to write at least one book that purported to define sociology as a discipline. Perhaps the last major work in this tradition was that written in 1937 by Talcott Parsons, *The Structure of Social Action*,[1] a book of great importance in our heritage, and to whose role I shall return. It is certainly true that, in the first half of the twentieth century, the various divisions of the social sciences established themselves and received recognition as disciplines. They each defined themselves in ways that emphasized clearly how they were different from other neighboring disciplines. As a result, few could doubt whether a given book or article was written within the framework of one discipline or another. It was a period in which the statement, "That is not sociology; it is economic history, or it is political science," was a meaningful statement.

I do not intend here to review the logic of the boundaries that were established in this period. They reflected three cleavages in objects of study that seemed obvious to scholars at the time and were strongly enunciated and defended as crucial. There was the cleavage past/present that separated idiographic history from the nomothetic trio of economics, political science, and sociology. There was the cleavage civilized/other or European/non-European that separated all four of the previous disciplines (which essentially studied the pan-European world) from anthropology and Oriental studies. And there was the cleavage — relevant only, it was thought, to the modern civilized world — of market, state, and civil society that constituted the domains respectively of economics, political science, and sociology.[2] The intellectual problem with these sets of boundaries is that the changes in the world-system after 1945 — the rise of the United States to world hegemony, the political resurgence of the non-Western world, and the expansion of the world-economy with its correlative expansion of the world university system — all conspired to undermine the logic of these three cleavages,[3] such that by 1970 there had begun to be in practice a serious blurring of the boundaries. The blurring has become so extensive that, in the view of many persons, in my view, it was no longer possible to defend these names, these sets of boundaries, as intellectually decisive or even very useful. As a result, the various disciplines of the social sciences have ceased to be disciplines, because they no longer represent obviously different fields of study with different methods and therefore with firm, distinctive boundaries.

The names have not for that, however, ceased to exist. Far from it! For the various disciplines have long since been institutionalized as corporate organizations, in the form of university departments, programs of instruction, degrees, scholarly journals, national and international associations, and even library classifications. The institutionalization of a discipline is a way of preserving and reproducing practice. It represents the creation of an actual human network with boundaries, a network that takes the form of corporate structures that have entrance requirements and codes providing for recognized paths of upward career mobility. Scholarly organizations seek to discipline not the intellect but the practice. They create boundaries that are far firmer than those created by disciplines as intellectual constructs, and they can outlast the theoretical justification for their corporate limits. Indeed, they have already done so. The analysis of sociology as an organization in the world of knowledge is profoundly different from the analysis of sociology as an intellectual discipline. If Michel Foucault may be said to have intended to analyze how academic disciplines are defined, created, and redefined in *The Archaeology of Knowledge*, Pierre Bourdieu's *Homo Academicus* is the analysis of how academic organizations are framed, perpetuated, and reframed within the institutions of knowledge.[4]

I am not going to follow either path at the moment. I do not believe, as I have said, that sociology is any longer a discipline (but neither are our fellow social sciences). I do believe they all remain very strong organizationally. And I believe that it follows that we all find ourselves in a very anomalous situation, perpetuating in a sense a mythical past, which is perhaps a dubious thing to do. However, I wish rather to turn my attention to sociology as a culture, that is, as a community of scholars who share certain premises. For I believe that it is in the debates in this domain that our future is being constructed. I shall argue that the culture of sociology is recent and vigorous, but also fragile, and that it can continue to thrive only if it is transformed.

The Heritage

What can we mean by the culture of sociology? I shall start by offering two comments. First, what we normally mean by a "culture" is a set of shared premises and practices, shared to be sure not by all members of the community all of the time but by most members most of the time; shared openly, but what is even more important shared subconsciously, such that the premises are seldom subject to discussion. Such a set of premises must necessarily be quite simple, and even banal. To the extent that the assertions are sophisticated, subtle, and learned, they would be unlikely to be shared by too many, and therefore to be able to create a worldwide community of scholars. I will suggest that there exists precisely such a set of simple premises shared by most sociologists, but not necessarily at all by persons who call themselves historians or economists.

Second, I think the shared premises are revealed — revealed, not defined — by who it is that we present as our formative thinkers. The standard list these days for sociologists around the world is Durkheim, Marx, and Weber. The first thing to note about this list is that if one posed the question of formative thinkers to historians, economists, anthropologists, or geographers, one would surely come up with a different list. Our list does not contain Jules Michelet or Edward Gibbon, Adam Smith or John Maynard Keynes, John Stuart Mill or Machiavelli, Kant or Hegel, Bronislaw Malinowski or Franz Boas.

So the question becomes, Where did our list come from? After all, if Durkheim did call himself a sociologist, Weber did so only in the very last period of his life, and even then ambiguously,[5] and Marx of course never did so. Furthermore, although I have met sociologists who call themselves Durkheimians, and others who call themselves Marxists, and still others who call themselves Weberians, I have never yet met any who said that they were Durkheimian-Marxist-Weberians. So in what sense can these three be said to be founding figures of the field? Yet book after book, and in particular textbook after textbook, says so.[6]

It was not always thus. This grouping is in fact largely the doing of Talcott Parsons and his formative work of the culture of sociology, *The Structure of Social Action*. Of course Parsons intended that we canonize the trio of Durkheim, Weber, and Vilfredo Pareto. Somehow, he was never able to persuade others of the importance of Pareto, who remains largely ignored. And Marx was added to the list, despite Parsons's best efforts to keep him off it. Nonetheless, I attribute the creation of the list essentially to Parsons. And that of course makes the list very recent. It is basically a post-1945 creation.

In 1937, when Parsons wrote, Durkheim was less central to French social science than he had been twenty years earlier and would be again after 1945.[7] And he was not a figure of reference in other major national sociological communities. It is interesting in this regard to look at the introduction that George E. G. Catlin wrote to the first English edition of *The Rules of Sociological Method.* In 1938, writing for a U.S. audience, Catlin pleaded for Durkheim's importance by classifying him in the same league as Charles Booth, Flexner, and W. I. Thomas, and said that, although his ideas were anticipated by Wundt, Espinas, Tönnies, and Simmel, he was nonetheless important.[8] This is not exactly the way Durkheim would be presented today. In 1937, Weber was not taught in German universities, and to be fair even in 1932 he was not the commanding figure he is today in German sociology. Nor had he yet been translated into English or French. As for Marx, he was scarcely ever even mentioned in most respectable academic circles.

R. W. Connell has shown in a recent survey what I had long suspected, that the pre-1945 textbooks may have mentioned these three authors, but only alongside a long list of others. Connell calls this "an encyclopedic, rather than a canonical, view of the new science by its practitioners."[9] It is the canon that defines the culture, and this canon had its heyday between 1945 and 1970, a very special period — one dominated by U.S. sociological practitioners, one during which structural-functionalism was by far the leading perspective within the sociological community.

The canon must begin with Durkheim, the most self-consciously "sociological" of the three, the founder of a journal called *L'Année Sociologique,* whose centenary we celebrate in 1998 as we celebrate the fiftieth anniversary of the International Sociological Association. Durkheim responded to the first and most obvious of questions about which any student of social reality doing empirical work must wonder. How is it that individuals hold particular sets of values and not others? And how is it that persons with "similar backgrounds" are more likely to hold the same set of values than persons of dissimilar backgrounds? We know the answer so well that it no longer seems to us a question.

Let us nonetheless review Durkheim's answer. He restates his basic arguments very clearly in the preface to the second edition of *The Rules of Sociological Method,* written in 1901. It was meant as a reply to the critics of the first edition, and in it he seeks to clarify what he is saying, since he feels he had been misunderstood. He declares three propositions. The first is that "social facts must be treated as things," a statement he insists is "at the very base of our method." He asserts that he is not thereby reducing social reality to some physical substratum but simply claiming for the social world "a degree of reality at least equal to that everyone accords" to the physical world. "The thing [he says] stands in opposition to the idea, just as what is known from the outside stands in opposition to what is known from the inside."[10] The second proposition is that "social phenomena [are] external to individuals."[11] And, finally, Durkheim insists that social constraint is not the same as physical constraint, because it is not inherent but imposed from the outside.[12] Durkheim further takes note that, for a social fact to exist, there must be individual interactions that result in "beliefs and modes of behaviour instituted by the collectivity; sociology can then be defined as the science of institutions, their genesis and their functioning."[13] Thus we are clearly talking of a social reality that is socially constructed, and it is this socially constructed reality that sociologists are to study — the science of institutions. Durkheim even anticipates our current concern with agency, because it is just at this point that he adds a footnote, arguing the limits of "permitted variation."[14]

These three declarations taken together constitute the argument for Durkheim's "basic principle, that of the objective reality of social facts. It is ... upon this principle that in the end everything rests, and everything comes back to it."[15]

I do not propose here to discuss my own views on these formulations of Durkheim. I do wish to suggest that his effort to carve out a domain for sociology, the domain of what he calls "social facts," a domain that is distinctive from the domains both of biology and of psychology, is indeed a basic premise of the culture of sociology. If you then say to me that there are persons among us who call themselves social psychologists, or symbolic interactionists, or methodological individualists, or phenomenologists, or indeed postmodernists, I say to you that these persons have nonetheless decided to pursue their scholarly endeavors under the label of sociology, and not of psychology or biology or philosophy. There must have been some intellectual reason for this. I suggest it is their tacit acceptance of the Durkheimian principle of the reality of social facts, however much they would like to operationalize this principle in ways quite different from those that Durkheim proposed.

In the preface to the first edition, Durkheim discusses how he wishes to be labeled. The correct way, he says, is not to call him either a "materialist" or an "idealist" but a "rationalist."[16] While that term in turn has been the subject of many centuries of philosophical debate and discord, it is certainly a label that almost all sociologists from Durkheim's time to at least 1970 would have embraced.[17] I would like therefore to restate Durkheim's argument as Axiom Number 1 of the culture of sociology: *there exist social groups that have explicable, rational structures.* Formulated in this simple way, I believe that there have been few sociologists who did not presume its validity.

The problem with what I am calling Axiom Number 1 is not the existence of these groups, but their lack of internal unity. This is where Marx comes in. He seeks to answer the question, How is it that social groups that are supposedly a unity (the meaning after all of "group") in fact have internal struggles? We all know his answer. It is the sentence that opens the first section of the *Communist Manifesto:* "The history of all hitherto existing society is the history of class struggles."[18] Of course, Marx was not so naive as to assume that the overt rhetoric of conflict, the explanations of the reasons for the conflict, was necessarily to be taken at face value or was in any sense correct, correct that is from the point of view of the analyst.[19] The rest of Marx's oeuvre is constituted by the elaboration of the historiography of the class struggle, the analysis of the mechanisms of functioning of the capitalist system, and the political conclusions one should draw from this framework of analysis. All this together constitutes Marxism, properly speaking, which is of course a doctrine and an analytic viewpoint that have been subject to great controversy within and outside the sociological community.

I do not propose to discuss either the merits of Marxism or the arguments of its opponents. I merely want to ask why it was that Parsons's attempt to exclude Marx from the picture failed so miserably, despite the Cold War and despite indeed the political preferences of the majority of the world's sociologists. It seems to me that Marx was discussing something so obviously central to social life that it simply could not be ignored, namely, social conflict.

Marx had a particular explanation of social conflict to be sure, one that centered on the fact that people had different relations to the means of production, some owning them and others not, some controlling their use and others not. It has been very fashionable for some time to argue that Marx was wrong about this, that the class struggle is not the only, or even the primary, source of social conflict. There have been various substitutes offered: status-groups, political affinity groups, gender, race. The list goes on. Once again, I shall not immediately discuss the validity of these alternatives to class, but confine myself to the observation that every substitute for "class" presumes the centrality of struggle and merely juggles the list of combatants. Is there anyone who has refuted Marx by saying, this is all nonsense, since there are no social conflicts?

Take so central an activity to the practice of sociologists as the opinion survey. What is it we do? We usually constitute what is called a representative sample, and we pose to this sample a series of questions about something. Normally, we presume that we will get a range of answers to these questions, although we may not have a clear idea in advance of what the range will turn out to be. If we thought everyone would answer the questions identically, there would be little point in doing the survey. When we get the answers to these questions, what is we do next? We correlate the answers with a set of basic variables, such as socioeconomic status, occupation, sex, age, education, and so on. Why do we do this? It is because we assume that often, even usually, each variable contains a continuum of persons along a certain dimension, and that the wageworkers and the businessmen, men and women, the young and the old, and so on, will tend to give different answers to the questions. If we didn't presume social variation (and most frequently the emphasis has in fact been on variation in socioeconomic status), we wouldn't be engaged in this enterprise. The step from variation to conflict is not a long one, and generally speaking those people who try to deny that variation leads to conflict are suspected of seeking to disregard an obvious reality for purely ideological reasons.

So there we are. We are all Marxists, in the diluted form of what I shall term Axiom Number 2 of the culture of sociology: *all social groups contain subgroups that are ranked in a hierarchy and are in conflict with each other.* Is this a dilution of Marxism? Of course it is, indeed a serious dilution. Is this however a premise of most sociologists? Of course it is as well.

Can we stop here? No, we can't. Having decided that social groups are real and that we can explain their mode of operation (Axiom Number 1), and having decided that they harbor within them repeated conflicts (Axiom Number 2), we face an obvious question: Why do not all societies simply blow up or split apart or destroy themselves in some other way? It seems clear that, although such explosions do indeed happen from time to time, they do not seem to happen most of the time. There does seem to be a semblance of "order" in social life, despite

Axiom Number 2. Here is where Weber comes in. For Weber has an explanation for the existence of order despite conflict.

We regularly identify Weber as the anti-Marx, one insisting on cultural as opposed to economic explanations, insisting on bureaucratization rather than accumulation as the central driving force of the modern world. But the key concept of Weber that serves to limit the impact of Marx, or at least to modify it seriously, is legitimacy. What does Weber say about legitimacy? Weber is concerned with the basis of authority. Why, he asks, do subjects obey those who give commands? There are various obvious reasons, such as custom and material calculation of advantage. But Weber says they are not enough to explain the commonness of obedience. He adds a third, crucial factor, the "belief in legitimacy."[20] At this point, Weber delineates his three pure types of authority or legitimate domination: legitimacy based on rational grounds, legitimacy based on traditional grounds, and legitimacy based on charismatic grounds. But since, for Weber, traditional authority is the structure of the past and not of modernity, and since charisma, however important a role it plays in historical reality and in Weberian analysis, is essentially a transitional phenomenon, always being eventually "routinized," we are left with "rational-legal authority" as the "specifically modern type of administration."[21]

The picture Weber offers us is that authority is administered by a staff, a bureaucracy, that is "disinterested," in the sense that it has no *parti pris* either vis-à-vis the subjects or vis-à-vis the state. The bureaucracy is said to be "impartial," that is, making its decisions according to the law, which is why this kind of authority is called rational-legal by Weber. To be sure, Weber admits that, in practice, the situation is a bit more complicated.[22] Nonetheless, if we now simplify Weber, we have a reasonable explanation for the fact that states are usually orderly, that is, that the authorities are usually accepted and obeyed, more or less, or to a certain extent. We shall call this Axiom Number 3, which can be stated as follows: *to the extent that groups/states contain their conflicts, it is in large part because lower-ranked subgroups accord legitimacy to the authority structure of the group on the grounds that this permits the group to survive, and the subgroups see long-term advantage in the group's survival.*

What I have been trying to argue is that the culture of sociology, which we all share, but which was strongest in the period of 1945– 70, contains three simple propositions — the reality of social facts, the perennity of social conflict, and the existence of mechanisms of legitimation to contain the conflict — which add up to a coherent minimal baseline for the study of social reality. I have tried to indicate the way in which each of the three propositions was derived from one of the three formative thinkers (Durkheim, Marx, and Weber), and I claim that is why we repeat the mantra that this trio represents "classical sociology." Once again, I repeat, this set of axioms is not a sophisticated and certainly not an adequate way of perceiving social reality. It is a starting point, one that most of us have internalized and one that operates largely at the level of unquestioned premises that may be assumed rather than debated. This is what I am calling "the culture of sociology." This is, in my view, our essential heritage. But again I repeat, it is a heritage of a construct that is recent, and if vigorous also fragile.

The Challenges

I shall now present six challenges that in my view raise very serious questions about the set of axioms I am calling "the culture of sociology." I shall present them in the order that they began to have an impact on the world of sociology, and more generally on social science, which was sometimes long after they were written. I wish to emphasize at the outset that these are challenges, not truths. Challenges are serious if they put forward credible demands on scholars to reexamine premises. Once we accept that the challenges are serious, we may be stimulated to reformulate the premises in ways that make them less vulnerable to the challenges. Or we may find ourselves forced to abandon the premises, or at the very least to revise them drastically. A challenge is thus part of a process, the beginning and not the end of the process.

The first challenge I shall present I associate with Sigmund Freud. This may seem surprising. For one thing, Freud was essentially a contemporary of Durkheim and Weber, not someone who came significantly later. For a second thing, Freud has in fact been well incorporated into the culture of sociology. Freud's topology of the psyche — the id, ego, and superego — has long been something we use to provide the intervening variables that explain how it is that Durkheim's social facts are internalized inside individual consciousnesses. We may not all use Freud's exact language, but the basic idea is there. In a sense, Freud's psychology is part of our collective assumptions.

I am not however interested now in Freud's psychology but in Freud's sociology. Here, we tend primarily to discuss a few important works, such as *Civilization and Its Discontents*,[23] and they are important to be sure. But we tend to ignore the sociological implications of his modes of diagnosis and therapy. I wish to discuss what I think is Freud's implicit challenge to the very concept of rationality. Durkheim called himself a rationalist. Weber made rational-legal legitimation the linchpin of his analysis of authority. And Marx was devoted to pursuing what he called scientific (that is, rational) socialism. Our formative thinkers were all children of the Enlightenment, even when, as in the case of Weber, they raised gloomy questions about where we were heading. (But the First World War caused much gloom for most of Europe's intellectuals.)

Freud was not at all a stranger to this tradition. Indeed, what was he about? He said to the world, and in particular to the medical world, that behavior that seems to us strange and irrational is in fact quite explicable, provided one understands that much of the individual's mind operates at a level Freud called the unconscious. The unconscious, by definition, cannot be seen or heard, even by the individual himself, but, said Freud, there are indirect ways of knowing what is going on in the unconscious. His first major work, *The Interpretation of Dreams*,[24] was precisely on this topic. Dreams reveal, said Freud, what the ego is repressing into the unconscious.[25] Nor are dreams the only analytic tool we have at our disposition. The whole of psychoanalytic therapy, the so-called talking cure, was developed as a series of practices that could help both the analyst and the analysand become aware of what was going on in the unconscious.[26] The method is quintessentially one derived from Enlightenment beliefs. It reflects the view that increased awareness may lead to improved decision making, that is, more rational behavior. But the road to this more rational behavior involves recognizing that so-called neurotic behavior is in fact "rational," once one understands what the individual intends by this behavior and therefore why it is occurring. The behavior may be in the opinion of the analyst suboptimal, but it is not thereby irrational.

In the history of psychoanalytic practice, Freud and the early analysts treated only, or at least primarily, adult neurotics. But following the logic of organizational expansion, later analysts were ready to analyze children and even to treat infants who had not reached the age of talking. And still others began to find ways of dealing with psychotics, that is, with persons presumably beyond the capacity to enter into straightforwardly rational discussion. Freud himself has some interesting things to say about acute neurotics and psychotics. In discussing what Freud calls the "metapsychology of repression," he indicates the multiple forms that repression can take, the various transference neuroses. For example, in anxiety hysteria, there might be first a drawing back from the impulse and then a flight to a substitutive idea, a displacement. But then the person might feel the need to "inhibit... the development of the anxiety which arises from the substitute." Freud then notes that "with each increase of instinctual excitation the protecting rampart round the substitutive idea must be shifted a little further outwards."[27] At this point, the phobia becomes still more complicated, leading to ever further attempts at flight.[28]

What is being described here is an interesting social process. Something has caused anxiety. The individual seeks to avoid the negative feelings and consequences by means of a repressive device. This does relieve the anxiety, but at a price. Freud suggests that the price is too heavy (or is it that it may be too heavy?). What the psychoanalyst is presumably trying to do is to help the individual confront what is causing the anxiety, and thereupon to be able to relieve the pain at a lower price. So the individual is trying rationally to reduce pain. And the psychoanalyst is trying rationally to lead the patient to perceive that there may be a better way (a more rational way?) to reduce pain.

Is the analyst right? Is this new way a more rational way to reduce pain? Freud ends this discussion of the unconscious by turning to still more difficult situations. Freud exhorts us to see "how much more radically and profoundly this attempt at flight, this flight of the ego, is put in operation in the narcissistic neuroses."[29] But even here, in what Freud regards as an acute pathology, he still perceives it as the same quest, the same rational quest for the reduction of pain.

Freud is very conscious of the limits of the role of the analyst. In *The Ego and the Id*, he warns quite clearly against the temptation to play "prophet, saviour and redeemer."[30] Freud manifests a similar sense of restraint in *Civilization and Its Discontents*. He is discussing the impossibility of fulfilling our necessary task of trying to be happy. He says: "There is no golden rule which applies to everyone: every man must find out for himself in what particular fashion he can be saved." He adds that choices pushed to an extreme lead to dangers and flights into neurosis, concluding that "the man who sees his pursuit of happiness come to nothing in later years can still find consolation in the yield of pleasure of chronic intoxication; or he can embark on the desperate attempt at rebellion seen in a psychosis."[31]

I am struck by several things in these passages of Freud. The pathologies he observes in the patient are described as flights from danger. I underline once again how rational it is to flee from danger. Indeed, even the most seemingly irrational flight of all, that into psychosis, is described as "a desperate attempt at rebellion," as though the person had little alternative. In desperation, he tried psychosis. And finally, there is only so much the analyst can do, not only because he is not, may not be, a prophet, but because "every man must find out for himself in what particular fashion he can be saved."

We are not in a congress of psychoanalysts. I have not raised these issues to discuss either the functioning of the psyche or the modalities of psychiatric treatment. I have intruded these passages from Freud because of the light they throw on our underlying presupposition of rationality. Something may be described as rational only if there are other things that may be described as irrational. Freud wandered into the arena of what was socially accepted as irrational, neurotic behavior. His approach was to uncover the underlying rationality of this seemingly irrational behavior. He continued into the even more irrational, the psychotic, and found there too an explanation we might call rational, once again the flight from danger. Of course, psychoanalysis is based on the assumption that there are better and less good modes of dealing with danger. The different responses of the individual exact different prices, to use Freud's economic metaphor.

Pushing, however, the logic of the search for the rational explanation of the seemingly irrational, Freud led us down a path whose logical conclusion is that nothing is irrational from the point of view of the actor. And who is any outsider to say that he or she is right and the patient is wrong? Freud is wary about how far analysts should go in imposing their priorities on a patient. "Every man must find out for himself in what particular fashion he can be saved." But if nothing is irrational, as seen from someone's point of view, whence the hosannas for modernity, for civilization, for rationality? This is such a profound challenge that I would argue we have not even begun to confront it. The only consistent conclusion we can draw is that there is no such thing as formal rationality, or rather that, in order to decide what is formally rational, one must necessarily spell out in the ultimate detail of complexity and specificity the end that is intended, in which case, everything depends on the point of view and the balance of concerns of the actor. In this sense, postmodernism in its most radical solipsistic versions takes this Freudian premise to its final destination, and without giving Freud the least bit of credit for this in the process, be it noted, probably because the postmodernists are unaware of the cultural origin of their assertions. But, of course, such postmodernists are not taking the Freudian challenge as a challenge, but as an eternal universal truth, the grandest of grand narratives, and with this kind of self-contradiction this extreme position self-destructs.

In the face of Freud's challenge, some have thrown up their hands with glee and have become solipsistic, and others have fallen back on repeating the mantra of rationality. We can afford to do neither. Freud's challenge to the very operationality of the concept of formal rationality forces us to take more seriously the Weberian pendant concept of substantive rationality, and to analyze it in greater depth than Weber was ready to do himself. What Freud has challenged, what in fact he has perhaps demolished, is the usefulness of the concept of *formal* rationality. Can there be such a thing as abstract formal rationality? Formal rationality is always someone's formal rationality. How then can there be a universal formal rationality? Formal rationality is usually presented as the utilization of the most effective means to an end. But ends are not so easy to define. They invite a Geertzian "thick description." And once given that, Freud is hinting, everyone is formally rational. *Substantive* rationality is precisely the attempt to come to terms with this irreducible subjectivity and to suggest that nonetheless we can make intelligent, meaningful choices, social choices. I shall return to this theme.

The second challenge with which I wish to deal is the challenge to Eurocentrism. This is very widespread today. It was seldom mentioned thirty years ago. One of the first persons to raise this issue publicly and among us was Anouar Abdel-Malek, whose denunciation of "Orientalism" (1963) predates that of Edward Said by more than a decade, and who has devoted his life work to suggesting what he has called an "alternative civilizational project."[32] I would like to discuss what he has argued, particularly in *Social Dialectics* (1981). I choose to discuss his work because Abdel-Malek goes beyond a mere denunciation of the misdeeds of the West to an exploration of alternatives. Abdel-Malek starts with the assumption that in the transformed geopolitical reality, "[p]repostulated universalism, as a recipe, simply would not do."[33] In order to arrive at what Abdel-Malek perceives of as "meaningful social theory" (43), he suggests we employ a nonreductionist comparativism, comparing what he sees as a world consisting of three interwoven circles — civilizations, cultural areas, and nations (or "national formations"). For him, there are only two "civilizations," the Indo-Aryan and the Chinese. Each contains multiple cultural areas. The Indo-Aryan contains Egyptian antiquity, Greco-Roman antiquity, Europe, North America, sub-Saharan Africa, the Arab-Islamic and Perso-Islamic zones, and major parts of Latin America. The Chinese includes China proper, Japan, Central Asia, Southeast Asia, the Indian subcontinent, Oceania, and the Asian-Islamic zone.

If the key factor for Abdel-Malek is "civilization," the key concept is "specificity," and this requires, in his words, adding a "geographical thread" to the historical (97). But having said that, he then adds that the central problem in general theory and epistemology is "to deepen and define the relations between the concept of time and the constellation of notions concerned particularly with the density of time in the domain of human societies" (156). Although one can compare civilizations in terms of production, reproduction, and social power, the crucial difference is relations with the time-dimension, wherein we find the greatest "density of manifest, explicit specificity. For here we are at the very heart of culture and thought." He speaks of "the all-pervading central constitutive influence of the time-dimension, the depth of the historical field" (171–72).

The geographical challenge thus turns out to be an alternative concept of time. Remember that, for Abdel-Malek, there are only two "civilizations" in the sense he is using it, and therefore only two relations to the time-dimension. On the one side is the Western vision of time, an "operational view," which he traces to Aristotle, "the rise of formal logic, the hegemony of analytical thinking," time as "a tool for action, not as a conception of man's place in historical duration" (179). And "on the other side of the river," we find a nonanalytic concept, where "time is master" and therefore cannot be "apprehended as commodity."[34] He concludes with a call for a "non-antagonistic yet contradictory dialectical interaction between the two banks of our common river" (185).[35] Where does this leave us? It leaves us with two banks of a common river — not at all the vision of Durkheim, Marx, and Weber. It leaves us with irreducible specificities about which we can nonetheless theorize. It leaves us with a civilizational challenge about the nature of time, an issue that was not even an issue for the classical culture of sociology. And this brings us directly to the third challenge.

The third challenge is also about time, not about two visions of time, but about multiple realities of time, about the social construction of time. Time may be the master, but if so, for Fernand Braudel, it is both a master we have constructed ourselves and yet one that it is difficult to resist. Braudel argues there are in fact *four* kinds of social time, but that, in the nineteenth century and most of the twentieth, the overwhelming majority of social scientists perceived only *two* of them. On the one hand, there were those who considered that time was essentially composed of a sequence of events, what Paul Lacombe had called *histoire événementielle*, a term best translated into English as "episodic history." In this view, time was the equivalent of a Euclidean line, which had an infinite number of points on it. These points were the "events," and they were located in a diachronic sequence. This is of course consonant with the ancient view that all is constantly changing at every moment, that explanation is sequential, and that experience is unrepeatable. It is at the basis of what we call idiographic historiography, but it is also the basis of atheoretical empiricism, both of which have been widespread in modern social science.

The alternative widespread view of time is that social processes are timeless, in the sense that what explains events are rules or theorems that apply across all of time and space, even if at the present moment we cannot explicate all these rules. In the nineteenth century, this view was sometimes referred to as "social physics," in an allusion to Newtonian mechanics, which provided the model of this kind of analysis. Braudel referred to this concept of time as *la très longue durée* (not to be confused with *la longue durée*). We might call this eternal time. Braudel discussed Claude Lévi-Strauss as his prime example of this approach, but of course the concept has been widely used by others. Indeed, one might say that it constitutes the prevalent usage within the culture of sociology and is what we usually mean when we speak of "positivism." Braudel himself says of this variety of social time: "if it exists, [it] can only be the time period of the sages."[36]

Braudel's basic objection to these two concepts of time is that neither of them takes time seriously. Braudel thinks that eternal time is a myth and that episodic time, the time of the event, is, in his famous phrase, "dust." He suggests that social reality in fact occurs primarily in two other kinds of time that have been largely ignored by both idiographic historians and nomothetic social scientists. He calls these times that of the *longue durée,* or structural time, long but not eternal, and that of the *conjoncture,* or cyclical, middle-range time, the time of cycles *within* structures. Both these times are constructs of the analyst, but they are also simultaneously social realities that constrain the actors. Perhaps you feel that Durkheim, Marx, and Weber were not entirely resistant to such Braudelian constructs. And to some extent, that is true. They were all three sophisticated and subtle thinkers and said much that we ignore today at our peril. But as the three were incorporated into what I am calling the culture of sociology, there was no room for socially constructed time, and hence Braudel represents a fundamental challenge to that culture. As the challenge to Eurocentrism forces us into a more complex geography, so the protest against ignoring social time forces us into a far longer time-perspective than we have been accustomed to use — but always one, I remind you, that is far less than infinite. No doubt the emergence in the 1970s of what we now call historical sociology was a response, at least in part, to the Braudelian challenge, but it has been absorbed as a specialty within sociology, and the implicit Braudelian demand for greater epistemological reconfiguration has been resisted.

The fourth challenge has come from outside social science. It has come from the emergence of a knowledge movement in the natural sciences and mathematics that today is known as complexity studies. There are a number of important figures in this movement. I shall concentrate on the one who has in my view stated the challenge most radically, Ilya Prigogine. Sir John Maddox, the former editor of *Nature,* took note of Prigogine's singular importance and asserted that the research community owes him a great debt "for his almost single-minded persistence over four decades with the problems of non-equilibrium and complexity."[37] Prigogine is of course a Nobel Prize laureate in chemistry, awarded for his work on so-called dissipative structures. But the two key concepts that resume his perspective are "the arrow of time" and "the end of certainties."[38]

Both concepts seek to refute the most fundamental assumptions of Newtonian mechanics, assumptions that Prigogine thinks survived even the revisions required by quantum mechanics and relativity.[39] The non-Newtonian concepts of entropy and probabilities are to be sure not recent ones. They were at the basis of chemistry, as it developed in the nineteenth century, and indeed in a sense justified the distinction between physics and chemistry. But, from the point of view of the physicists, the resort to such concepts indicated the intellectual inferiority of chemistry. Chemistry was incomplete, precisely because it was insufficiently deterministic. Not only does Prigogine refuse to accept the lesser merit of such concepts, but he goes much further. He wishes to argue that physics itself must be based on them. He is intent on spearing the dragon in its inner rampart, asserting that irreversibility, far from being noxious, is a "source of order" and "plays a fundamental constructive role in nature" (26–27).[40] Prigogine makes it quite clear that he does not wish to deny the validity of Newtonian physics. It deals with integrable systems and holds within its "domain of validity" (29). However, this domain is limited, since "[i]ntegrable systems are the exception" (108).[41] Most systems "involve both deterministic processes (between bifurcations) and probabilistic processes (in the choice of the branches)" (69), and the two processes together create a historical dimension recording the successive choices.

Just as we are not in a congress of psychoanalysts, so we are not in a congress of physicists. If I raise this challenge here among us, it is largely because we have been so accustomed to assuming that Newtonian mechanics represented an epistemological model that we ought to emulate that it is important to recognize that this epistemological model is under severe challenge within the very culture in which it originated. But, even more important, it is because this reformulation of dynamics inverts completely the relation of social science to natural science. Prigogine reminds us of Freud's assertion that humanity has known three successive hurts to its pride: when Copernicus showed that the earth was not the center of the planetary system; when Darwin showed that humans were a species of animal; and when he, Freud, showed that our conscious activity is controlled by our unconscious. To this Prigogine adds: "We can now invert this perspective: We see that human creativity and innovation can be understood as the amplification of laws of nature already present in physics and chemistry" (71). Notice what he has done here. Prigogine has reunited social science and natural science, not on the nineteenth-century assumption that human activity can be seen as simply a variant of other physical activity, but on the inverted basis that physical activity can be seen as a process of creativity and innovation. This is surely a challenge to our culture, as it has been practiced. Furthermore, Prigogine also speaks to the issue of rationality that we have raised. He calls for a "return to realism" that is not a "return to determinism" (131).[42] The rationality that is realistic is precisely the rationality that Weber was calling "substantive," that is, the rationality that is the result of realistic choice.[43]

The fifth challenge that I wish to discuss is that of feminism. Feminists say to the world of knowledge that it has been biased in multiple ways. It has ignored women as subjects of human destiny. It has excluded women as students of social realities. It has utilized a priori assumptions about gender differences that are not based on realistic research. It has ignored the standpoint of women.[44] All of these charges seem to me to be just in terms of the historical record. And the feminist movement, within sociology and within the larger domain of the world of social knowledge, has had some impact in recent decades in rectifying these biases, although of course there is still a long way to go before these issues become nonissues.[45] However, in all this aspect of the work of feminists, they have not been challenging the culture of sociology. Rather they have been utilizing it and simply saying that most sociologists (and more broadly, social scientists) have not been respecting the very rules they established for the practice of social science.

This is no doubt a very important thing to have done. Yet I think there is something even more important, wherein feminists have very definitely been challenging the culture of sociology. This has been the assertion that there been a masculinist bias not only in the domain of social knowledge (where, so to speak, it might have been theoretically expectable), but also in the domain of knowledge of the natural world (where in theory it should not have existed). In this assertion, they have attacked the legitimacy of the claim to objectivity in its *sanctum sanctorum*, a claim that is central to the classical culture of sociology. Just as Prigogine was not satisfied to be permitted to have chemistry as an exception to the determinism of physics, but has insisted that physics itself is not and cannot be deterministic, so feminists are not satisfied with having social knowledge defined as a domain in which social biases are expectable (if undesirable); they are insisting that this applies equally to the knowledge of natural phenomena. I shall deal with this issue by discussing a few feminist scholars whose background (that is, whose initial training) was in the natural sciences and who therefore lay claim to be able to speak to this issue with the necessary technical knowledge of, training in, and sympathy for natural science.

The three I have chosen are Evelyn Fox Keller, trained as a mathematical biophysicist; Donna J. Haraway, trained as a hominid biologist;

and Vandana Shiva, trained as a theoretical physicist. Keller relates her realization in the mid-1970s that what had previously seemed to her a patently absurd question suddenly took precedence in her intellectual hierarchy: "How much of the nature of science is bound up with the idea of masculinity, and what would it mean for science if it were otherwise?" She then indicates how she will answer this query: "My subject . . . [is] how the making of men and women has affected the making of science." Thus far, we are no further than the sociology of knowledge or the sociology of science. And Keller says quite correctly that posing the question merely in this way will result in a "marginal" impact at most on the culture of natural science. What needs to be shown is that gender affects the "production of scientific theory."[46]

Can this be done? Keller looks to the intervening variable of the psyches of the scientists. She speaks of "the intrapersonal dynamics of 'theory choice.' "[47] Keller has no difficulty showing how the founders of Baconian science suffused their work with masculinist metaphors, involving a virile mastery and domination of nature, and that the claim of scientists to be different from natural philosophers on the basis that only scientists eschewed the projection of subjectivity simply does not stand the test of analysis.[48] Keller thus observes "androcentrism" in science but refuses to draw the conclusion either of rejecting science per se or of calling for the creation of a so-called radically different science. Rather, she says:

> My view of science — and the possibilities of at least a partial sorting of cognitive from ideological — is more optimistic. And, accordingly, the aim of these essays is more exacting: it is the reclamation, from within science, of science as a human instead of a masculinist project, and the renunciation of the division between emotional and intellectual labor that maintains science as a male preserve.[49]

Donna Haraway starts from her concerns as a hominid biologist and attacks the two somewhat different attempts of R. M. Yerkes and E. O. Wilson to transform biology "from a science of sexual organisms to one of reproducing genetic assemblages."[50] The object of both theories, she argues, is human engineering, in two successively different forms, the differences merely reflecting changes in the larger social world. She asks about both theories: Human engineering in the interests of whom? She calls her work one "about the invention and reinvention of nature — perhaps the most central arena of hope, oppression, and contestation for inhabitants of the planet earth in our times" (1). She insists she is speaking not about nature as it is, but about the stories we are told about nature and experience, in whose telling biologists play a key role.

I will not try to reproduce her arguments here, but simply draw attention to the conclusions she wishes to draw from this critique. Like Keller, she refuses to draw from her critique of "biological determinism" an exclusively "social constructionist" view (see 134–35). Rather she sees the social development of the twentieth century as one in which we have all become "chimeras, theorized and fabricated hybrids of machine and organism," to which she gives the name of cyborgs. She says that hers is "an argument for *pleasure* in the confusion of boundaries and for *responsibility* in their construction" (150). The boundary breakdowns she sees are those of human and animal, or human plus animal (or organism) and machine; of the physical and nonphysical.

She warns against "universal, totalizing theory," which she calls "a major mistake that misses most of reality," but she also claims that "taking responsibility for the social relations of science and technology means refusing an anti-science metaphysics, a demonology of technology" (181).[51] The theme of responsibility is central to this challenge. She rejects relativism not in the name of "totalizing visions" but in the name of "partial, locatable, critical knowledges sustaining the possibility of webs of connections called solidarity in politics and shared conversations in epistemology" (191).[52]

Vandana Shiva's critique is focused less on scientific methods proper than on the political implications that are drawn from science's position in the cultural hierarchy. She speaks as a woman of the South, and thus her critique rejoins that of Abdel-Malek.[53]

She opposes to the idea of "man's empire over nature" the concept of the "democracy of all life," which she says is the basis of "most non-Western cultures."[54] Shiva sees the preservation of biodiversity and the preservation of human cultural diversity as intimately linked and is therefore particularly concerned about the consequences of the contemporary biotechnological revolution.[55]

I am struck by two constants in the challenge as formulated by Keller, Haraway, and Shiva. One is that the critique of natural science as it has been practiced is never translated into a rejection of science as a knowledge activity, but rather into a scientific analysis of scientific knowledge and practice. And, second, that the critique of natural science as it has been practiced leads to a call for responsible social judgment. Perhaps you feel that the case for gender bias in natural science is not proven. Here, I think Sandra Harding makes the appropriate response: "Improbable as [attempts to show how Newton's and Einstein's laws of nature might participate in gender symbolization] may sound, there is no reason to think them in principle incapable of success."[56] The key phrase is "in principle." It is on this note of appeal to the most basic practice of science, submitting all claims to empirical verification, that the challenge of feminism to science stands. By its doubts about any a priori assumption that gender is irrelevant to scientific practice, feminism poses a fundamental challenge to the culture of sociology. Whether it poses an equal challenge to the culture of natural science, one it will take into account, remains to be seen.[57]

The sixth and last challenge with which I shall deal is perhaps the most surprising of all, and the one least discussed. It is that modernity, the centerpiece of all our work, has never really existed. This thesis has been put forth with most clarity by Bruno Latour, the title of whose book is the message: "We have never been modern." Latour starts his book with the same argument as that of Haraway, that impure mixtures are constitutive of reality. He speaks of the proliferation of "hybrids," what she calls "cyborgs." For both, hybrids are a central phenomenon, increasing over time, underanalyzed, and not at all terrifying. What is crucial for Latour is overcoming the scholarly and social segmentation of reality into the three categories of nature, politics, and discourse. For him the networks of reality are "simultaneously real, like nature, narrated, like discourse, and collective, like society."[58]

Latour is often misread as a variety of postmodernist. It is hard to see how an attentive reader could in fact make this error. For he attacks with equal vigor those he calls antimodern, those he calls modern, and those he calls postmodern. For him, all three groups assume that the world in which we have been living for the last several centuries and in which we are still living has been "modern" in the definition that all three groups in common give to modernity: "an acceleration, a rupture, a revolution in time [in contrast to] an archaic and stable past" (10).

Latour argues that the word "modern" hides two sets of quite different practices: on the one hand, the constant creation by "translation" of new hybrids of nature and culture; and, on the other, a process of "purification," separating two ontological zones, humans and nonhumans. The two processes, he argues, are not separate and cannot be analyzed separately, because paradoxically it is precisely by forbidding hybrids (purification) that it becomes possible to create hybrids, and conversely it is by conceiving of hybrids that we limit their proliferation.[59] To sort out the so-called modern world, Latour recommends an "anthropology," by which he means "tackling everything at once."[60]

Latour conceives of the world in which we live as based on what he call a Constitution, which renders the moderns "invincible" by proclaiming that nature is transcendent and beyond human construction, but that society is not transcendent and therefore humans are totally free.[61] Latour believes that, if anything, the opposite is true.[62] The whole concept of modernity is a mistake:

> No one has ever been modern. Modernity has never begun. There has never been a modern world. The use of the present perfect tense[63] is important here, for it is a matter of a retrospective sentiment, of a rereading of our history. I am not saying we are entering a new era; on the contrary we no longer have to continue the headlong flight of the post-post-postmodernists; we are no longer obliged to cling to the avant-garde of the avant-garde; we no longer seek to be even cleverer, even more critical, even deeper into the "era of suspicion." No, instead we discover that we have never begun to enter the modern era. Hence the hint of the ludicrous that always accompanies postmodern thinkers; they claim to come after a time that has not even started! (47)

There is something new, however; it is that we have reached a point of saturation.[64] And this brings Latour to the question of time, which as you may see by now is at the center of most of the challenges:

> If I explain that revolutions attempt to abolish the past but cannot do so, I again run the risk of being taken for a reactionary. This is because for the moderns — as for their antimodern enemies, as well as for their false postmodern enemies — time's arrow is unambiguous; one can go forward, but then one has to break with the past; one can choose to go backward, but then one has to break with modernizing avant-gardes, which have broken radically with their own past. . . . If there is one thing we are incapable of carrying out, we now know, it is a revolution, whether it be in science, technology, politics or philosophy. But we are still modern when we interpret this fact as a disappointment. (69)

We have all, says Latour, never ceased to be "amoderns" (90). There are no "cultures," just as there are no "natures"; there are only "natures-cultures" (103–4). "Nature and Society are not two distinct poles, but one and the same production of successive states of societies-natures, of collectives" (139). It is by recognizing this and making it the center of our analyses of the world that we can go forward.

We are at the end of our recital of the challenges. I remind you that for me the challenges are not truths but mandates for reflection about basic premises. Do you have some doubts about each of the challenges? Most probably. So do I. But together, they constitute a formidable attack on the culture of sociology and cannot leave us indifferent. Can there be such a thing as formal rationality? Is there a civilizational challenge to the Western/modern view of the world that we must take seriously? Does the reality of multiple social times require us to restructure our theorizing and our methodologies? In what ways do complexity studies and the end of certainties force us to reinvent the scientific method? Can we show that gender is a structuring variable that intrudes everywhere, even into zones that seem incredibly remote, such as mathematical conceptualization? And is modernity a deception — not an illusion, but a deception — that has deceived first of all social scientists?

Can the three axioms, derived as I have suggested from Durkheim/ Marx/Weber, the axioms that constitute what I have called the culture of sociology, deal adequately with these questions, and if not, does the culture of sociology thereby collapse? And if it does, with what can we replace it?

The Perspectives

I should like to deal with the promise of social science in terms of three prospects that seem to me both possible and desirable for the twenty-first century: the epistemological reunification of the so-called two cultures, that of science and the humanities; the organizational reunification and redivision of the social sciences; and the assumption by social science of centrality in the world of knowledge.

What conclusions can we draw from my analysis of the culture of sociology and the challenges it has been facing? First, quite simply, the ultraspecialization that sociology, and indeed all the other social sciences, has been suffering has been both inevitable and self-destructive.[65] We must nonetheless continue to struggle against it, in the hope of creating some reasonable balance between depth and breadth of knowledge, between the microscopic and the synthetic vision. Second, as Neil

Smelser has put it so well recently, there are no "sociologically naive actors."[66] But do we have sociologically well-informed actors? That is, are our actors rational? And what world do our actors know?

It seems to me that the social facts with which we deal are social in two senses: they are shared perceptions of reality, shared more or less by some medium-large group but with different shadings for every individual viewer. And they are socially constructed perceptions. But let us be clear. It is not the analyst whose social construction of the world is of interest. It is that of the collectivity of actors who have created social reality by their cumulated actions. The world is as it is because of all that has preceded this moment. What the analyst is trying to discern is how the collectivity has constructed the world, using of course his own socially constructed vision.

The arrow of time is thus ineluctable, but also unpredictable, since there are always bifurcations before us, the outcome of which is inherently indeterminate. Furthermore, although there is but one arrow of time, there are multiple times. We cannot afford to neglect either the structural *longue durée* or the cyclical rhythms of the historical system we are analyzing. Time is far more than chronometry and chronology. Time is also duration, cycles, and disjunction.

On the one hand, a real world does exist, indubitably. If *it* doesn't exist, *we* don't exist, and that is absurd. If we don't believe this, we should not be in the business of studying the social world. Solipsists cannot talk even to themselves, since we are all changing at each instant, and therefore, if one adopts the standpoint of a solipsist, our own views of yesterday are as irrelevant to our created visions of today as are the views of others. Solipsism is the greatest of all forms of hubris, greater even than objectivism. It is the belief that our ratiocinations create what we perceive and that we thereby perceive what exists, that which we have created.

But, on the other hand, it is also true that we can only know the world through our vision of it, a collective social vision no doubt, but a human vision nonetheless. This is obviously as true of our vision of the physical world as it is of our vision of the social world. In that sense, we all depend on the glasses with which we engage in this perception, the organizing myths (yes, the grand narratives) that William McNeill calls "mythistory,"[67] without which we are helpless to say anything. It follows from these constraints that there are no concepts that are not plural; that all universals are partial; and that there exists a plurality of universals. And it also follows that all verbs that we use must be written in the past tense. The present is over before we can pronounce it, and all statements need to be located in their historical context. The nomothetic temptation is every bit as dangerous as the idiographic temptation and constitutes a pitfall into which the culture of sociology has more frequently led too many of us.

Yes, we are at the end of certainties. But what does this mean in practice? In the history of thought, we have been constantly offered certainty. The theologians offered us certainties as seen by prophets, priests, and canonized texts. The philosophers offered us certainties as rationally deduced or induced or intuited by them. And the modern scientists offered us certainties as verified empirically by them using criteria they invented. All of them have claimed that their truths were validated visibly in the real world, but that these visible proofs were merely the outward and limited expression of deeper, more hidden truths for whose secrets and discovery they were the indicated intermediaries.

Each set of certainties has prevailed for some times in some places, but none of them everywhere or eternally. Enter the skeptics and nihilists who pointed to this wide array of contradictory truths and derived from the doubts this sowed the proposition that no claimed truth is more valid than any other. But if the universe is in fact intrinsically uncertain, it does not follow that the theological, the philosophical, and the scientific enterprises have no merit, and it surely does not follow that any of them represents merely a gigantic deception. What does follow is that we would be wise to formulate our quests in the light of permanent uncertainty and look upon this uncertainty not as unfortunate and temporary blindness nor as an insurmountable obstacle to knowledge but rather as an incredible opportunity to imagine, to create, to search.[68] Pluralism becomes at this point not an indulgence of the weak and ignorant but a cornucopia of possibilities for a better universe.[69]

In 1998, a group composed largely of physical scientists published a book they entitled *Dictionnaire de l'ignorance* (Dictionary of ignorance), arguing that science plays a bigger role in creating zones of ignorance than in creating zones of knowledge. I cite the blurb they placed on the back of the book:

> In the process of science enlarging our field of knowledge, we become aware, paradoxically, that our ignorance grows as well. Each new problem we resolve tends to cause the appearance of new enigmas, such that

the processes of research and discoveries renew themselves constantly. The frontiers of knowledge seem to widen ceaselessly, giving birth to previously unsuspected questions. But these new problems are salutary. Creating new challenges to science, they oblige it to advance in a perpetual movement without which, perhaps, its light would be quickly extinguished.[70]

One of the problems about the creation of new ignorances is that there is no plausible reason to presume that they can be best treated only in or by the narrow domain within which these ignorances were uncovered. The physicist may expose new ignorances that require for their resolution concerns previously designated as biological or philosophical. And this is, as we know, certainly true of the new ignorances sociologists uncover. The protection of one's turf in the face of new ignorances is the worst of scholarly sins, and the greatest possible deterrence to clarity.

It is this issue of turf that underlies the organizational problems of the social sciences. The institutionalization of the nominal divisions of the social sciences is extremely strong today, despite all the genuflection before the rosy glow of "interdisciplinarity." Indeed, I would argue that interdisciplinarity is itself a lure, representing the greatest support possible to the current list of disciplines, by implying that each has some special knowledge that it might be useful to combine with some other special knowledges in order to solve some practical problem.

The fact is that the three great cleavages of nineteenth-century social science: past/present, civilized/others, and state/market/civil society are all three totally indefensible as intellectual markers today. There are no sensible statements one can make in the so-called fields of sociology, economics, or political science that are not historical, and there are no sensible historical analyses one can undertake that do not make use of the so-called generalizations that are in use in the other social sciences. Why then continue to pretend that we are engaged in different tasks?

As for civilized/other, the civilized are not civilized and the other are not other. There are of course specificities, but they are legion, and the racist simplifications of the modern world are not only noxious but intellectually disabling. We must learn how to deal with the universal and the particular as a symbiotic pair that will never go away, and that must inform all of our analyses.

And finally the distinction of state/market/civil society is quite simply an implausible one, as any real actor in the real world knows. The market is constructed and constrained by the state and the civil society. The state is a reflection of both the market and the civil society. And the civil society is defined by the state and the market. One cannot separate these three modes of expression of actors' interests, preferences, identities, and wills into closeted arenas about which different groups of people will make scientific statements, *ceteris paribus*.

I continue, however, to share the Durkheimian premise that psychology and social science are two separate enterprises, and that psychology is closer to, perhaps an intrinsic part, of biology. I note that most psychologists, from the behaviorists to the Freudians, seem to share this view. The group most resistant to this separation is in fact to be found within sociology.

If then none of our existing modes of dividing the social sciences today into separate organizations of knowledge makes sense, what shall we do? On the one hand, those who have studied what is called the sociology of organizations have shown us time and again how resistant organizations are to imposed change, how fiercely and cleverly their leaders act to defend interests that they will not avow but seem very real to those in power. It is difficult to force the pace of transformation. It is perhaps Quixotic even to try. On the other hand, there are processes internal to each of our organizations that are destroying the boundaries without the intrusion of any deliberate reform process. Individual scholars are seeking peers with which to create the small groups and networks they find necessary to do their work. And increasingly such networks are paying no attention whatsoever to disciplinary labels.

Furthermore, as specialization proliferates, those who hold the budgetary purse strings are growing increasingly restive about the seeming irrationality of the overlaps, especially given the worldwide pressures to reduce rather than increase expenditures on higher education. It is the accountants who may force our pace, and quite possibly in ways that are not intellectually optimal. Thus, it seems to me, it is urgent that the scholars engage in organizational exploration, allowing for wide experimentation and being quite tolerant of each other's efforts, in order to see what kinds of organizational realignments might work best. Perhaps micro-macro should be institutionalized as a mode of organizing groups of scholars. I am not sure. Up to a point, it is in use in the natural sciences already, and in practice (if not in theory), social scientists are using it too. Or perhaps we should be dividing ourselves according to the temporalities of change with which we are dealing — short-term, middle-term, long-term. On none of these dividing lines do I have a fixed view at this point. I feel we should try them out.

What I am very clear about is that we must open ourselves up collectively and recognize our blinkers. We must read far more widely than we now do, and we must strongly encourage our students to do so. We should recruit our graduate students far more widely than we do, and we must let them play a major role in determining where we can help them grow. And it is crucial for us to learn languages. A scholar who cannot *read* three to five major scholarly languages is severely handicapped. English is surely crucial, but English alone means that one has access to at most 50 percent of what is written, and as the decades go by, the percentage will diminish because the areas of greatest growth in the production of scholars will be increasingly non-English in their written production. Increased reading knowledge of languages goes hand in hand with increased internationalization of our corps of scholars, even if they are not identical.

I do not know what kind of restructuring will take place, but I am skeptical that there will ever be a one hundredth anniversary of any of the existing international social science associations, at least under the same name.

I have saved for the last what I think is the most fascinating perspective of all, and perhaps the most important. Ever since the so-called divorce between philosophy and science consummated in the late eighteenth century, the social sciences have been the poor relation — neither fish nor fowl, and scorned by both sides in this war of the "two cultures." And the social scientists have internalized this image, feeling they had no fate other than to align themselves either with the scientists or with the humanists. Today the situation has radically changed. In the physical sciences, there is a strong and growing knowledge movement, complexity studies, that talks of the arrow of time, of uncertainties, and believes that human social systems are the most complex of all systems. And in the humanities, there is a strong and growing knowledge movement, cultural studies, that believes that there are no essential aesthetic canons and that cultural products are rooted in their social origins, their social receptions, and their social distortions.

It seems to me clear that complexity studies and cultural studies have moved the natural sciences and the humanities respectively onto the terrain of social science. What had been a centrifugal field of forces in the world of knowledge has become a centripetal one, and social science is now central to knowledge. We are in the process of trying to overcome the "two cultures," of trying to reunite into a single domain the search for the true, the good, and the beautiful. This is cause for rejoicing, but it will be a very difficult row to hoe.

Knowledge, in the face of uncertainties, involves choices — choices by all matter, and of course choices by social actors, among them the scholars. And choices involve decisions about what is substantively rational. We can no longer even pretend that scholars can be neutral, that is, divested of their social reality. But this in no way means that anything goes. It means that we have to weigh carefully all the factors, in all the domains, to try to arrive at optimal decisions. And that in turn means we have to talk to each other and to do so as equals. Yes, some of us have more specific knowledge about specific areas of concern than others, but no one, and no group, has all the knowledge necessary to make substantively rational decisions, even in relatively limited domains, without taking into account the knowledge of others outside these domains. Yes, no doubt, I would want the most competent brain surgeon, if I needed brain surgery. But competent brain surgery involves some judgments that are juridical, ethical, philosophical, psychological, and sociological as well. And an institution like a hospital needs to bring these wisdoms into a blended substantively rational view. Furthermore, the views of the patient are not irrelevant. It is the brain surgeon more than anyone else who needs to know this, as does the sociologist or the poet. Skills do not dissolve into some formless void, but skills are always partial and need to be integrated with other partial skills. In the modern world, we have been doing very little of this. And our education does not prepare us sufficiently for this. Once we realize that functional rationality does not exist, then and only then can we begin to achieve substantive rationality.

This is what I believe Ilya Prigogine and Isabelle Stengers mean when they speak of the "reenchantment of the world."[71] It is not to deny the very important task of "disenchantment," but to insist that we must put the pieces together again. We dismissed final causes too fast. Aristotle was not that foolish. Yes, we need to look at efficient causes, but we need also to look at final causes. The scientists generalized a tactic useful for disentangling themselves from theological and philosophical control systems into a methodological imperative, and this has been disabling.

Finally, the world of knowledge is an egalitarian world. This has been one of the great contributions of science. Anyone is authorized to challenge the veracity of existing statements of truth, provided that he or she furnishes some empirical evidence for the counterstatement and offers it to everyone for collective evaluation. But since the scientists refused to be social scientists, they neglected to observe, or even realize, that this virtuous insistence on egalitarianism in science was not possible, was not even credible, in an inegalitarian social world. To be sure, politics arouses fears in scholars, and they seek safety in insulation. Scholars are afraid of the powerful minority, the minority in power. They are afraid of the powerful majority, the majority who might come into power. It will not be easy to create a more egalitarian world. Nonetheless, to achieve the objective that natural science bequeathed the world requires a far more egalitarian social setting that we now have. The struggle for egalitarianism in science and in society are not two separate struggles. They are one and the same, which points once again to the impossibility of separating the search for the true, the good, and the beautiful.

Human arrogance has been humanity's greatest self-imposed limitation. This, it seems to me, is the message of the story of Adam in the Garden of Eden. We were arrogant in claiming to have received and understood the revelation of God, to know the intent of the gods. We were even more arrogant in asserting that we were capable at arriving at eternal truth through the use of human reason, so fallible a tool. And we have been continuously arrogant in seeking to impose on each other, and with such violence and cruelty, our subjective images of the perfect society.

In all these arrogances, we have betrayed first of all ourselves, and closed off our potentials, the possible virtues we might have had, the possible imaginations we might have fostered, the possible cognitions we might have achieved. We live in an uncertain cosmos, whose single greatest merit is the permanence of this uncertainty, because it is this uncertainty that makes possible creativity — cosmic creativity, and with that of course human creativity. We live in an imperfect world, one that will always be imperfect and therefore always harbor injustice. But we are far from helpless before this reality. We can make the world less unjust; we can make it more beautiful; we can increase our cognition of it. We need but to construct it, and in order to construct it we need but to reason with each other and struggle to obtain from each other the special knowledge that each of us has been able to seize. We can labor in the vineyards and bring forth fruit, if only we try.

My close collaborator, Terence K. Hopkins, wrote me a note in 1980, which I will take as our conclusion: "There's no place left to go but up, and up, and up, which translates into higher and higher and higher intellectual standards. Elegance. Precision. Short compass. Being right. Enduring. That's all."

Notes

Uncertainty and Creativity

1. These theses have been argued at some length in two recent books: Immanuel Wallerstein, *After Liberalism* (New York: New Press, 1995), and Terence K. Hopkins and Immanuel Wallerstein, coords., *The Age of Transition: Trajectory of the World-System, 1945–2025* (London: Zed Press, 1996).

2. Ilya Prigogine, *La fin des certitudes* (Paris: Odile Jacob, 1996); English trans.: *The End of Certainty* (New York: Free Press, 1997).

1. Social Science and the Communist Interlude

1. In Pasternak's original novel, Zhivago is greeted only by his family, who explain that they have "given away" two of the three floors of "living space" (the new term) to various Soviet institutions. But in this version, too, Zhivago expresses his sense that this is more just, that the rich have previously had too much of everything.

2. The ANC and South Africa

1. For an elaboration of these ideas, see Immanuel Wallerstein, "The French Revolution as a World-Historical Event," in *Unthinking Social Science* (Cambridge: Polity Press, 1991), 7–22.

2. The argument in the following paragraphs summarizes an extensive analysis in Terence K. Hopkins and Immanuel Wallerstein, coords., *The Age of Transition: Trajectory of the World-System, 1945–2025* (London: Zed Press, 1996).

3. See Fernand Braudel, *Capitalism and Civilization, 15th to 18th Century*, 3 vols. (New York: Harper and Row, 1981–84).

3. The Rise of East Asia

1. This is precisely the subject of Terence K. Hopkins and Immanuel Wallerstein, coords., *The Age of Transition: Trajectory of the World-System, 1945–2025* (London: Zed Press, 1996).

2. For an early, detailed analysis of these processes, see Folker Fröbel, "The Current Development of the World-Economy: Reproduction of Labor and Accumulation of Capital on a World Scale," *Review* 5, no. 4 (spring 1982): 507–55.

3. I resume here material that has been argued at length in Immanuel Wallerstein, *After Liberalism* (New York: New Press, 1995).

4. Of course, other regions of the world were also reacting at the same time. Ethiopia had defeated Italy in 1896. Mexico had its revolution in 1910. There were a succession of events/revolutions in the Ottoman Empire/Turkey, Persia, Afghanistan, and the Arab world in the beginning of the twentieth century. The Indian National Congress was founded in 1886, and the South African Native National Congress (to become later the ANC) in 1912. But the East Asian events had particularly wide resonance.

5. I previously argued this in more detail in "Japan and the Future Trajectory of the World-System: Lessons from History," in *Geopolitics and Geoculture: Essays on the Changing World-System* (Cambridge: Cambridge University Press, 1991), 36–48.

6. In particular, see chapters 8 and 9 of Hopkins and Wallerstein, *Age of Transition*.

Coda: The So-called Asian Crisis

1. This has been long discussed by economic historians and recently spelled out in great detail by Giovanni Arrighi in *The Long Twentieth Century* (London: Verso, 1994).

2. I have analyzed this whole process both in "Crisis as Transition," in Samir Amin et al., *Dynamics of Global Crisis* (New York: Monthly Review Press, 1982), 11–54, and in *Geopolitics and Geoculture: Essays in World-Economy* (Cambridge: Cambridge University Press, 1991), esp. part 1.

3. Henry Kissinger, "How U.S. Can End Up as the Good Guy," *Los Angeles Times,* February 8, 1998.

4. See Robert E. Ward and Dankwart A. Rustow, eds., *Political Modernization in Turkey and Japan* (Princeton, N.J.: Princeton University Press, 1964).

5. See the analysis in Terence K. Hopkins and Immanuel Wallerstein, coords., *The Age of Transition: Trajectory of the World-System, 1945–2025* (London: Zed Press, 1996).

4. States? Sovereignty?

1. R. H. Tawney, *Equality,* 4th ed. (London: George Allen and Unwin, 1952), 109.

2. Juan Carlos Lerda, "Globalization and the Loss of Autonomy by the Fiscal, Banking and Monetary Authorities," *CEPAL Review* 58 (April 1996): 76–77. The text goes on: "It is worth asking, for example, whether the international financial markets' growing intolerance — of arbitrary manipulation of the exchange rate, or of sustained high public deficits — really affects domestic authorities' autonomy (by tightening the restrictions on governments) or if it is not rather a force for good which will prevent greater evils in the future (such as the accumulation of large exchange rate slippages which give rise to financial traumas with considerable negative effects in the real sphere of the economy when devaluation inevitably occurs)."

3. Henry Kaufman, "After Drexel, Wall Street Is Headed for Darker Days," *International Herald Tribune,* February 24–25, 1990 (reprinted from *New York Times*).

4. See the detailed analysis of the crisis in the structures of the capitalist world-economy in Terence K. Hopkins and Immanuel Wallerstein, coords., *The Age of Transition: Trajectory of the World-System, 1945–2025* (London: Zed Press, 1996).

6. Liberalism and Democracy

1. I have outlined the ways in which entrepreneurs have always depended on the states in chapter 4, above. See also Fernand Braudel, *Civilisation matérielle, économie et capitalisme, XVᵉ–XVIIIᵉ siècles* (Paris: Armand Colin, 1979); Eng. trans.: *Capitalism and Civilization, 15th to 18th Century*, 3 vols. (New York: Harper and Row, 1981–84).

2. I have outlined how and why this has been done over the centuries in "The Bourgeois(ie) as Reality and Concept," in Etienne Balibar and Immanuel Wallerstein, *Race, Nation, Class: Ambiguous Identities* (London: Verso, 1991), 135–52.

3. I do this in "The French Revolution as a World-Historical Event," in *Unthinking Social Science* (Cambridge: Polity Press, 1991), 7–22, and also in part 2 of *After Liberalism* (New York: New Press, 1995).

4. See the theorization of *égaliberté* in Etienne Balibar, "Trois concepts de la politique: Émancipation, transformation, civilité," in *La crainte des masses* (Paris: Galilée, 1997), 17–53.

5. This is a theme that I have pursued in detail in *After Liberalism*, especially but not only in part 4. See also my "Marx, Marxism-Leninism, and Socialist Experiences in the Modern World-System," in *Geopolitics and Geoculture* (Cambridge: Cambridge University Press, 1991), 84–97, and chapter 1, above.

6. For the detailed arguments, see my chapters 7 and 8 in Terence K. Hopkins and Immanuel Wallerstein, coords., *The Age of Transition: Trajectory of the World-System, 1945–2025* (London: Zed Press, 1996).

7. Integration to What? Marginalization from What?

1. See Frederic Lane, *Profits and Power* (Albany: State University of New York Press, 1979).

2. I spell out the historical relationship of the states to the entrepreneurs in chapter 4, above.

3. The historical evolution of this program and its social underpinnings are analyzed in detail in my *After Liberalism* (New York: New Press, 1995), esp. part 2, "The Construction and Triumph of Liberal Ideology," 71–122.

4. See Georges Haupt, *Le congrès manqué: L'internationale à la veille de la première guerre mondiale* (Paris: François Maspéro, 1965).

5. A. Kriegel and J.-J. Becker, *1914: La guerre et le mouvement ouvrier français* (Paris: Armand Colin, 1964), 123.

6. But see Terence K. Hopkins and Immanuel Wallerstein, coords., *The Age of Transition: Trajectory of the World-System, 1945–2025* (London: Zed Press, 1996).

8. Social Change?

1. The argument that follows is an abbreviated summary of the explanation I offer in some detail in "The West, Capitalism, and the Modern World-System," *Review* 15, no. 4 (fall 1992): 561–619.

2. I have done this in the three volumes of *The Modern World-System* (vols. 1 and 2: New York: Academic Press, 1974, 1980; vol. 3: San Diego: Academic Press, 1989) as well as in many other writings.

3. I here summarize arguments to be found in *After Liberalism* (New York: New Press, 1995) and in Terence K. Hopkins and Immanuel Wallerstein, coords., *The Age of Transition: Trajectory of the World-System, 1945–2025* (London: Zed Press, 1996).

9. Social Science and Contemporary Society

1. See my "The West, Capitalism, and the Modern World-System," *Review* 15, no. 4 (fall 1992): 561–619.

2. Steven Shapin, *A Social History of Truth: Civility and Science in Seventeenth-Century England* (Chicago: University of Chicago Press, 1994).

3. See Richard Olson, *The Emergence of the Social Sciences, 1642–1792* (New York: Twayne Publishers, 1993).

4. Max Weber, *Economy and Society* (New York: Bedminster Press, 1968); subsequent references to this work in the text will be cited there and will give volume number and page number.

5. See my "The French Revolution as a World-Historical Event," in *Unthinking Social Science* (Cambridge: Polity Press, 1991), 7–22.

6. See two chapters in my *After Liberalism* (New York: New Press, 1995): "Liberalism and the Legitimation of Nation-States: An Historical Interpretation," 93–107 and "The Concept of National Development: Elegy and Requiem," 108–22.

7. Sigmund Freud, *Civilization and Its Discontents* (London: Hogarth Press, 1951); subsequent references to this work in the text will be cited there.

8. Giovanni Arrighi et al., "1989, Continuation of 1968," *Review* 15, no. 2 (spring 1992): 221–42.

9. See my "Peace, Stability, and Legitimacy: 1990–2025/2050," in *After Liberalism*, 25–45.

10. Differentiation and Reconstruction in the Social Sciences

1. These statements are all drawn from Ilya Prigogine, "La fin de la certitude," in *Représentation et complexité*, ed. E. R. Larreta (Rio de Janeiro: Educam/UNESCO/ISSC, 1997), 61–84; subsequent references to this work in the text will be cited there. Prigogine's paper was given at a colloquium convened by the Senior Board of the International Social Science Council, in conjunction with others, to discuss the implications of the work of Prigogine for the social sciences.

11. Eurocentrism and Its Avatars

1. E. J. Jones, *The European Miracle: Environment, Economics, and Geopolitics in the History of Europe and Asia* (Cambridge: Cambridge University Press, 1981).

2. Cited in Anouar Abdel-Malek, *La dialectique sociale* (Paris: Seuil, 1972), 89; Eng. trans.: *Social Dialectics* (London: Macmillan, 1981).

3. Heinrich Rickert, *The Limits of Concept Formation in the Physical Sciences* (Cambridge: Cambridge University Press, 1986 [1913]).

4. Abdel-Malek, *La dialectique sociale;* Edward Said, *Orientalism* (New York: Pantheon Books, 1978).

5. See Wilfred Cantwell Smith, "The Place of Oriental Studies in a University," *Diogenes* 16 (1956): 106–11.

6. Xiaomei Chen, "Occidentalism as Counterdiscourse: 'He Shang' in Post-Mao China," *Critical Inquiry* 18, no. 4 (summer 1992): 687.

7. See J. B. Bury, *The Idea of Progress* (London: Macmillan, 1920); and Robert A. Nisbet, *History of the Idea of Progress* (New York: Basic Books, 1980).

8. See various authors in Stephen K. Sanderson, ed., *Civilizations and World Systems: Studying World-Historical Change* (Walnut Creek, Calif.: Altamira, 1995).

9. See my "The West, Capitalism, and the Modern World-System," *Review* 15, no. 4 (fall 1992): 561–619.

10. Adam Smith, *Inquiry into the Nature and Causes of the Wealth of Nations* (New York: Modern Library, 1937 [1776]), 13.

11. Per contra, see Samir Amin, "The Ancient World-Systems versus the Modern Capitalist World-System," *Review* 14, no. 3 (summer 1991): 349–85.

12. See Immanuel Wallerstein, *After Liberalism* (New York: New Press, 1995); Terence K. Hopkins and Immanuel Wallerstein, coords., *The Age of Transition: Trajectory of the World-System, 1945–2025* (London: Zed Press, 1996).

13. See my "Capitalist Civilization," *Chinese University Bulletin* 23 (1992), reprinted in *Historical Capitalism, with Capitalist Civilization* (London: Verso, 1995).

14. See Joseph Needham, *Science and Civilisation in China* (Cambridge: Cambridge University Press, 1954–), multiple volumes in progress.

12. The Structures of Knowledge

1. Immanuel Wallerstein et al., *Open the Social Sciences: Report of the Gulbenkian Commission on the Restructuring of the Social Sciences* (Stanford, Calif.: Stanford University Press, 1996).

2. Ilya Prigogine, *La fin des certitudes* (Paris: Odile Jacob, 1996), 67.

13. The Rise and Future Demise of World-Systems Analysis

1. See the discussion in Immanuel Wallerstein et al., *Open the Social Sciences: Report of the Gulbenkian Commission on the Restructuring of the Social Sciences* (Stanford, Calif.: Stanford University Press, 1996).

2. See my "The Unintended Consequences of Cold War Area Studies," in N. Chomsky et al., *The Cold War and the University: Toward an Intellectual History of the Postwar Years* (New York: New Press, 1997), 195–231.

3. I have argued the nature of such risks in my article "Hold the Tiller Firm: On Method and the Unit of Analysis," in *Civilizations and World Systems: Studying World-Historical Change*, ed. Stephen K. Sanderson (Walnut Creek, Calif.: Altamira, 1995), 239–47.

14. Social Science and the Quest for a Just Society

1. Cited in Alexander Koyré, *From the Closed World to the Infinite Universe* (Baltimore: Johns Hopkins University Press, 1957), 276.

2. Cited in Roger Hahn, *Laplace as a Newtonian Scientist* (a paper delivered at a Seminar on the Newtonian Influence held at the Clark Library, April 8, 1967) (University of California, Los Angeles: William Andrews Clark Memorial Library, 1967), 15.

3. Immanuel Wallerstein, "History in Search of Science," *Review* 19, no. 1 (winter 1996): 11–22.

4. See Immanuel Wallerstein et al., *Open the Social Sciences: Report of the Gulbenkian Commission on the Restructuring of the Social Sciences* (Stanford, Calif.: Stanford University Press, 1996).

5. "The crystal has been shattered," Ivar Ekeland tells us. "The qualitative approach is not a mere stand-in for quantitative methods. It may lead to great theoretical advances, as in fluid dynamics. It also has a significant advantage over quantitative methods, namely, stability" (*Mathematics and the Unexpected* [Chicago: University of Chicago Press, 1988], 73).

6. Ilya Prigogine, *La fin des certitudes* (Paris: Odile Jacob, 1996), 83, 177.

7. I have no place to argue this here, but I have spelled this out previously in "Peace, Stability, and Legitimacy, 1990–2025/2050," in *After Liberalism* (New York: New Press, 1995), 25–45.

15. The Heritage of Sociology, the Promise of Social Science

1. Talcott Parsons, *The Structure of Social Action*, 2d ed. (Glencoe, Ill.: Free Press, 1949 [1937]).

2. Immanuel Wallerstein et al., *Open the Social Sciences: Report of the Gulbenkian Commission on the Restructuring of the Social Sciences* (Stanford, Calif.: Stanford University Press, 1996), chap. 1.

3. Ibid., chap. 2.

4. Michel Foucault, *The Archaeology of Knowledge* (New York: Pantheon, 1972); Pierre Bourdieu, *Homo Academicus* (Stanford, Calif.: Stanford University Press, 1988).

5. If one looks at one of the very last articles that Weber wrote, "Science as a Vocation," delivered as a speech in 1918, one notices that Weber specifically identifies himself in the second sentence as a "political economist." In fact, in the German text, the word he uses to describe himself is *Natiönalokonom*, which is close to, but not quite, a political economist. Further on in the text, however, he refers to work that "sociologists must necessarily undertake." In this latter sentence, one is not sure to what degree he is referring to himself (Max Weber, "Science as a Vocation," in *From Max Weber: Essays in Sociology*, ed. H. H. Gerth and C. Wright Mills [New York: Oxford University Press, 1946 (1919)], 129, 134).

6. One recent example is by a Canadian sociologist, Ken Morrison: *Marx, Durkheim, Weber: Formations of Modern Social Thought* (London: Sage, 1995). Its blurb reads: "Every undergraduate course focuses on Marx, Durkheim and Weber as the base of the classical tradition in sociological theory."

7. On the relative decline of Durkheim, and especially of the *L'Année Sociologique*, see Terry N. Clark, "The Structure and Functions of a Research Institute: The *Année Sociologique*," *European Journal of Sociology* 9 (1968): 89–91.

8. George E. G. Catlin, introduction to Emile Durkheim, *The Rules of Sociological*

Method, trans. Sarah A. Solovay and John H. Mueller, 8th ed. (Glencoe, Ill.: Free Press, 1964 [1938], xi–xii).

9. R. W. Connell, "Why Is Classical Theory Classical?" *American Journal of Sociology* 102, no. 6 (May 1967): 1514.

10. Emile Durkheim, *The Rules of Sociological Method,* trans. W. D. Halls (Glencoe, Ill.: Free Press, 1982 [1938]), 35–36.

11. To the view that society is based on a substratum of individual consciousnesses, Durkheim responds: "Yet what is so readily deemed unacceptable for social facts is freely admitted for other domains of nature. Whenever elements of any kind combine, by virtue of this combination they give rise to new phenomena. One is therefore forced to conceive of these phenomena as residing, not in the elements, but in the entity formed by the union of these elements.... Let us apply this principle to sociology. If, as is granted to us, this synthesis *sui generis,* which constitutes every society, gives rise to new phenomena, different from those which occur in consciousnesses in isolation, one is forced to admit that these specific facts reside in the society itself that produces them and not in its parts — namely its members" (Durkheim, *Rules* [1982], 38–40).

12. "What is exclusively peculiar to social constraint is that it stems not from the unyieldingness of certain patterns of molecules, but from the prestige with which certain representations are endowed. It is true that habits, whether unique to individuals or hereditary, in certain respects possess this same property. They dominate us and impose beliefs and practices upon us. But they dominate us from within, for they are wholly within each one of us. By contrast, social beliefs and practices act upon us from the outside; thus the ascendancy exerted by the former as compared with the latter is basically very different" (ibid., 44).

13. Ibid., 45.

14. "Despite the fact that beliefs and social practices permeate us in this way from the outside, it does not follow that we receive them passively and without causing them to undergo modification. In thinking about collective institutions, in assimilating ourselves to them, we individualise them, we more or less impart to them our own personal stamp. Thus in thinking about the world of the senses each one of us colours it in his own way, and different people adapt themselves differently to an identical physical environment. This is why each one of us creates to a certain extent *his own* morality, *his own* religion, *his own* techniques. Every type of social conformity carries with it a whole gamut of individual variations. It is nonetheless true that the sphere of permitted variations is limited. It is non-existent or very small as regards religious and moral phenomena, where deviations may easily become crimes. It is more extensive for all matters relating to economic life. But sooner or later, even in this last case, one encounters a limit that must not be overstepped" (ibid., 47, n. 6).

15. Ibid., 45.

16. Ibid., 32–33.

17. In his recent discussion of rational choice theory, William J. Goode notes: "Ordinarily, sociologists begin with behavior whose aims and goals seem to be clear enough, and we try to find out which variables explain most of the variance. However, if those variables fail to predict adequately, if for example people choose consistently to act in ways that lower the likelihood that they will achieve what they claim is their material, moral, or esthetic goal, we do not suppose that these people are irrational. Instead, we look at them more closely to locate the 'underlying rationality' of what they are really

seeking" (William J. Goode, "Rational Choice Theory," *American Sociologist*, 28, no. 2 [summer 1997]: 29).

18. Karl Marx and Friedrich Engels, *The Communist Manifesto* (New York: International Publishers, 1948 [1848]), 9. In the 1888 preface added by Engels, he restates the "fundamental proposition which forms [the] nucleus [of the *Manifesto*]....That in every historical epoch, the prevailing mode of economic production and exchange, and the social organization necessarily following from it, form the basis upon which is built up, and from which alone can be explained, the political and intellectual history of that epoch; that consequently the whole history of mankind (since the dissolution of primitive tribal society, holding land in common ownership) has been a history of class struggles, contests between exploiting and exploited, ruling and oppressed classes; that the history of these class struggles forms a series of evolutions in which, nowadays, a stage has been reached where the exploited and oppressed class — the proletariat — cannot attain its emancipation from the sway of the exploiting and ruling class — the bourgeoisie — without at the same time, and once and for all, emancipating society at large from all exploitation, oppression, class distinctions, and class struggles" (ibid., 6).

19. In discussing what happened in France in the period 1848–51, Marx says: "And as in private life one differentiates between what a man thinks and says of himself and what he really is and does, so in historical struggles one must distinguish still more the phrases and fancies of parties from their real organizations and their real interests, their conceptions of themselves from their reality" (Karl Marx, *The 18th Brumaire of Louis Napoleon* [New York: International Publishers, 1963 (1852)], 47).

20. "[Custom and material advantage] do not form a sufficiently reliable basis for a given domination. In addition there is normally a further element, the belief in *legitimacy*. Experience shows that in no instance does domination voluntarily limit itself to material or affectual or ideal motives as a basis for its continuance. In addition every such system attempts to cultivate the belief in its legitimacy. But according to the kind of legitimacy which is claimed, the type of obedience, the kind of administrative staff developed to guarantee it, and the mode of exercising authority, will all differ fundamentally" (Max Weber, *Economy and Society*, ed. Guenther Roth and Claus Wittich [New York: Bedminster Press, 1968], 213).

21. Ibid., 217.

22. "In general, it should be kept clearly in mind that the basis of every authority, and correspondingly of every kind of willingness to obey, is a *belief*, a belief by virtue of which persons exercising authority are lent prestige. The composition of this belief is seldom altogether simple. In the case of 'legal authority,' it is never purely legal. The belief in legality comes to be established and habitual, and this means that it is partly traditional. Violation of the tradition may be fatal to it. Furthermore, it has a charismatic element, at least in the negative sense that persistent and striking lack of success may be sufficient to ruin any government, to undermine its prestige, and to prepare the way for charismatic revolution" (ibid., 263).

23. Sigmund Freud, *Civilization and Its Discontents* (New York: W. W. Norton, 1961 [1930]).

24. Sigmund Freud, *The Interpretation of Dreams* (New York: Basic Books, 1955 [1900]).

25. "We have learnt from psycho-analysis that the essence of the process of repression lies, not in putting an end to, in annihilating, the idea which represents an instinct,

but in preventing it from becoming conscious" (Sigmund Freud, "The Unconscious," in *Standard Edition* [1957 (1915)], 14:166).

26. "A gain in meaning is a perfectly justifiable ground for going beyond the limits of direct experience. . . . Just as Kant warned us not to overlook the fact that our perceptions are subjectively conditioned and must not be regarded as identical with what is perceived though unknowable, so psycho-analysis warns us not to equate perceptions by means of consciousness with the unconscious mental processes which are their object. Like the physical, the psychical is not necessarily in reality what it appears to us to be" (ibid., 14:167, 171).

27. Ibid., 14:182.

28. "The ego behaves as if the danger of a development of anxiety threatened it not from the direction of an instinctual impulse but from the direction of a perception, and it is thus enabled to react against the external danger with the attempts at flight represented by phobic avoidances. In this process repression is successful in one particular; the release of anxiety can to some extent be dammed up, but only at a heavy sacrifice of personal freedom. Attempt at flight from the demands of instinct are, however, in general useless, and in spite of everything, the result of phobic flight remains unsatisfactory" (ibid., 14:184).

29. Ibid., 14:203.

30. "The battle with the obstacle of an unconscious sense of guilt is not made easy for the analyst. Nothing can be done against it directly, and nothing indirectly but the slow procedure of unmasking its unconscious repressed roots, and of thus gradually changing it into a *conscious* sense of guilt. . . . It depends principally on the intensity of the sense of guilt; there is often no counteracting force of a similar order of strength which the treatment can oppose to it. Perhaps it may depend, too, on whether the personality of the analyst allows of the patient's putting him in the place of his ego ideal, and this involves a temptation for the analyst to play the part of prophet, saviour and redeemer to the patient. Since the rules of analysis are diametrically opposed to the physician's making use of his personality in any such manner, it must be honestly confessed that here we have another limitation to the effectiveness of analysis; after all analysis does not set out to make pathological reactions impossible, but to give the patient's ego *freedom* to decide one way or the other" (Sigmund Freud, *The Ego and the Id* [New York: W. W. Norton, 1960 (1923)], 50–51).

31. Freud, *Civilization*, 34, 35–36.

32. Anouar Abdel-Malek, *Civilisations and Social Theory*, vol. 1 of *Social Dialectics* (London: Macmillan, 1981 [1972]), xii; subsequent references to this work in the text will be cited there.

33. "The initial inspiration . . . lies and remains deeply rooted in the transformation of the world in our time, in the rise to contemporaneity of the Orient — Asia and Africa, together with Latin America. . . . The central difficulty facing social theory at the time of Yalta, the climax of Western hegemony, was how to generate ways and means of tackling the hitherto marginalised societies and cultures belonging within the non-Western civilisational moulds. Prepostulated universalism, as a recipe, simply would not do. It was neither able to interpret, from the inside, the specificities at work, nor was it acceptable to the major formative tendencies within the national schools of thought and action. . . . A non-temporal social theory can only obtain in the subjectivist epistemological productions of professional ideologists, divorced from the real concrete world,

from the objective dialectics of human societies in given historical periods and places, and from the geo-historical formative influences deeply at work in the hidden part of the iceberg" (ibid., xi, xiii).

34. "On the other side of the river, the conceptions of the Orient were structured through a different process realised in a totally different environment. If we study the historical-geographical constitution of the nations and societies of the Orient — Asia, around China; the Islamic area in Afro-Asia — it will be clear immediately that we have before us the oldest sedentary and stable societies of socioeconomic formations in the history of mankind. A group of societies came to be established around the major rivers, facing wide openings to the ocean and sea, thus enabling the pastoral groups to move toward a more stable, agricultural-sedentary mode of production and social existence. . . . It is crucial here to consider the relevance of 'durability,' of 'societal maintenance' through centuries and millennia to these objective basic elements. . . . Time is master. Therefore the conception of time can be said to have developed as a non-analytical vision, as a unitary, symbiotic, unified and unifying conception. Man could no longer 'have' or 'lack' time; time, the master of existence, could not be apprehended as commodity. On the contrary, man was determined and dominated by time" (ibid., 180–81).

35. Abdel-Malek is not rejecting all of Western modernity. Indeed, he adds this warning to the Orient in its confrontation with the West: "If the Orient wishes to become master of its own destiny, it would do well to ponder the old saying of the martial arts in Japan: 'Do not forget that only he who knows the new things while knowing the ancient things, can become a true master'" (ibid., 185).

36. Fernand Braudel, "History and the Social Sciences: The *Longue Durée*," in *Economy and Society in Early Modern Europe*, ed. P. Burke (London: Routledge and Kegan Paul, 1972), 35.

37. Sir John Maddox, blurb on cover of Ilya Prigogine, *The End of Certainty* (New York: Free Press, 1997).

38. *The End of Certainty* is the title given to the English translation of Prigogine's work in 1997. But the original French title was *La fin des certitudes* (Paris: Odile Jacob, 1996), and I think the plural form is more consonant with his argument.

39. "As is well known, Newton's law [relating force and acceleration] has been superseded in the twentieth century by quantum mechanics and relativity. Still, the basic characteristics of his laws — determinism and time symmetry — have survived. . . . By way of such equations [such as Schrödinger's equation], laws of nature lead to certitudes. Once initial conditions are given, everything is determined. Nature is an automaton, which we can control, at least in principle. Novelty, choice, and spontaneous action are real only from our human point of view. . . . The concept of a passive nature subject to deterministic and time-reversible laws is quite specific to the Western world. In China and Japan, nature means 'what is by itself'" (Prigogine, *End of Certainty*, 11–12; subsequent references to this work in the text will be cited there). Note here the similarity to Abdel-Malek's insistence on two different civilizational relations to the time-dimension.

40. "Probability plays an essential role in most sciences, from economics to genetics. Still, the idea that probability is merely a state of mind has survived. We now have to go a step further and show how probability enters the fundamental laws of physics, whether classical or quantum. . . . [Arguments that entropy is a measure of ignorance] are untenable. They imply that it is our ignorance, our coarse graining, that leads to the second law [of thermodynamics]. For a well-informed observer, such as the demon imagined

by Laplace, the world would appear as perfectly time-reversible. We would be the father of time, of evolution, and not its children. . . . Our own point of view is that the laws of physics, as formulated in the traditional way, describe an idealized, stable world that is quite different from the unstable, evolving world in which we live. The main reason to discard the banalization of irreversibility is that we can no longer associate the arrow of time with an increase in disorder. Recent developments in nonequilibrium physics and chemistry point in the opposite direction. They show unambiguously that the arrow of time is a source of *order*. The constructive role of irreversibility is even more striking in far-from-equilibrium situations where nonequilibrium leads to new forms of coherence" (ibid., 16–17, 25–26).

41. "[O]ur position is that classical mechanics is incomplete because it does not include irreversible processes associated with an increase in entropy. To include these processes in its formulation, we must incorporate instability and nonintegrability. Integrable systems are the exception. Starting with the three-body problem, most dynamical systems are nonintegrable" (ibid., 108).

42. "Our thinking constitutes a return to realism, but emphatically not a return to determinism. . . . Chance, or probability, is no longer a convenient way of accepting ignorance, but rather part of a new, extended rationality. . . . In accepting that the future is not determined, we come to the end of certainties. Is this an admission of defeat for the human mind? On the contrary, we believe that the opposite is true. . . . Time and reality are irreducibly linked. Denying time may either be a consolation or a triumph of human reason. It is always a negation of reality. . . . What we have tried to follow is indeed a narrow path between two conceptions that both lead to alienation: a world ruled by deterministic laws, which leaves no place for novelty, and a world ruled by a dice-playing God, where everything is absurd, acausal, and incomprehensible" (ibid., 131, 155, 183, 187–88). Heed the words "narrow path" in the last sentence.

43. It is interesting at this point to return to Braudel to see how his formulations, written three decades earlier, use language that is very similar to that of Prigogine. He wishes to describe his attempts to blend "unity and diversity in the social sciences" by a term he says he borrows from Polish colleagues, that of "complex studies" (Fernand Braudel, "Unity and Diversity in the Human Sciences," in *On History* [Chicago: University of Chicago Press, 1980 (1960)], 61). He describes *histoire événementielle*, the kind he considers to be dust, as "linear" history (Fernand Braudel, "History and Sociology," in *On History*, 67). And he tells us to embrace Georges Gurvitch's view of global society, in a model that reminds us of bifurcations: "[Gurvitch] sees the future of both [the Middle Ages in the West and our contemporary society] as hesitating between several different destinies, all radically different, and this seems to me a reasonable assessment of the variety of life itself; the future is not a single path. So we must renounce the linear" (Fernand Braudel, "The History of Civilizations: The Past Explains the Present," in *On History*, 200).

44. I cite two summary statements of what feminist scholarship is about. Constance Jordan (*Renaissance Feminism: Literary Texts and Political Models* [Ithaca, N.Y.: Cornell University Press, 1990], 1): "Feminist scholarship is predicated on the assumption that women have experienced life differently from men and that difference is worth studying." And Joan Kelly (*Women, History, and Theory: The Essays of Joan Kelly* [Chicago: University of Chicago Press, 1984], 1): "Women's history has a dual goal: to restore women to history and to restore history to women."

45. See Joan Kelly again (*Women,* 1): "In seeking to add women to the fundaments of historical knowledge, women's history has revitalized theory, for it has shaken the conceptions of historical study. It has done this by making problematical three of the basic concerns of historical thought: (1) periodization, (2) categories of social analysis, and (3) theories of social change."

46. Evelyn Fox Keller, *Reflections on Gender and Science* (New Haven: Yale University Press, 1985), 3–5.

47. Ibid., 10. Keller writes: "[Reading laws of nature for their personal content uncovers] the personal investment scientists make in impersonality; the anonymity of the picture they produce is revealed as itself a kind of signature.... Attention to the intrapersonal dynamics of 'theory choice' illuminates some of the subtler means by which ideology manifests itself in science — even in the face of scientists' best intentions.... The fact that Boyle's law is not wrong must, however, not be forgotten. Any effective critique of science needs to take due account of the undeniable successes of science as well as of the commitments that have made such successes possible.... Boyle's law does give us a reliable description,... [one] that stands the tests of experimental replicability and logical coherence. But it is crucial to recognize that it is a statement about a particular set of phenomena, prescribed to meet particular interests and described in accordance with certain agreed-upon criteria of both reliability and utility. Judgments about which phenomena are worth studying, which kinds of data are significant — as well as which descriptions (or theories) of those phenomena are most adequate, satisfying, useful, and even reliable — depend critically on the social, linguistic, and scientific practices of the judgments in question.... [S]cientists in every discipline live and work with assumptions that feel like constants ... but are in fact variable, and, given the right kind of jolt, subject to change. Such parochialities ... can only be perceived through the lens of difference, by stepping outside the community" (ibid., 10–12).

48. "[I]t is a thesis of this book that the ideology of modern science, along with its undeniable success, carries within it its own form of projection: the projection of disinterest, of autonomy, of alienation. My argument is not simply that the dream of a completely objective science is in principle unrealizable, but that it contains precisely what it rejects: the vivid traces of a reflected self-image" (ibid., 70).

49. Ibid., 178.

50. Donna J. Haraway, *Simians, Cyborgs, and Women: The Reinvention of Nature* (New York: Routledge, 1991), 45; subsequent references to this work in the text will be cited there.

51. For Haraway, this "means embracing the skilful task of reconstructing the boundaries of daily life, in partial connection with others, in communication with all of our parts.... This is a dream not of a common language, but of a powerful infidel heteroglossia" (ibid., 181).

52. She concludes that "bodies as objects of knowledge are material-semiotic generative nodes. Their *boundaries* materialize in social interaction. Boundaries are drawn by mapping processes; 'objects' do not pre-exist as such. Objects are boundary projects. But boundaries shift from within; boundaries are very tricky. What boundaries provisionally contain remains generative, productive of meanings and bodies. Siting (sighting) boundaries is a risky practice. Objectivity is not about dis-engagement, but about mu-

tual *and* usually unequal structuring, about taking risks in a world where 'we' are permanently mortal, that is, not in 'final' control" (ibid., 200–201).

53. "The White Man's Burden is becoming increasingly heavy for the earth and especially for the South. The past 500 years of history reveal that each time a relationship of colonization has been established between the North and nature and people outside the North, the colonizing men and society have assumed a position of superiority, and thus of responsibility for the future of the earth and for other peoples and cultures. Out of the assumption of superiority flows the notion of the white man's burden. Out of the *idea* of the white man's burden flows the *reality* of the burdens imposed by the white man on nature, women and others. Therefore, decolonizing the South is intimately linked to the issue of decolonizing the North" (Vandana Shiva, in Maria Mies and Vandana Shiva, *Ecofeminism* [New Delhi: Kali for Women, 1993], 264).

54. Ibid., 265.

55. "While science itself is a product of social forces and has a social agenda determined by those who can mobilize scientific production, in contemporary times scientific activity has been assigned a privileged epistemological position of being socially and politically neutral. Thus science takes on a dual character: it offers technological fixes for social and political problems, but absolves and distances itself from the new social and political problems it creates.... The issue of making visible the hidden links between science technology and society and making manifest and vocal the kind of issues that are kept concealed and unspoken is linked with the relationship between the North and the South. Unless and until there can be social accountability of the science and technology structures and the systems to whose needs they respond, there can be no balance and no accountability in terms of relationships between North and South.... To question the omnipotence of science and technology's ability to solve ecological problems is an important step in the decolonization of the North" (ibid., 272–73).

56. Sandra Harding, *The Science Question in Feminism* (Ithaca, N.Y.: Cornell University Press, 1986), 47. Harding writes: "In social inquiry we... want to explain the origins, forms, and prevalence of apparently irrational but culturewide patterns of human belief and action.... Only if we insist that science is analytically separate from social life can we maintain the fiction that explanations of irrational social belief and behavior could not ever, in principle, increase our understanding of the world physics explains.... Counting objects and partitioning a line are common social practices, and these practices can generate contradictory ways of thinking about the objects of mathematical inquiry. It may be hard to imagine what gender practices could have influenced the acceptance of particular concepts in mathematics, but cases such as these show that the possibility cannot be ruled out a priori by the claim that the intellectual, logical content of mathematics is free of all social influence" (ibid., 47, 51).

57. Jensen says in a review of five books on these questions: "Except primatology, mainstream sciences have virtually ignored feminist attempts to rename nature and reconstruct science. Beyond suggesting models and taxonomies that are less hierarchical, more permeable, and more reflexive than the male prototypes... it is not clear what feminist revisions and reconstruction of science will entail. Feminist practices may generate new ways of being in the world... and thereby give birth to new ways of knowing and describing the world. Or, perhaps the ultimate achievement of the new epistemologies will be to map the limits of language and knowledge; to chart the embeddedness of knowledge in structures of (gendered) power-relations" (Sue Curry Jensen, "Is Science

a Man? New Feminist Epistemologies and Reconstructions of Knowledge," *Theory and Society* 19, no. 2 [April 1990]: 246).

58. Bruno Latour, *We Have Never Been Modern* (Cambridge, Mass.: Harvard University Press, 1993), 6; subsequent references to this work in the text will be cited there.

59. "What link is there between the work of translation or mediation and that of purification? This is the question on which I should like to shed light. My hypothesis — which remains too crude — is that the second has made the first possible: the more we forbid ourselves to conceive of hybrids, the more possible their interbreeding becomes — such is the paradox of the moderns.... The second question has to do with premoderns, with the other types of culture. My hypothesis — once again too simple — is that by devoting themselves to conceiving of hybrids, the other cultures have excluded their proliferation. It is this disparity that would explain the Great Divide between Them — all the other cultures — and Us — the westerners — and would make it possible finally to solve the insoluble problem of relativism. The third question has to do with the current crisis: if modernity were so effective in its dual task of separation and proliferation, why would it weaken itself today by preventing us from being truly modern? Hence the final question, which is also the most difficult one: if we have stopped being modern, if we can no longer separate the work of proliferation from the work of purification, what are we going to become? My hypothesis — which, like the previous ones, is too coarse — is that we are going to have to slow down, reorient and regulate the proliferation of monsters by representing their existence officially" (ibid., 12).

60. "If an anthropology of the modern world were to exist its task would consist in describing in the same way how all the branches of our government are organized, including that of nature and the hard sciences, and in explaining how and why these branches diverge as well as accounting for the multiple arrangements that bring them together" (ibid., 14–15). The subtitle of the original French version, which was left off the English title, is *Essai d'anthropologie symétrique* (see Bruno Latour, *Nous n'avons jamais été modernes: Essai d'anthropologie symétrique* [Paris: La Découverte, 1991]).

61. "Because it believes in the total separation of humans and nonhumans, and because it simultaneously cancels out this separation, the Constitution has made the moderns invincible. If you criticize them by saying that nature is a world constructed by human hands, they will show you that it is transcendent, that science is a mere intermediary allowing access to Nature, and that they keep their hands off. If you tell them that Society is transcendent and that their laws infinitely surpass us, they will tell you that we are free and that our destiny is in our own hands. If you object that they are being duplicitous, they will show you that they never confuse the Laws of Nature with imprescriptible human freedom" (Latour, *We Have Never Been Modern*, 37). I have corrected a howler of a mistranslation by referring to the French original (Latour, *Nous n'avons jamais été modernes*, 57). In the English text, the third sentence reads, quite incorrectly: "If you tell them that we are free and that our destiny is in our own hands, they will tell you that Society is transcendent and its laws infinitely surpass us."

62. Latour further clarifies this paradox by looking at its expression in the world of knowledge: "Social scientists have for long allowed themselves to denounce the belief system of ordinary people. They call this belief system 'naturalization.' Ordinary people imagine that the power of gods, the objectivity of money, the attraction of fashion, the beauty of art, come from some objective properties intrinsic to the nature of things.

Fortunately, social scientists know better and they show that the arrow goes in the other direction, from society to the objects. Gods, money, fashion and art offer only a surface for the projection of our social needs and interests. At least since Emile Durkheim, such has been the price of entry into the sociology profession. The difficulty, however, is to reconcile this form of denunciation with another one in which the directions of the arrows are exactly reversed. Ordinary people, mere social actors, average citizens, believe they are free and that they can modify their desires, their motives and their rational strategies at will.... But fortunately, social scientists are standing guard, and they denounce, debunk and ridicule this naive belief in the freedom of the human subject and society. This time they use the nature of things — that is the indisputable results of the sciences — to show how it determines, informs and moulds the soft and pliable wills of the poor humans" (Latour, *We Have Never Been Modern*, 51–53).

63. Again an error in the translation. The English text reads "past perfect tense," but this is a mistranslation. The French text reads *passé composé*.

64. "[T]he moderns have been victims of their own success.... Their Constitution could absorb a few counter-examples, a few exceptions — indeed, it thrived on them. But it is helpless when the exceptions proliferate, when the third estate of things and the Third World join together to invade all its assemblies, *en masse*.... [T]he proliferation of hybrids has saturated the constitutional framework of the moderns" (Latour, *We Have Never Been Modern*, 49–51).

65. See Deborah T. Gold (introduction to "Cross-Fertilization of the Life Course and Other Theoretical Paradigms," section 3 of *The Gerontologist* 36, no. 2 [April 1996]: 224): "For the last several decades, sociology has become a discipline of ultra-specialization. Although sociologists may think we are giving our graduate students a broad sociological education, in truth, by example, we encourage students to narrow their areas of expertise. Unfortunately, this parochialism means that many sociologists are unaware of what is current in specializations not their own. If sociology continues this approach, we can hardly expect to inspire a 21st century Talcott Parsons or Robert Merton who could take a broader perspective. Instead, sociologists in the future are likely to configure their areas of expertise even more narrowly." It is worthy of note that this peroration was published in a quite specialized journal, *The Gerontologist*.

66. "We might even say that the model of sociologically naive actors — as in rational choice and game theoretical models — are misguided for almost all occasions. Our typifications and explanations must involve the continuous interaction of institutionalized expectations, perceptions, interpretations, affects, distortions, and behavior" (Neil Smelser, *Problematics of Sociology* [Berkeley: University of California Press, 1997], 27).

67. William McNeill, *Mythistory and Other Essays* (Chicago: University of Chicago Press, 1986).

68. "Historian, the one who knows? No, the one who searches" (Lucien Febvre, "Par manière d'introduction," in G. Friedmann, *Humanisme du travail et humanités*, Cahiers des Annales 5 [Paris: A. Colin, 1950], v).

69. It seems to me that uncertainty is the essential issue Neil Smelser was addressing in his 1997 presidential address to the American Sociological Association when he discussed "ambivalence," a term he borrowed from Merton. He discussed it primarily as a psychological constant in terms of actors' motivations rather than as a structural constant of the physical world. He does however draw a conclusion with which I heartily agree: "We might even suggest that ambivalence forces us to reason even more than preferences

do, because conflict may be a stronger motive for thinking than is desire" (Neil Smelser, "The Rational and the Ambivalent in the Social Sciences," *American Sociological Review* 63, no. 1 [February 1998]: 7).

70. Michel Cazenave, dir., *Dictionnaire de l'ignorance* (Paris: Bibliothèque Sciences Albin Michel, 1998).

71. "[The concept of the disenchantment of the world] is paradoxically due to the glorification of the earthly world, henceforth worthy of the kind of intellectual pursuit Aristotle reserved for heaven. Classical science denied becoming, natural diversity, both considered by Aristotle attributes of the sublunar, inferior world. In this sense, classical science brought heaven to earth.... The radical change in the outlook of modern science, the transition toward the temporal, the multiple, may be viewed as the reversal of the movement that brought Aristotle's heaven to earth. Now we are bringing earth to heaven" (Ilya Prigogine and Isabelle Stengers, *Order out of Chaos: Man's New Dialogue with Nature* [Boulder, Colo.: New Science Library, 1984], 305–6).

Permissions

The University of Minnesota Press and the author gratefully acknowledge permission to reprint the following essays in this book.

"Uncertainty and Creativity: Premises and Conclusions" was first published in *American Behavioral Scientist* 42, no. 3 (November–December 1998): 320–22. Reprinted by permission of Sage Publications, Inc.

Chapter 1, "Social Science and the Communist Interlude, or Interpretations of Contemporary History," was first published in *Polish Sociological Review*, no. 1 (1997).

Chapter 2, "The ANC and South Africa: The Past and Future of Liberation Movements in the World-System," was first published in *Economic and Political Weekly* 31, no. 39 (September 28, 1996).

Chapter 3, "The Rise of East Asia, or The World-System in the Twenty-First Century," was first published in *Capitalism and Evolution,* edited by M. Itoh et al. (Cheltenham: Edgar Elgar Publishing, 1999).

The Coda to chapter 3, "The So-called Asian Crisis: Geopolitics in the *Longue Durée,*" was first published in *Economia Global e Gestão* (1999).

Chapter 4, "States? Sovereignty? The Dilemmas of Capitalists in an Age of Transition," was first published in *State and Sovereignty in the Global Economy,* edited by D. Solinger et al. (London: Routledge, 1999).

Chapter 5, "Ecology and Capitalist Costs of Production: No Exit," was first published in *Ecology and the World-System,* edited by W. Goldfrank et al. (Westport, Conn.: Greenwood Press, 1997). Greenwood Press is an imprint of Greenwood Publishing Group, Inc., Westport, Connecticut.

Chapter 6, "Liberalism and Democracy: *Frères Ennemis?*" was first published in *Acta Politica* 32, no. 2 (summer 1997).

Chapter 7, "Integration to What? Marginalization from What?" was first published in *Scandinavian Political Studies* 20, no. 4 (1997).

Chapter 8, "Social Change? Change Is Eternal. Nothing Ever Changes," was first presented as the keynote address at the III Portuguese Congress of Sociology, Lisbon, February 7, 1996. The theme of the Congress was "Practices and Processes of Social Change." Copyright Immanuel Wallerstein.

Chapter 9, "Social Science and Contemporary Society: The Vanishing Guarantees of Rationality," was first published in *International Sociology* 11, no. 1 (March 1996).

Chapter 10, "Differentiation and Reconstruction in the Social Sciences," was first presented at Research Council, International Sociological Association, Montreal, August 6, 1997. Copyright Immanuel Wallerstein.

Chapter 11, "Eurocentrism and Its Avatars: The Dilemmas of Social Science," was first published in *New Left Review*, no. 226 (November–December 1997).

Chapter 12, "The Structures of Knowledge, or How Many Ways May We Know?" was first published in *World Views and the Problem of Synthesis* (Yellow Book of *Einstein Meets Magritte*) (Dordrecht: Kluwer, 1998). Reprinted with kind permission by Kluwer Academic Publishers.

Chapter 13, "The Rise and Future Demise of World-Systems Analysis," was first published in *Review* 21, no. 1 (1998).

Chapter 14, "Social Science and the Quest for a Just Society," was first published in *American Journal of Sociology* 102, no. 5 (March 1997). Reprinted with permission of the University of Chicago Press. Copyright 1997 by The University of Chicago. All rights reserved.

Chapter 15, "The Heritage of Sociology, the Promise of Social Science," was first published in *Current Sociology* 47, no. 3 (1999). Reprinted with permission of Sage Publications Ltd.

Index

In this index, certain terms that comprise the very subject matter of the entire book are not included because they are to be found passim: social science, world-system, historical system, modern world-system, capitalist world-economy, historical capitalism.

Words are given in their noun form and include therein their use as adjectives. Names of countries include the noun form that indicates persons coming from that country. Names of university subject matters are included insofar as they refer to the subject matter, but do not include other common uses of the same term. The phrase "economic stagnation" would not be indexed under "economics."

Immanuel Wallerstein is Distinguished Professor of Sociology and director of the Fernand Braudel Center for the Study of Economies, Historical Systems, and Civilizations at Binghamton University. He is the author of, among many other titles, *The Modern World-System* (3 vols.); *The Capitalist World-Economy; Historical Capitalism, with Capitalist Civilization; The Politics of the World-Economy: The States, the Movements, and the Civilizations; Africa and the Modern World; Race, Nation, Class: Ambiguous Identities* (with Etienne Balibar); *Geopolitics and Geoculture: Essays on the Changing World-System; Unthinking Social Science: The Limits of Nineteenth-Century Paradigms; After Liberalism; Open the Social Sciences: Report of the Gulbenkian Commission on the Restructuring of the Social Sciences* (with others); and *Utopistics, or Historical Choices for the Twenty-First Century.*